⊰Christian Character Curriculum⊱

⊰Christian Character Curriculum⊱

Special thanks to you who have supported PEARABLES from the beginning:

Our dear parents and...
Kent & Sherry
Kurt & Aronda
Lawrence & Mary Greider
Anne White

Paul & Miriam Annon
Art Director/World Challenge Ministries

ISBN-13 978-0-9792446-7-4

First Published January 1993
Fourth Printing September 1999
Copyright PEARABLES 1993, 1999
PEARABLES
P.O. Box 272000
Fort Collins, CO 80527

CONTENTS

Unit 1 - FAITH Pages 13-46

Lesson:
1. Faith
2. Faith in God ... Who is God?
3. God is King!
4. Our Lord's Kingdom
5. How to Enter the Kingdom of Heaven
6. Loyalty
7. Loyalty ... Loving God
8. Loyalty ... Being Steadfast
9. Loyalty ... Faithfulness vs. Faithlessness
10. Loyalty ... Being Faithful
11. Trust ... Are We to Put our Trust in Men?
12. Trust ... In God!
13. Trust ... Confidence
14. Trust ... Reliance
15. Trust ... Hope
16. Allegiance
17. Allegiance ... We are Servants
18. Allegiance ... Being an Obedient Servant
19. Allegiance ... Obeying
20. Allegiance ... Being in Subjection to God
21. Allegiance ... Being Humble Servants
22. Loyal Subjects ... Listening!
23. Allegiance ... Doing the Will of the Father
24. Conviction
25. Being Fully Persuaded ... Not Doubting
26. REVIEW
PEARABLES Kingdom Story ... Faith

Unit 2 - VIRTUE Pages 47-92

Lesson:
1. Virtue
2. The Virtuous Woman
3. Ruth ... Known for Her Virtue!
4. Righteousness ... God's
5. Righteousness ... God's Righteous Ones
6. Righteousness ... What the Righteous Do
7. Righteousness ... More of what the Righteous Do
8. Righteousness ... Purity
9. Righteousness ... What the Righteous Should Follow After
10. Righteousness ... Righteous Lot
11. Moral Excellence
12. Moral Excellence ... Discernment
13. Moral Excellence ... Judging Vs. Condemnation
14. Moral Excellence ... Judging Between Good and Evil
15. Moral Excellence ... Being Upright
16. Valor
17. Valor ... Fearing God
18. Valor ... We are Not to Fear Men
19. Valor ... The Courage of David Pt. 1
20. Valor ... The Courage of David Pt. 2
21. Boldness
22. Boldness ... Waxing Bold
23. Boldness ... In Word
24. Boldness ... Even in Bonds
25. Goodness
26. Goodness ... Being Competent or Serviceable
27. Goodness ... Being Sound and Whole
28. Goodness ... Being Kind
29. REVIEW
PEARABLES Kingdom Story ... Virtue

Unit 3 - KNOWLEDGE Pages 93-128

Lesson:
1. Knowledge
2. Knowing God's Word
3. Enlightenment
4. Being Illuminated
5. Understanding
6. Understanding ... We are to Get it!
7. Understanding ... Those Who are Void of Understanding
8. Understanding ... Qualities of those With Understanding
9. Wisdom
10. Wisdom ... Cry For it!
11. Wisdom ... God's, Not Man's
12. Wisdom ... Vain Philosophies
13. Being Void of Understanding
14. Foolishness
15. A Fool and His Folly
16. More Folly of a Fool
17. Discretion
18. Prudence
19. REVIEW
    PEARABLES Kingdom Story ... Knowledge

Unit 4 - TEMPERANCE Pages 129-150

Lesson:
1. Temperance
2. Controlling the Lusts of the Flesh
3. Lasciviousness
4. Concupiscence and Gluttony
5. Pleasures
6. Covetousness
7. Saying "No"
8. Dying to Ourselves
9. REVIEW
    PEARABLES Kingdom Story ... Temperance

Unit 5 - PATIENCE Pages 151-184

Lesson:
1. Patience
2. Being Patient
3. Forbearance
4. Forbearing
5. Endurance
6. Enduring Afflictions
7. Being Afflicted
8. Enduring Tribulations
9. Through Tribulations
10. God is Longsuffering
11. Longsuffering
12. Suffering Long
13. Sufferings for Righteousness
14. Suffering With Patience
15. Persecutions
16. Enduring Persecutions
17. Bearing Trials
18. Being Tried
19. REVIEW
    PEARABLES Kingdom Story ... Patience

Unit 6 - GODLINESS Pages 185-218

Lesson:
1. Godliness
2. Following Godliness
3. Being Godly
4. God Has Set Us Apart
5. Guarding Our Hearts
6. Company We Keep
7. Who We Associate With
8. Living For God
9. Training children to Be Godly
10. Instructing Children to Godliness
11. Teaching Our Children to Train Their Children
12. Piety
13. Being Devoted to God
14. Holiness
15. Being Holy
16. Being Holy as He is Holy
17. We are Told to Walk Pleasing to God
18. Being Blameless
19. True Religion
20. REVIEW
    PEARABLES Kingdom Story ... Godliness

Unit 7 - BROTHERLY KINDNESS
Pages 219-246

Lesson:
1. Brotherly Kindness
2. God, Our Father
3. The Family of God
4. Who are Our Brothers?
5. Considering Needs
6. Preferring Others Above Ourselves
7. Submitting to One Another
8. Kindness
9. God's Kindness
10. Being Gentle
11. Being Hospitable
12. Being Gracious
13. Forbearing
14. REVIEW
    PEARABLES Kingdom Story ...
    Brotherly Kindness

Unit 8 - CHARITY   Pages 247-269

Lesson:
1. Charity
2. Following Charity
3. Charity Above All
4. We are Commanded to Have Love
5. God's Love
6. God's Love for Us as a Parent Loves His Child
7. Loving Our Enemies
8. Loving God
9. Loving Each Other
10. REVIEW
    PEARABLES Kingdom Story ...
    Charity

Notes   **Pages 270-300**

CHARACTER TRAINING

This curriculum is designed for home schooling families whose conviction for home schooling is based upon the Bible. There are some people who are disgusted with Public Education because of poor academics, not to mention drugs and the growing popularity of gangs. These are things that bring fear to every parent's heart and are good reasons to pull their children from these institutions, but we as Christians, have Biblical convictions because of God's Word.

The Bible states that we are to train our children:

Deut. 6:6-9 And these words, which I command thee this day, shall be in thine heart; and thou shalt teach them diligently unto thy children, and shalt talk of them when thou sittest in thine house, and when thou walkest by the way, and when thou liest down, and when thou risest up. And thou shalt write them upon the posts of thy house, and on thy gates.

Deut. 11:19-20 And ye shall teach them your children, speaking of them when thou sittest in thine house, and when thou walkest by the way, when thou liest down, and when thou risest up. And thou shalt write them upon the door posts of thine house, and upon thy gates.

Deut. 31:12-13 Gather the people together, men, and women, and children, and thy stranger that is within thy gates, that they may hear, and that they may learn, and fear the Lord your God, and observe to do all the words of this law; And that their children, which have not known anything, may hear, and learn to fear the Lord your God, as long as ye live in the land whither ye go over Jordan to possess it.

Psalm 78:1-8 Give ear, O my people, to my law; incline your ears to the words of my mouth. I will open my mouth in a parable; I will utter dark sayings of old. Which we have heard and known, and our fathers have told us. We will not hide them from their children, shewing to the generation to come the praises of the Lord, and his strength, and his wonderful works that he hath done. For he hath established a testimony in Jacob, and appointed a law in Israel, which he commanded our fathers that they should make them known to their children; That the generation to come might know them, even the children which should be born; who should arise and declare them to their children; That they might set their hope in God, and not forget the works of God, but keep his commandments; and might not be as their fathers, a stubborn and rebellious generation; a generation that set not their heart aright, and whose spirit was not steadfast with God.

Isaiah 28:9-10 Whom shall he teach knowledge ? and whom shall he make to understand doctrine ? Them that are weaned from the milk, and drawn from the breasts. For precept must be upon precept, precept upon precept; line upon line, line upon line; here a little, and there a little.

Joel 1:3 Tell ye your children of it, and let your children tell their children, and their children another generation.

These scriptures do not tell us to train our children up in the latest Math, English, Spelling or

Science, but in the instruction of God's holy Word. The most important thing we can give our children in the way of education is a character that is formed from the Word of God. If our children have a character that reflects obedience to God's Word, our children will be able to succeed in Math, English, etc., but the emphasis should be on their character!

We are training our children to be the next generation of women and men of God. They are to be the next generation of vessels that will serve our Lord. It is up to us as parents to instill in them:

> 1) That God is our Ruler who we will obey.
> 2) That we will submit to Him and the Word of God.
> 3) That there is nothing else on this earth that will come above the first two.

Most of the generation of parents today were trained up by the Public Education System. We have no idea how to train our children as we ourselves were not homeschooled nor trained continuously. The big question many of us have is HOW ?

This curriculum is a step by step learning process that hopefully, will guide parents in forming Godly character in their children through the Word of God. It is intended to be used for any age group, with all the children participating together. If a child is to learn the Word of God starting at the age he is weaned, (Isaiah 28:9) then even a child of three can start learning to develop a Godly character based on the Bible. He might not have the concentration of a six year old, but if the Word says to teach them His Word from the time they are weaned, then this is what we should do!

This curriculum contains Daily Lessons that are easy to follow and understand. Each lesson will give you detailed instructions. There are also eight new PEARABLES Kingdom Stories that the children can be read that will reinforce each characteristic being taught. The only things you will need with this curriculum are:

> 1) A King James Bible (To go with the Strong's Concordance)
> 2) A dictionary
> 3) A Strong's Exhaustive Concordance of the Bible (Optional, as all the words and definitions are already listed.)

You can use this curriculum again and again. Each time you do, you will reinforce and solidify the Biblical characteristics that we, as Christians, all want our children to develop.

May the Lord richly bless you in your endeavor to serve Him and to train your children up in the way they should go!

A. B. Leaver & Friends
PEARABLES

PEARABLES
Doctrinal Statement of Faith

We believe in the One True God who loved the world so much that He sent His only Son to be sacrificed for our sins. That whoever believes in Jesus, His Son, may not perish but have everlasting life. We believe in the Holy Spirit who was given to us after Jesus was resurrected from the dead to be our Comforter and Teacher.

We believe that salvation is a free gift from God, and that only your believing makes you righteous. We believe that the Word of God is God's own Word and infallible. That we are to read the Word of God and obey His Word, not because this is what is going to GET us into heaven, but because we love God.

We believe that we are to go into all the world and preach the gospel of salvation, which is that all men are sinners and only through believing in Jesus Christ as God's Son and our Savior, will they enter into heaven, because only HIS blood cleanses us from all unrighteousness.

We believe that Jesus is returning someday and has prepared a place for those that love Him and we are to look to that day, for our redemption draws near!

We at PEARABLES, hope that you will realize that we are not perfect, nor claim to be near perfection, but hope that you will know that we are growing everyday with the help of God and His Word. Please feel free to come to us if you do not understand some of the teachings in this curriculum. We are trying to stay as narrow as possible in accordance to God's Word, but all of us are in a growing stage until He comes and we hope that you will be patient with us as we have not "attained" the full knowledge of God's TRUTH. If you find something that you feel is in error, please write us and we would be happy to respond. We want to always be open to Biblical Truth!

Love in Christ,

PEARABLES

"Whereby are given unto us exceeding great and precious promises; that by these ye might be partakers of the divine nature, having escaped the corruption that is in the world through lust. And beside this, giving all diligence, add to your faith virtue; and to virtue knowledge; and to knowledge temperance; and to temperance patience; and to patience godliness; and to godliness brotherly kindness; and to brotherly kindness charity. For if these things be in you, and abound, they make you that ye shall neither be barren nor unfruitful in the knowledge of our Lord Jesus Christ!"
-2 Peter 1:4-8

Lesson One
FAITH

READ: (Whenever READ is printed, ask the children that are old enough to read, to find the scripture and read it out loud for all to hear.) 2 Peter 1:4-8. ("Whereby are given unto us exceeding great and precious promises; that by these ye might be partakers of the divine nature, having escaped the corruption that is in the world though lust. And beside this, giving all diligence, add to your faith virtue; and to virtue knowledge; and to knowledge temperance; and to temperance patience; and to patience godliness; and to godliness brotherly kindness; and to brotherly kindness charity. For if these things be in you, and abound, they make you that ye shall neither be barren nor unfruitful in the knowledge of our Lord Jesus Christ.")

PARENT: We are going to learn what the Bible teaches us about faith, virtue, knowledge, temperance, patience, godliness, brotherly kindness, charity and diligence. The scripture says that if we have these things in us we will never be barren or unfruitful in the knowledge of our Lord Jesus Christ. Can you tell me what BARREN means?

DICTIONARY: BARREN

(Barren: 1. Not producing offspring; childless or fruitless. 2. Not producing vegetation, unproductive. 3. Unprofitable.)

PARENT: What will happen to us if we do not develop these things. We are going to start with the first thing listed in 2 Peter which is Faith. What is faith?

DICTIONARY: FAITH

(FAITH: 1. Confident belief in the truth, value, or trustworthiness of a person, idea, or thing. 2. Belief that does not rest on logical proof or material evidence; 3. Loyalty to a person or thing; allegiance; 4. Belief and trust in God and in the doctrines expressed in the Scriptures or other sacred works; religious conviction.)

PARENT: What are some characteristics of faith? (Belief, Loyalty, Trust, Allegiance, Conviction)

Have children read the following scriptures on Faith:

READ: Matthew 9:20-22

How many years did the woman have her disease in Matthew 9:20-22?
What did she say that showed an attribute of faith? (If I but touch his garment, I shall be whole.)
Which characteristics did she show? (Belief, trust, conviction)
What made her whole? (vs. 22)

READ: Matthew 9:27-30

What question did Jesus ask the blind men? (Matthew 9:28)
Which characteristic of faith did He talk about? (Believing.)
What did he say to the blind men when he touched them? (According to your faith be it unto you)
Did the blind men have faith? (Yes, for their eyes were opened.)

READ: Matthew 15:22-28

What was the matter with the woman in Matthew 15:22?
Why did Jesus not immediately help her? (Vs. 24 I am not sent but unto the lost sheep of the house of Israel.)
What did she say that made Jesus know she had faith? (Vs. 27 And she said, "Truth, Lord; yet the dogs eat of the crumbs which fall from their masters' table".)
What did Jesus praise her of? (Vs. 28 O woman, great is thy faith!!!)

ACTIVITY

Have the children pick one of the three stories about faith and have them draw a picture pertaining to it.

Lesson Two
FAITH
Faith in God... Who is God?

STRONG'S: Have children look up first the word FAITH that is listed in alphabetical order. Have them find the word FAITH listed in 2 Peter 1:5. Go to the right of the scripture and you will see a number. It is # 4102. Turn to the back of the Strong's and find the Greek Dictionary. Go to number 4102 and read: pistis; from 3982; persuasion, i.e. credence; conviction (of religious truth, or the truthfulness of God), espec. reliance upon Christ for salvation; constancy in such profession; assurance, belief, believe, faith, fidelity.

PARENT: Who are we to have faith in?... (God) Who gives faith? ... (God)

READ: Luke 17:5-6 And the apostles said unto the Lord, Increase our faith, and the Lord said, If ye had faith as a grain of mustard seed, ye might say unto this sycamore tree, Be thou plucked up by the root, and be thou planted in the sea; and it should obey you.

PARENT: Notice that the apostles asked Jesus to increase their faith. We must also ask Jesus to increase our faith. Have you lately been able to cast sycamore trees into the sea, just by telling it to do so? How much faith does it take to do this? (Faith the size of a mustard seed.) How much faith do you think we have now, what size? ... Do we need a lot of faith? Can we get this faith ourselves? (No, the Lord has to increase it.) Faith means to believe. What does it mean to believe something?

DICTIONARY: BELIEVE and BELIEF.

(BELIEVE: 1. To accept as true or real. 2. To have confidence in; trust.)

(BELIEF: 1. The mental act, condition, or habit of placing trust or confidence in a person or thing; FAITH.)

PARENT: We are to believe in God. We need to find out WHO it is that we believe in. What do we know about God? (Urge the children to think about WHO God is? What do they know about Him?)

READ: Genesis 1:26,27: We are made in the image (form) of God.
        Genesis 5:3   "
        1 Corinthians 11:7   "
        James 3:9   "

PARENT: God is so very wonderful. God is not a man. His ways are much higher than our ways.

READ: Numbers 23:19

PARENT: God does not change! Isn't this a wonderful thing? God will stay the same yesterday, today and forever! As this world changes for the worst, God will remain Holy and good.

READ: Malachi 3:16

PARENT: God is too wonderful for us to understand.

READ: 1 Kings 8:27
        Jeremiah 23:24

READ: John 4:23-24

PARENT: God is GOOD. God is righteous and true and everything that is Holy!

READ:
Psalms 25:8
Psalms 34:8
Psalms Psalm 86:5
Psalms 100:5

PARENT: God is LOVE.

READ: 1 John 4:8

PARENT: God and His ways are incomprehensible to our human minds. He is GOD, the One True God. In the Old Testament God was called "THE MOST HIGH". How wonderful that we serve the living God who is also FATHER to us!

Lesson Three
FAITH
God is King!

PARENT: Most of us have never been under the rule of a King. Here in America, we do not have a King but a President. We do not have someone that rules over us. What is a King?...

DICTIONARY: KING

(KING: 1. A male monarch. 2. One that is the most powerful or eminent of a particular group, category, or place. 3. God or Christ. (This is in the New American Heritage Dictionary!!!))

DICTIONARY: MONARCH

(MONARCH: 1. A sole and absolute ruler of a state. 2. A sovereign, such as a king or emperor. 3. One that presides over and rules.)

PARENT: God is a King. In fact, He is King of all the earth and universe.

READ:
Psalms 24:10
Psalms 29:10
Psalms 74:12
Psalms 95:3
Psalms 98:6
Psalms 145:11-13
Daniel 6:26
Malachi 1:14
1 Timothy 6:15-16

PARENT: God is the King of everything. Can you think of things that Kings do?... Kings rule over subjects. One word that tells what a king does is "reign".

DICTIONARY: REIGN
(1. The exercise of sovereign power, as by a monarch. 2. The term during which sovereignty is held. 3. Dominance or widespread influence.)

PARENT: You will find that Kings have certain laws that they make for the people in their Kingdom to obey. Our King, Our Heavenly Father, has laws and rules that He wrote down in the Bible for us to follow. We need to read the Bible and live by the rules which He tells us to obey. Jesus fulfilled the Laws that God gave to the children of Israel, but we are to still obey our King in that Jesus came and gave rules to follow for His Kingdom. They are written throughout the Bible. Legalism is a term applied to people who are trying to follow the Levitical Laws written in the Books of Exodus, Leviticus and Deuteronomy. Legalism is not when people are trying to obey Jesus' teachings and commands in the Word of God. We are commanded by our King to obey His teachings! Our God wants to be the King of our lives. We need to have faith that He is our King and let Him rule!

READ: Revelation 19:11-16

(I saw heaven opened, and behold a white horse; and He that sat upon him was called Faithful and True, and in righteousness He doth judge and make war. His eyes were as a flame of fire, and on His head were many crowns; and He had a name written, that no man knew, but He Himself. And He was clothed with a vesture dipped in blood; and His name is called The Word of God. And the armies which were in heaven followed Him upon white horses, clothed in fine linen, white and clean. And out of His mouth goeth a sharp sword, that with it He should smite the nations; and He shall rule them with a rod of iron; and He treadeth the winepress of the fierceness and wrath of Almighty God. He hath on His vesture and on His thigh a name written, KING OF KINGS, AND LORD OF LORDS.)

QUESTIONS

What is He wearing that makes you think He is a King? (Crowns)
What will He rule the nations with?
What is this King called? (Faithful and True.)
What is His name?
Are there armies in heaven?
Do people dress in heaven? In what?
What is Our King's clothing dipped in?
Who is King of Kings and Lord of Lords?
Who is the Word of God? (John 1, Jesus is the Word.)

ACTIVITY

Have the children each draw a picture of our Mighty King according to the description of the scripture.

Lesson Four
FAITH
Our Lord's Kingdom

PARENT: *God is a King! What or where is His Kingdom? . . . If we believe in God as our King, He must have a Kingdom. Let's see what the Bible says about this.*

READ: Matthew 3:2
          Matthew 4:17
          Matthew 10:7

STRONG'S: HAND in the above scriptures.

(The Greek number is 1448. To make near, approach, be at hand, come near, be (come, draw) nigh.)

PARENT: *Jesus was telling people that the Kingdom of Heaven was near! But where was His Kingdom? Many of the Jewish people of His day knew the scriptures about a Messiah or Savior coming to set up a Kingdom. They expected the Messiah to be coming with many armies and with power and great might. In our last lesson we read a scripture in Revelation 19:11-16. This sure does sound like our King coming in great power and glory! Isaiah 9:6-7 says: For unto us a child is born, unto us a son is given; and the government shall be upon His shoulder; and His name shall be called Wonderful, Counselor, The mighty God, The everlasting Father, The Prince of Peace. Of the increase of His government and peace there shall be no end, upon the throne of David, and upon His kingdom, to order it, and to establish it with judgment and with justice from henceforth even for ever. The zeal of the Lord of hosts will perform this. Also Jeremiah 23:5 says: Behold, the days will come, saith the Lord, that I will raise unto David a righteous Branch, and a King shall reign and prosper, and shall execute judgment and justice in the earth. In His days Judah shall be saved, and Israel shall* be called, THE LORD OUR RIGHTEOUSNESS.

They expected the Messiah to come and set up a Kingdom with great power and might, not like Jesus was doing. They had forgotten the scriptures that said He would come first as a lowly, humble servant. Zechariah 9:9 says: Rejoice greatly, O daughter of Zion; shout, O daughter of Jerusalem; behold, thy King cometh unto thee; He is just, and having salvation; lowly, and riding upon an ass, and upon a colt the foal of an ass. WHERE IS JESUS' KINGDOM, THEN?

READ: Luke 17:20-21
John 18:36

PARENT: The Kingdom of Heaven is within us. We are subjects of the King here on earth, even though His visible Kingdom is not yet here. We are ambassadors for Christ until He returns in all His glory!

STRONG'S: Heaven

(Greek # 3772. Ouranos; the sky; heaven (as the abode of God); by impl. happiness, power, eternity; spec. the Gospel (Christianity); air, heaven, sky.)

PARENT: After finding the definition of Heaven in the Strong's, you could also call God's Kingdom the Kingdom of the Gospel; or the Kingdom of God; or the Kingdom of Eternity! Can you think of some other names to rightly describe it?

READ: Revelation 21
Revelation 22:1-5

QUESTIONS

What will be on the new earth? (The holy city, the new Jerusalem, Rev. 21:2.)
What does it look like? (Rev. 21:11, It has the glory of God. The light of the city is like a jasper stone, clear as crystal. It has a wall, great and high, with twelve gates with the names of the twelve tribes of the children of Israel written on them. It has twelve foundations with the twelve apostles names on them. The city is pure gold, vs. 18. The foundations are garnished with all manner of precious stones.)
Is there a temple in the New Jerusalem? (Rev. 21:22 says NO, for the Lord God Almighty and the Lamb are the temple of it.)
Is there a sun or moon? (No, for the glory of God illuminates it.)

Lesson Five
FAITH
How To Enter the Kingdom of Heaven

PARENT: How are we going to be able to be in the Kingdom of Heaven? ... Can anyone get into heaven? ... I want to be able to have God as my King. What does the Bible say about entering into the Kingdom of heaven?

READ: Matthew 18:3-4
John 3:3-13
John 3:14-21

(And as Moses lifted up the serpent in the wilderness, even so must the Son of man be lifted up; That whosoever believeth in Him should not perish, but have eternal life. For God so loved the world, that He gave His only begotten Son, that whosoever believeth in Him should not perish, but have everlasting life. For God sent not His Son into the world to condemn the world; but that the world through Him might be saved. He that believeth on Him is not condemned; but he that believeth not is condemned already, because he hath not believed in the name of the only begotten Son of God.)

PARENT: Do you know what it means to

believe? (The dictionary definition was to accept as true or real or to have confidence in ... to trust.)

STRONG'S: BELIEVETH (The word used in the above scripture is Greek, 4100. To have faith, to entrust (espec. one's spiritual well-being to Christ); believe, COMMIT, put in trust with. It says it is from the root of 4102, which is FAITH.)

PARENT: According to what the word believeth here means, if you believe you also will commit yourself to that belief. One of the characteristics of faith is fidelity. What is fidelity?... That means you will be faithful to whom you believe in. If you believe in the Son of God, you will be loyal to Him. If you believe, you will give your allegiance, fealty, loyalty to Him and will be a devoted subject of the King of the Kingdom of Heaven!

READ: Mark 16:16
Acts 14:22
John 6:40-47
John 11:25-27
John 12:44-48

PARENT: 1 John 5 says: Whosoever believeth that Jesus is the Christ is born of God; and every one that loveth Him that begat loveth Him also that is begotten of Him. By this we know that we love the children of God, when we love God, and keep His commandments. For this is the love of God, that we keep His commandments; and His commandments are not grievous. For whatsoever is born of God overcometh the world; and this is the victory that overcometh the world, even our faith. Who is he that overcometh the world, but He that believeth that Jesus is the Son of God?

QUESTIONS

How do we become born of God or in other words, born again? (Believing Jesus is the Messiah or Christ.)
If we love Jesus, do we love God?
How do we love others? (When we love God and obey His Word.)
How do we love God? (By obeying His Word.)
If we love God, would we want to obey?
Would it be a sad thing to do?
How do we overcome the world? (Believing that Jesus is the Son of God.)
What does "overcometh the world" mean? (It means to subdue, conquer, prevail, get the victory!)

Lesson Six
FAITH
Loyalty

PARENT: To become a subject of the Kingdom of Heaven, what must we do? ... When we believe that Jesus is the Son of God, we have become subjects of the King of Heaven and earth, of God! We read that one of the characteristics of faith was loyalty. What does it mean to be loyal? ...

DICTIONARY: Loyal; Loyalty

(Loyal: 1. STEADFAST in allegiance to one's homeland, government, or KING!. 2. FAITHFUL to a person, ideal, or custom. 3. Of or PROFESSING loyalty.)

(Loyalty: 1. The state or quality of being loyal. 2. Feelings of devoted attachment and affection. 3. Fidelity.)

READ: Proverbs 24:21

PARENT: Does a person that is "given to change" seem loyal? ... We need to make sure that we are not given to change! This means that we are to remain loyal to God and stand fast in this.

READ: 2 Timothy 4:16-18

(At my first answer no man stood with me, but all men forsook me; I pray God that it may not be laid to their charge. Notwithstanding the Lord stood with me, and strengthened me; that by me the preaching might be fully known, and that all the Gentiles might hear; and I was delivered out of the mouth of the lion. And the Lord shall deliver me from every evil work, and will preserve me unto His heavenly Kingdom; to whom be glory for ever and ever. Amen.)

QUESTIONS

According to this scripture, did Paul have any believers with him that remained loyal? (Everyone forsook him, forsook meaning to leave him altogether, abandon, to desert him.)
Who remained loyal to Paul? (God stood with Him.)
It says that the Lord shall deliver him from every evil work ... do you think this shows again how God stood with Paul?
Was Paul a loyal subject to God, the King?
Is God loyal to His people?
Loyalty is a characteristic of God! Do we need to be loyal to Him?
Which is it more important to be loyal to... other people and friends, or to God?
If people you are around want to do something that would not please God, are you going to be loyal to God or go and do what the others are doing?
When no one is around, and temptation comes, who will see if you are loyal?
If being loyal is a characteristic of believing, if you believe will you be loyal? (We must learn to be loyal!)

ACTIVITIES

Sit with the children and ask them ways that they can be loyal to God. Then, ask them each to tell in what ways they HAVE been loyal in their lives.

⌘ ⌘ ⌘ ⌘

Lesson Seven
FAITH
Loyalty... Loving God

PARENT: We learned that one of the definitions of loyalty was to feel devoted affections or LOVE! You are loyal to someone because you believe in them... or love them.

We are to love God!

READ: Deuteronomy 10:12
Deuteronomy 13:3
Joshua 22:5
Psalms 31:23
Psalms 145:20
Mark 12:29-34

PARENT: How much are we to love God? ... According to the Word of God, we are to love Him with ALL our hearts, ALL our minds, and ALL our souls. Does this sound to you as if we are to be lukewarm in our love for God? ... God is demanding ALL of us. He wants us to be saturated in Him. He wants us to love Him with EVERYTHING in our being!

What would you say if someone told you you were taking the Bible and Christianity too far? Does that thought go along with Mark 12:29-34? Can you believe in God too much?

Every single bit of us is suppose to love God. ALL of each of us is to be committed to God!

STRONG'S: Love (Found in Mark 12:29-34)

(Love, Greek # 25; agapao: to love; beloved.)

DICTIONARY: Love

(1. An intense affectionate concern for another person. 2. To delight in. 3. To thrive on; need.)

READ: Romans 5:5
Romans 8:28
2 Thessalonians 3:5
Jude 21

PARENT: These scriptures also tell us to love God. If we love God, He will reign over our hearts and help us to be loyal subjects to Him. His Word tells us that everything will work together for good, to them that love Him. What do you think this means? ...

We are going to read some more scriptures that tell us about HOW we can love God. We can love Him by telling Him we love Him with our words. But there is more to loving someone than by just SAYING you love them. We also must love God through our actions. How we live our lives shows if we are loyal subjects or not. God commands us to love one another also. This is not just saying you love other Christians but to love them enough to speak the Truth in love! How much do you love someone if you know they are going to hell, and you don't tell them how they can enter into the Kingdom of Eternal Life? ...

READ: 1 John 2:3-5
1 John 2:15-16
1 John 3:16-24
1 John 4:16-21
1 John 5:1-4
2 John 5-6

QUESTIONS

What is the great commandment? (That we love one another)
What is the world's way of loving one another? (Not offending... Talk about the I'm OK, You're OK philosophy. There are no absolutes... love is relative ...)
What is God's way of loving one another? (You will obey God's Word. If we obey God's Word, the love of God is perfected in us. If we obey God's Word we will love each other!)
How do we love God? (1 Jn 5:2)
If we love the world and its things, do we love God? (1 Jn 2:15)
If we see other believers in need and do nothing about it, do we love God? (1Jn 3:17)
If I just say with my mouth that I love God and my actions don't show it, do I love Him? (This is called giving lip service.)

Lesson Eight
FAITH
Loyalty ... Being Steadfast

PARENT: As we are learning to be loyal subjects of our King, we are learning there are characteristics of being loyal. In the last lesson we learned that if you are loyal to God you will love God. What are some of the ways we can love God? ... Do you remember any of the characteristics of being loyal? Steadfast, faithful, professing loyalty. Feelings of devoted attachment. Fidelity.
The characteristic that we need to learn about today is being STEADFAST. What does this mean? ...

DICTIONARY: Steadfast

(1. Fixed or unchanging; steady. 2. Firmly loyal or constant; unswerving!)

READ: Daniel 6:26

PARENT: God is steadfast! He is steadfast in all that He does and He is loyal! We need to be steadfast to God. The following scriptures talk about us being steadfast.

READ: Psalms 78:6-8
1 Corinthians 15:58
Hebrews 3:12-14

PARENT: According to God's Word, we are to be steadfast in our Loyalty to Him and in our Believing in Him. God wants us to be firm in what we believe and unchanging.

READ: Matthew 25:31-46

(When the Son of man shall come in His glory, and all the holy angels with Him, then shall He sit upon the throne of His glory; and before Him shall be gathered all nations; and He shall separate them one from another, as a shepherd divideth his sheep from the goats; And He shall set the sheep on His right hand, but the goats on the left. Then shall the King say unto them on His right hand, Come, ye blessed of my Father, inherit the kingdom prepared for you from the foundation of the world; For I was an hungred, and ye gave Me meat; I was thirsty, and ye gave Me drink; I was a stranger, and ye took Me in; Naked, and ye clothed Me; I was sick and ye visited Me; I was in prison, and ye came unto Me. Then shall the righteous answer Him, saying, Lord, when saw we thee an hungred, and fed thee ? or thirsty, and gave thee drink ? When saw we thee a stranger, and took thee in ? or naked, and clothed thee ? Or when saw we thee sick, or in prison, and came unto thee ? And the King shall answer and say unto them, Verily I say unto you, Inasmuch as ye have done it unto one of the least of these my brethren, ye have done it unto Me. Then shall He say also unto them on the left hand, Depart from Me, ye cursed, into everlasting fire, prepared for the devil and his angels; For I was an hungred, and ye gave Me no meat; I was thirsty, and ye gave Me no drink; I was a stranger, and ye took Me not in; naked, and ye clothed Me not; sick, and in prison, and ye visited Me not. Then shall they also answer Him, saying, Lord, when saw we thee an hungred, or athirst, or a stranger, or naked, or sick, or in prison, and did not minister unto thee ? Then shall He answer them, saying, Verily I say unto you, Inasmuch as ye did it NOT to one of the least of these, ye did it not to me. And these shall go away into everlasting punishment; but the righteous into life eternal.)

QUESTIONS

What will our King say to His steadfast, loyal subjects? (MT 25:34)
Which animal does the Word liken those set on the right hand of our King? (Sheep)
What are the sheep; steadfast servants or disloyal ones?
Did these loyal servants only say that they were loyal?
What did they do for the least of our King's subjects?
Did the sheep KNOW that they had been doing these things to the Lord when they were doing it unto their brothers and sisters in Christ? (No!)
Why were they doing these things? (Because they were loving one another.)
What did the Word call those on the left?
Did they call the King "Lord"?
Was He really their Lord?
What will happen to the goats? (MT 25:46)
If we love God, will we want to take care of the least in the Kingdom of Heaven?
What does our King call the goats? (MT 25:41 ... Ye cursed)
Why are they cursed?

Lesson Nine
FAITH
Loyalty ... Faithfulness vs. Faithlessness

PARENT: In the last lesson we talked about being steadfast. Today we are going to read about Jesus' disciples.

READ: Matthew 26:32-35
Matthew 26:69-75

PARENT: According to these scriptures Peter denied the Lord three times. Was Peter faithful?

... The Bible talks about denying the Lord. When you deny someone you refuse to believe or refuse to recognize or acknowledge. Deny also means to disavow or disown.

READ: Matthew 10:32-33
        2 Timothy 2:12
        Titus 1:16
        Jude 4

PARENT: We see with these scriptures that we are not to deny Jesus either in word or in deed! We wouldn't be very faithful subjects if we did deny Him! What do you think happened to Peter then? According to Luke 22:31-34 it says: "And the Lord said, Simon, Simon, behold, Satan hath desired to have you, that he may sift you as wheat; But I have prayed for thee, that thy faith fail not; and when thou art converted, strengthen thy brethren. And he said unto Him, Lord, I am ready to go with thee, both into prison, and to death! And He said, I tell thee, Peter, the cock shall not crow this day, before that thou shalt thrice deny that thou knowest me..." According to Matthew 10:32-33 Jesus shall deny those who deny Him, but look at how Jesus knew this ahead of time and prayed for Peter. Jesus protected Peter from Satan so that he didn't lose his faith and after Peter was converted he strengthened the others! (Converted meaning turned about; revert).

READ: Matthew 17:16-18
        Mark 9:14-24
        Luke 9:40-41
        John 20:27

PARENT: Did you know that the opposite of faithless is believing? We need to ask the Lord to help us with our unbelief. He can help us to believe. Even the disciples had a hard time, and they walked and talked with Jesus. We need to learn to be steadfast and loyal and faithful to God. If we are first faithful to Him, we then have it in our characters to be faithful to men on earth. If we are faithful to God who sees us in our private times when no one else is looking, then it will be in our hearts to be faithful when others are. We won't be faithful BECAUSE people are looking, but because we LOVE God!

QUESTIONS

Does God see us in the dark? (Jeremiah 23:23-24 Yes!)
Does He know what we think? (1 Chr. 28:9 Yes!)
Will God know it if we are not faithful?
Why did Peter deny Jesus?
Do you think he was afraid of the soldiers and religious leaders, that they might come and get him also?
What does the Bible say Peter did when he realized what he had done? (Lk. 22:62 He wept bitterly.)
Are you going to try to never deny Jesus?
If we love Him, will we deny Him?
If we love Him, will we be faithful?

ACTIVITIES

Talk with the children about the sheep and goat scripture ... Ask them how the goats denied the Lord ...

Lesson Ten
FAITH
Loyalty ... Being Faithful

PARENT: Now we know that we are not to be faithless or deny the Lord! We need to know what the Bible says about being faithFUL. When you grow up and have a wife or husband of your own, you must know that you are to be faithful to them. This means that you will grow up and

Your eyes should only be for the one to whom you are married to. If you only look to YOUR mate, you will be called faithful! In the same way, we are to be faithful to God! If we love Him with ALL our hearts, ALL our souls, and ALL our minds we will be faithful to Him. We will not be UNfaithful by loving other things besides Him. When we love the world and the things in the world, we are not being faithful to God. Remember the Scripture we read that said: 1John 2:15 Love not the world, neither the things that are in the world. If any man love the world, the love of the Father is not in him. We need to be faithful to God first ... Then we can be faithful to others!

READ: Luke 12:34-48
        Luke 16:11-13
        Luke 19:12-27

PARENT: If we look at these scriptures in the light of those who were faithful and those who were not, we can see that the Lord is calling those servants GOOD who are faithful. The Lord also is rewarding those who are faithful in these scriptures! But, our hearts should not be wanting to be faithful for the reason that we GET something, but rather because we LOVE God. God will reward those of us who have been faithful. The Word tells us: 1 Corinthians 2:9 But as it is written, Eye hath not seen, nor ear heard, neither have entered into the heart of man, the things which God hath prepared for them that love him. But we cannot deceive God if our hearts do not love Him, and we are only doing things for a reward. I sure want to love Him, don't you?

READ: 1 Corinthians 4:1-2
        Ephesians 1:1
        Colossians 4:7-9

QUESTIONS

Are we all ministers of Christ? (Minister here means servant; a servant of Christ according to the Strong's. Yes! We are all called to be servants!)

Are we suppose to be faithful?
What does Paul call the believers in Eph. 1:1? (The faithful in Jesus.)
What did Paul call Tychicus and Onesimus? (Beloved and Faithful!)
How can we be faithful to God? ...

Lesson Eleven
FAITH
Trust ... Are We to Put our Trust in Men?

PARENT: What does it mean to trust someone? Is there anyone that you think you trust? Today we are going to learn about trust according to what the Bible tells us.

DICTIONARY: Trust
(1. Firm reliance on the integrity, ability, or character of a person or thing; confident belief; faith. 2. The person or thing in which confidence is placed. 3. Custody or care. 4. Something committed into the care of another. 5. The condition and resulting obligation of having confidence placed in one. 6. Reliance and assurance on something in the future; hope.)

PARENT: We are going to be learning this week about Trust, Confidence, Reliance, Assurance and Hope. The Bible is going to teach us that we are to put our trust in no man, but in God alone.

READ: Jeremiah 17:5-10
        2 Corinthians 1.9

PARENT: These scriptures tell us that we are to not trust in ANYONE but God! Men's hearts are deceitfully wicked and full of sin. This is why

God sent Jesus to die for us so that we could have a relationship with God the Father. We are so sinful that our sin separated us from God, but God loved us SO much that He gave His own son to die for us and to bridge the gap. Now if you believe in Jesus, God sees Jesus' blood that covers our wickedness and now we can come boldly before God. Not pridefully, but BOLDLY through the righteous one who is JESUS! This is what TRUST is all about! We should never trust men, but GOD.

STRONG'S: Trust (In Jer. 17, and 2 Cor. 1:9)

(Trust. Hebrew #982; To trust; be confident or sure; be bold (confident, secure, sure).
(Greek #3982; To convince; assent, rely, agree, assure, believe, have confidence, obey, persuade, trust, yield.)

PARENT: What do you think this means in regard to men? Do you think that people will let you down?... Do you think God will ever let us down? ... Can we trust God? According to the Bible, we are to trust God completely, but not men.

READ: Luke 18:9-14

QUESTIONS

What does the Bible have to say about people that trust in other men? (They are cursed. Jer. 17:5)
What does it say about those who trust in the Lord? (They are blessed!)
What does the Word of God have to say about people's hearts? (Jer.17:9 says that they are deceitfully wicked.)
Does God know the hearts of men? (Yes, but men can't. Jer. 17:9-10)
Does God reward people according to what they DO? (Yes, Jer.17:10 says, "I the Lord search the heart, I try the reins, even to give every man according to his ways, and according to the fruit of his doings.")
Does the Bible teach us to trust in ourselves? Can we trust OURSELVES? (2 Cor. 1:9 says No! For we had the sentence of death in ourselves!)
Who was the parable in Luke 18 spoken for? (Vs. 9 says Jesus said it to the religious which trusted in themselves that they were righteous, and despised others.)
What is a Pharisee? (It was a religious leader that knew the Bible very well but denied that Jesus was the Messiah.)
What was a publican? (Publicans were tax-gatherers and greatly despised amongst the religious leaders in Jesus' day. They were known to be great sinners, asking for more money for taxes than was due, and pocketing the excess.)
Are we to despise others?
If we do, are we a publican or a pharisee?
Which did Jesus say it is better to be? (Vs. 14 says: I tell you, this man went down to his house justified rather than the other; for every one that exalteth himself shall be abased; and he that humbleth himself shall be exalted.)

ACTIVITIES

Have the children illustrate for you what a publican looks like, and what a Pharisee looks like.

Lesson Twelve
FAITH
Trust ... In God!

PARENT: We are learning that we need to trust in God. But HOW much are we to trust in Him? Let's read the following scriptures and see what God's Word has to say about trusting Him.

READ: Proverbs 3:5-8

(Trust in the Lord with all thine heart; and lean not unto thine own understanding. In all thy ways acknowledge Him, and He shall direct thy paths. Be not wise in thine own eyes; fear the Lord, and depart from evil. It shall be health to thy navel, and marrow to thy bones.)

PARENT: According to this scripture, we are suppose to trust Him with ALL our hearts. We are not suppose to think that we have any right answers without God. This is the opposite of what the world is telling us today. The people who do not obey God believe that each person can decide for themselves what is right and wrong. They also believe that there is no REAL right or wrong, that it depends on the situation at hand. We, as Christians, know better than this. God's Word tells us what is right and wrong. If we learn to acknowledge God in all that we do, we will learn to do the right things, not wrong! We should pray and ask God to tell us always what He wants us to do. We also need to read the Bible to find out what He tells us to do.

READ: Proverbs 28:25
Proverbs 29:25
Proverbs 30:5
1 Timothy 4:10

PARENT: We have read that God will be a shield to us. If we trust in the Lord our God, He will take care of us. We need to remember that no matter what we will trust in God. We must never fear what men may do to us if we follow God, but rather what may happen if we DENY Him.

QUESTIONS

In Proverbs 28:25 it talks about something that stirs up strife, what is it? (A proud heart.) How does a proud heart stop someone from trusting in the Lord?
In Proverbs 29:25 what brings a snare? (The fear of man. Remember Matthew 10:28, "And fear not them which kill the body, but are not able to kill the soul; but rather fear him which is able to destroy both soul and body in hell.")
If we trust in the Lord will we be in danger? (No, we will be safe.)
What will God be to us? (He will be a shield, Prov. 30:5)
According to 1 Timothy 4:10, will we be liked by the world if we trust in the living God? (No, we will suffer reproach.)

READ: Daniel 3

ACTIVITY

Talk about how Shadrach, Meshach, and Abednego were not afraid of what men could do to them, but rather TRUSTED in God.

Lesson Thirteen
FAITH
Trust ... Confidence

PARENT: We are learning that we need to trust in God with ALL our hearts. Part of trust is having confidence in God. What does it mean to have confidence in someone?

DICTIONARY: Confidence

(1. Trust in a person or thing. 2. An intimate and trusting relationship. 3. Something confided, such as a secret. 4. A feeling of assurance or certainty.)

PARENT: Today we are living in a world that says Self-confidence is everything. All around us people are going to psychologists to learn how to have more confidence IN THEMSELVES! The problem is, they are wasting their time, because the Bible tells us this is foolishness. We are not to be confident in ourselves, but in God! We learned what the Bible says about Trusting in ourselves... The same thing goes for having confidence in ourselves.

READ:	Psalms 118:8-9
	Proverbs 25:19
	Philippians 3:3-4
	Philippians 3:12-13

PARENT: Even Paul did not have confidence in himself. His confidence was that he was reaching for the high calling of God in Christ Jesus! In Jesus we have our confidence.

READ:	Proverbs 3:25-26
	Proverbs 14:26
	Ephesians 3:11-12
	2 Thessalonians 3:3-4
	Hebrews 3:6;14
	Hebrews 10:32-39
	1 John 2:28

PARENT: We need to know that our confidence is in the FEAR of the Lord. Proverbs 1:7 says that the fear of the Lord is the beginning of knowledge; but fools despise wisdom and instruction. How will we understand what the fear of the Lord is? Proverbs 2:1-7 says: My son, if thou wilt receive my words, and hide my commandments with thee; so that thou incline thine ear unto wisdom, and apply thine heart to understanding; yea, if thou criest after knowledge, and liftest up thy voice for understanding; if thou seekest her as silver, and searchest for her as for hid treasures; THEN shalt thou understand the fear of the Lord and find the knowledge of God. For the Lord giveth wisdom; out of His mouth cometh knowledge and understanding. We will have confidence in God when we do what the Word of God tells us to do!

QUESTIONS

Shall we be afraid of sudden things that happen to us that make us fear? (No! God will be our confidence.)

Where is our confidence, according to Proverbs 14:26? (It is in the FEAR of the Lord.)

In whom do we have access to the Father? (Through Jesus, Eph. 3:11-12)

Again, who is our confidence in then? (In Jesus.)

The Lord is faithful ... What does the scripture in 2 Thessalonians tell us that God will do? (He will establish us, that means to grow us up in Him, and He will keep us from evil.)

Is it anything that we do that keeps us from evil? (We have to BELIEVE in Him, and He will do the rest!)

If we BELIEVE in Him, how are we to be CONFIDENT in God? (We must have confidence that He will do all the things He says He will do!)

In Hebrews 10:32-39, Paul was writing to the believers telling them not to lose their confidence. What happened to them? (They were a people of great reproach and afflictions in the world, and according to vs.34, lost many of their material goods.)

What does Paul encourage them not to do? (Not to go backwards into the world and its ways; vs. 38-39.)

How do you think you are going to feel when you are hated and afflicted because of your life for the Lord? (Remember that we are not to throw away our confidence in the Lord! But TRUST in God, even through the afflictions of this life!)

How may we have confidence? (1 John 2:28 says that we MUST abide in Him! Then we will not be ashamed when He comes.)

MEMORIZE
Proverbs 2:1-5

Lesson Fourteen
FAITH
Trust ... Reliance

PARENT: We are learning that we must ask God to develop in us Faith and all the attributes that go along with it. Yesterday, we learned that we were to only have confidence in God, not ourselves. Part of trust means to rely. We are to learn to rely on God for everything in our lives. Do you know what it means to RELY on someone? Let's look in the dictionary and find out what RELY means.

DICTIONARY: Rely

(Rely: 1. To depend. 2. To trust confidently. 3. Reckon.)

PARENT: If we rely on God, then we depend on Him. We will trust in Him CONFIDENTLY!

READ: 2 Chronicles 13:18
          2 Chronicles 16:7-8

PARENT: According to these scriptures, God knows EXACTLY if we are relying on Him or not! Those who rely on Him, God rewards. Can you imagine that people would rather rely on MEN than on God? ... Are we suppose to trust men? ... Who is our confidence suppose to be in? ...

READ: Psalms 27:1-5

(The Lord is my light and my salvation; whom shall I fear? The Lord is the strength of my life; and whom shall I be afraid? When the wicked, even mine enemies and my foes, came upon me to eat up my flesh, they stumbled and fell. Though a host should encamp against me, my heart shall not fear; though war should rise against me, in this will I be confident. One thing I desired of the Lord, that will I seek after; that I may dwell in the house of the Lord all the days of my life, to behold the beauty of the Lord, and to enquire in his temple. For in the time of trouble He shall hide me in his pavilion; in the secret of His tabernacle shall he hide me; He shall set me up upon a rock.)

PARENT: When we read the Scriptures here it says that we should fear NO ONE with God being the strength of our lives! If we love God we will only seek HIM all the days of our lives. We should not fear but have confidence in the Lord. We never know what the future brings, but there is a scripture that says: Those who desire to live godly in Christ Jesus WILL suffer persecution. If we are persecuted are we to FEAR those who persecute us? ... We must only FEAR God, never men. We must TRUST in the Lord with all our hearts, and not lean on our own understanding! We should know Psalms 27:1-5 very well. Then, when we are persecuted we can remember what the Word of God says about being CONFIDENT in Him!

READ: Daniel 6

QUESTIONS

In Daniel 6:3 it talks about Daniel's character. Why was Daniel preferred? (He had an excellent spirit.)
Vs. 4 gives more information about Daniel. What was he like? (He was FAITHFUL, and they could find no fault or error in him.)
How was Daniel persecuted?
What makes you KNOW that Daniel was "framed"? (Vs. 10-11, They gathered to find him praying and making supplication to God.)
According to vs. 16, did the king have faith? How?
What did God do for Daniel? (He sent an angel that shut the lions' mouth.)
What did God find in Daniel and the king? (Innocency.)
Did God save Daniel's persecutors from the mouths of the lions?
Why? (They were faithless and didn't BELIEVE in God!)
What does vs. 26 say God is? (He is the living God and He is STEADFAST!)
Did Daniel RELY on God?

Will God's kingdom ever be destroyed? (No! Vs. 26)
What does vs. 27 say God does? (He delivers and rescues, and He works signs and wonders in heaven and in earth!!!)

Lesson Fifteen
FAITH
Trust ... Hope

PARENT: Today we are going to be talking about hope. Hope is also a characteristic of Trust. What are some things that you hope? ... Do we hope that Jesus will return soon? ... Let's find out what the Bible says about hope ...

READ: Psalms 31:23-24
Psalms 33:18
Psalms 39:7
Psalms 42: 5,11
Psalms 71:5
Proverbs 10:28
Proverbs 14:32

PARENT: We are to hope in the Lord. According to the Strong's, this HOPE in the Hebrew means: 1. Flee for protection; to put trust, make refuge. 2. To wait in, to be patient, tarry, trust, wait. 3. Expectation, hope. 4. Expectancy; hope, live, thing that I long for! Let's read in the New Testament about HOPE.

READ: Acts 24:15
Romans 8:24-25
Romans 12:12
Romans 15:13
Colossians 1:4-5
Titus 2:12-13
Hebrews 6:11-20
1 Peter 3:15

1 John 3:2-3

PARENT: These scriptures show us that we are to have HOPE in the Lord and His Kingdom that is coming; in the resurrection into life after death; and the hope of the Lord returning! We have HOPE while the rest of the world has no hope. The rest of the world is fearful of something happening to their earthly bodies and have a terrible fear of their flesh dying, while we have HOPE that after this life we go on into living with the LORD!

STRONG'S: Hope

(Greek #1680; elpis; to anticipate with pleasure; expectation or confidence; faith; hope.)

QUESTIONS

In Acts, what is the scripture talking about in relation to hope? (That there shall be a resurrection of the dead, of both the just and unjust.)
According to Romans 8, what are we saved by? (We are saved by HOPE! This also means Belief, Faith!)
What do we rejoice in, in Ro. 12:12? (We rejoice in HOPE!)
What is God the God of? (The God of HOPE, Ro. 15:13)
What are we to abound in? (Hope! Ro. 15:13)
What is "that blessed hope" that is talked about in Titus 2:12-13? (The hope of eternal life! Tit.3:7 says: That being justified by His grace, we should be made heirs according to the hope of eternal life.)
Do we know what eternal life will be like for sure? (No, no one has ever gone on into eternal life and come back to tell us about it except Jesus. Jesus says that those who believe in Him will live forever in His Kingdom, so we know this is true, but we don't have knowledge of what will EXACTLY happen.)
In our hope, what are our lives suppose to be like?

Lesson Sixteen
FAITH
Allegiance

PARENT: Another characteristic of Faith is ALLEGIANCE. A few years ago, it use to be popular to say the pledge of allegiance in the public schools. It started, "I pledge allegiance to the flag, of the United States of America, and to the Republic for which it stands, One Nation, Under God, indivisible, with liberty and justice for all." What are they saying? ... That they promise to be loyal to the flag of America and to the Nation.

DICTIONARY: Allegiance

(1. Loyalty to a nation, sovereign, or cause. 2. The obligation of a vassal to his overlord. 3. Liege; fidelity. A subject owing allegiance and services to a lord. 4. Obligation to give such allegiance and services to a lord or monarch. 5. Loyalty.)

PARENT: Isn't this interesting? Part of Faith is that we become VASSALS to an overlord and to that lord we are obliged to give our allegiance and services! What does it mean to be a VASSAL?

DICTIONARY: Vassal and Vassalage
(Vassal: 1. A person who holds land from a feudal lord and receives protection in return for homage and allegiance. 2. One subject or subservient to another; a subordinate or dependent. 3. Servant.)

(Vassalage: 1. The condition of being a vassal. 2. The service, homage, and fealty required of a vassal. 3. A position of subordination or subjection; servitude.)

PARENT: Again, we are reminded that when we BELIEVE in Jesus we then step into a Kingdom! We become a vassal or subject of the King of Everything! We will give our service with our lives to the King. We will pledge allegiance to God!!!

READ

World Book Encyclopedia has this to say about VASSALS ... A man must first become a vassal. The ceremony by which he became a vassal was called homage. The future vassal promised to fight for the lord and became his man. The vassal promised to honor the Lord and in exchange the lord would take care of all his physical needs and honor his vassal. If either broke his promise, he was considered guilty of perfidy, a serious crime.

This is an example of ALLEGIANCE! In the same way, when we give God our total allegiance we will HONOR Him!

READ: Psalms 71:8
        Psalms 91:14-16
        Psalms 149:4-9

PARENT: We are to honour God, and isn't it surprising that He will honour us? These scriptures tell us that God honours men that are His! Just like the relationship between a vassal and his lord. We need to glorify God and honour Him because he is so wonderful and great. He doesn't like it when we do not honour Him as God above everything. We are going to read a story about a man that did not know that the Most High ruled in the kingdom of men but he certainly found out the hard way!

READ: Daniel 4

QUESTIONS

What did Daniel say would happen to the king? (Vs. 25-26)
Did it happen?
Why was this going to happen? (Vs. 25 So the king would know that God rules over all)
What did the king say that showed he was

prideful? (Vs. 30 Is not this great Babylon, that I have built for the house of the kingdom by the might of MY power, and for the HONOUR of MY majesty?!)
What happened to the king? (Vs. 30-33)
Did Nebuchadnezzar finally honour God?
What did he say? (vs. 37)
Does God want us to be prideful?
What does God think of pride? (Proverbs 16:5 says: Every one that is proud in heart is an abomination to the Lord; though hand join in hand, he shall not be unpunished. And Proverbs 16:18 says: Pride goeth before destruction, and an haughty spirit before a fall.)

❖❖❖❖❖❖❖

Lesson Seventeen
FAITH
Allegiance ... We are Servants!

PARENT: Did you know that we are to be servants to God? ... We are to let Him be our master, and we are to have no one else be our master but Jesus!

READ: Matthew 23:8-12

PARENT: According to this Scriptures, the greatest among all of us will be those who SERVE others! If we try to exalt ourselves we shall be abased or put down. If we humble ourselves we will be exalted by God. In the world, people who are famous or those who want to be the center of attention, probably will be exalted by men. There are many people who are famous in the world's entertainment, but do you think that God thinks they are important according to His Word's standards? ... Which do you think our Father thinks more of, people who humbly try to obey His Word and are meek and humble and are not famous in the world, but rather are hated by the world, ... or people who are exalted according to the world's standards but do not obey His Word? ... I think I'd rather be associated with the first type of people, wouldn't you?

READ: Psalms 113:1
Psalms 119:91
Psalms 134:1
Psalms 135:1
Isaiah 66:14
Romans 6:16-22
1 Corinthians 7:22
Philippians 1:1
1 Peter 2:16

PARENT: These scriptures show that we are indeed now servants of the Most High God and His Son, Jesus Christ! We are to learn to be His servants and develop a servant heart! But! There is something very important that we need to remember. Read the following scripture:

John 15:13-15 "Greater love hath no man than this, that a man lay down his life for his friends. Ye are my friends, if ye do whatsoever I command you. Henceforth I call you not servants; for the servant knoweth not what his lord doeth; but I have called you friends; for all things that I have heard of my Father I have made known unto you."

This scripture puts another aspect to being His servants. The disciples still called themselves servants in the scriptures we read above, but Jesus looks upon us in a much more loving way than servants. God calls those who love Him His children. Children are much closer to Him than servants! They are family. Maybe what the Word of God is telling us is that we are to be SERVING God! Don't we want to love one another enough that we can be SERVING each other in any way we can. When you willingly serve someone because of love and not because of money, we are again... LOYAL SUBJECTS of a King! Not servants,... but SUBJECTS that SERVE Him!!!

READ:
- Deuteronomy 6:13
- Psalm 2:11
- Psalm 100:2
- Matthew 4:10
- John 12:26
- Acts 27:23 (Please note that Paul is saying he serves God, not the angel.)

PARENT: It seems very clear that it was common knowledge that God's people were to serve Him. We need to develop an attitude of being servants to God and to His people. Remember the Scriptures about the sheep and the goats. The sheep were serving others whenever they visited the sick, or took in strangers, or in any way they helped other believers. Remember ... We need to learn to have the attitude of the sheep!

QUESTIONS

How can we be Jesus' friends? (By obeying His commandments.)
What is the difference of being servants and serving?
Are we God's servants?
Do we need to serve Him?
How do we serve Him?

ACTIVITIES

Have the children each make a list of things they can do to be helping others in their lives now ... , in the future ...

Lesson Eighteen
FAITH
Allegiance ... Being an Obedient Servant

PARENT: The Bible has some very interesting things to say about faithful, obedient servants and those servants who are unfaithful. Today we are going to study what the Bible says about DISOBEDIENCE.
What does it mean to be disobedient? ... Have you ever been disobedient? ... What happened when you were? ... We must learn to make it a HABIT to be obedient. First, we are to be obedient to God ... If you are obeying God, you will find that God tells children to also obey their parents. So if you obey God ... you will OBEY your parents!!! This is a commandment of God in His Word.

READ:
- Ephesians 2:2
- Ephesians 5:6
- Colossians 3:5-7
- 2 Timothy 3:2
- Titus 1:16
- 2 Thessalonians 1:8-9
- 1 Peter 2:7-8
- 1 Peter 4:17

PARENT: These scriptures talk about disobedience. What do you think about the scriptures that mention the "children of disobedience"? ... Who do you think they are talking about? ... We are to be children of OBEDIENCE, not disobedience. If we disobey God's Word, we are not being Loyal Subjects. We have not given him our allegiance then, have we? We also are not faithful servants.

Lets read some scriptures about those servants who are not faithful...

READ: Luke 19:12-26

QUESTIONS

In this scripture, which of these servants were faithful?
In what way were they faithful?
What did the Lord call the servant that was not faithful? (Thou wicked servant.)
Is it good to be faithful in a little?
What will happen if we are faithful in a little?

READ: Luke 16:1-13

QUESTIONS

Was it an honest thing that this steward did?
What is this steward called? (An unjust steward, vs. 8)
Was this steward unjust in much? (Yes. Read vs. 10)
Are we to be faithful in all the things we do each day?
What scripture makes us think this? (Vs.11)
Can we be serving both God and the world? (Vs. 13, NO!)
Do we have to make a decision which we will serve?

READ: Genesis 2 & 3
Romans 5:19

QUESTIONS

Were Adam and Eve obedient to God?
What happened to everyone because of their disobedience?
What did God tell Adam? (Gen. 2:16-17)
Who tempted Eve?
If other people tempt us to disobey God, should we listen to them?
Whose fault was it that Eve was disobedient? (Hers, she listened to the wicked advice of the serpent.)
Did Eve accept the blame? (No, she blamed the serpent.)
According to Romans 5:19, what happened to all men? (Many were made sinners.)
Because of Jesus, what can happen to all who believe in Him? (We can be made righteous.)
If you were Adam or Eve, do you think you would have eaten the fruit?

ACTIVITIES

Have the children illustrate the garden and what happened to Adam and Eve.

Lesson Nineteen
FAITH
Allegiance ... Obeying!

PARENT: We are learning to give our allegiance to our Father, God! In the last lesson we talked about disobedience. Because of disobedience, the Fall of all man-kind happened and we were made sinners. The Lord wants us to become obedient children. We are not born obedient, but we can LEARN to obey. Just like your parents want you to obey them, so does God, as your Father, want you to obey Him. We need to learn that no matter what anyone else around us is doing, we will try to obey God. Does what we do SAVE us? ... No, it is BELIEVING that saves us through God's grace. But those who believe, God will train them to obey Him, just like your parents are training you to obey them! To give our allegiance to God means that when He tells us to do something we will listen and Do what He says.

READ: Mark 1:27
Mark 4:41

PARENT: According to these scriptures, demons obey Jesus and so do the elements, such as the wind and sea. How much more should WE obey Him, when Jesus died for you and I?!!!

READ: Acts 5:29-32

PARENT: When we give our allegiance to God, we have decided to only let GOD rule us. Peter said in this scripture that we ought to obey God rather than men. We need to also follow their example and remember this. When anyone is telling us to do anything other than what the Word of God tells us, we must find out what God says to do and DO His will! This scripture also tells us that God gives His Holy Spirit to those that obey Him. The Holy Spirit will guide us and help us to know what God would will, through His Holy Word.

READ: Romans 2:7-9
Romans 6:17
Philippians 2:12
Hebrews 5:8-9
1 Peter 1:13-14

PARENT: In the scriptures, it is very clear that we need to learn to be obedient. God wants us to obey Him because in obedience is safety. It is like parents who yell "STOP!!" when they see their children in danger. Obedient children will immediately stop and will be safe. Disobedient children will continue on in what they are doing and will come to harm.

READ: Matthew 9:9

QUESTIONS

According to this scripture, did Matthew question Jesus when Jesus told Him to follow Him?
What happened to Matthew? (Matthew became one of the twelve disciples of Jesus.)
Was there any hesitation in Matthew to follow Jesus?
How can we be like Matthew?

READ: John 12:25-26

QUESTIONS

What does this scripture mean "He that loveth his life shall lose it; and he that hateth his life in this world shall keep it unto life eternal"?
Are we called, just like Matthew, to follow Jesus?
If we serve Him, are we following Him?
Will God honour those who serve Jesus?

READ: Genesis 6, 7, 8, & 9

ACTIVITIES

Discuss with the children the obedience of Noah in the midst of a perverse and disobedient generation.

Lesson Twenty
FAITH
Allegiance ... Being in Subjection to God

PARENT: We have been learning about obeying God. This is a very important part of our FAITH. Giving our allegiance to God is what we will do when we have FAITH in Him.
Today, we are going to learn what it means to be in subjection to God.

DICTIONARY: Subjection

(1. To subjugate 2. To submit for consideration. 3. To submit to the discipline or authority of; make amenable. 4. To render liable to something; expose. 5. To cause to experience or undergo.)

STRONG'S: Subjection

(Greek #5293; To subordinate; to obey; be under obedience, put under; subdue unto; be, make subject to; be put in subjection; submit self unto.)

PARENT: What do you think subjection means now? If we put this towards God, it means to obey or to be in obedience to Him, to be subject to God ... We could also say it means to be His loyal subjects, couldn't we? ... To submit ourselves unto God. There is a scripture which says, "It's no longer I that liveth, but Christ who liveth in me!" We need to be to the point where we know our Heavenly Father's will through His Word and His Spirit, that we will be in subjection to Him as much as possible!!

READ: 2 Corinthians 9:13
Hebrews 2:8
Hebrews 12:9

PARENT: According to these scriptures, we are to be in subjection to God. Another word that would describe what subjection means is SUBMIT, or SUBMISSION.

READ: Romans 10:3
James 4:7

PARENT: These scriptures point to submitting to God, but we are also suppose to submit to one another ...

READ: Ephesians 5:21
1 Peter 5:5

PARENT: In order to submit ourselves one to another, we must be HUMBLE. HUMILITY is a very important thing we must attain.
The opposite character trait of humility is pride. What do you think God thinks of PRIDE? ...
Let's read what His Word has to say about it.

READ: Proverbs 8:13
Proverbs 11:2

QUESTIONS

Does God like pride?
Is pride evil?
When pride comes, what comes with it? (Shame.)
What is with the lowly or humble? (Wisdom)

READ: Proverbs 13:10
Proverbs 16:18
Proverbs 29:23

QUESTIONS

What comes with pride? (Contention!)
With those who have much counsel or are well-advised comes what? (Wisdom!)
What comes after pride? (Destruction.)
What brings about a fall? (A haughty spirit!)
What will uphold the humble of spirit? (Honour.)

PARENT: Can a prideful person be in subjection to God? ... Does God like pride in men? ... We need to be of a humble and contrite spirit. Only a person that is humble can be in subjection to another. This would mean that you would have to put someone else's wishes above your own. This would be hard to do if you didn't love the one who you were submitting to. But, we love God more than ANYTHING and if you love someone, you will want to please them. Obeying God pleases Him!

Lesson Twenty One
FAITH
Allegiance ... Being Humble Servants

PARENT: What did we learn about PRIDE? The opposite of pride is ... ? Humility, being humble.

DICTIONARY: Humble

(1. Having or showing feelings of humility rather than of pride; aware of one's short comings; modest; meek. 2. Showing deferential respect. 3. Lacking high station; lowly; unpretentious.)

READ: Psalms 138:6
Psalms 147:6
Psalms 149:4
Proverbs 3:34
Proverbs 11:2
Proverbs 15:33
Proverbs 29:23
Isaiah 29:19
Isaiah 66:2
Matthew 11:29
Matthew 18:2-4
Matthew 23:12
Luke 14:10
Luke 22:24-27

PARENT: God really likes people to be lowly in their hearts. He wants us to be meek and humble. This way He can lead us and we can be His people. We then can be loyal subjects to Him. The danger of pride is that when pride is in your heart one thinks that HE can do everything HIMSELF. It is also exalting SELF rather than the Lord. Jesus was meek and lowly. He is our example and if the King of all Kings is meek and humble, what MORE that WE should be!

READ: John 13:14-17
Romans 12:3

PARENT: We are to think SOBERLY. What does this mean?

STRONG'S: Soberly

(Greek #4993, 4996; Moderately, with sound mind; self-controlled; sobriety; soberness.)

DICTIONARY: Sober

(1. Straightforward in character; serious or grave; sedate. 2. Plain or subdued. 3. Without frivolity, excess, exaggeration, or speculative imagination. 4. Rational.)

PARENT: Does this mean that we are to not be a happy people? Of course not! We are to have joy in the Lord! In fact, the Joy of the Lord is our STRENGTH!!!! We are not to think more highly than we ought. Again, if our Savior was meek and humble then so ought we to be.

READ: Exodus 3:1-14

QUESTIONS

What was the attitude of Moses when God told Him what to do? (Vs.11 says Moses asked, "Who am I?" He was of a humble attitude before God.)
How did Moses respond to God? (He listened to God with a humble spirit, ready to obey.)

READ: Exodus 4:1-19

Did it sound like the children of Israel were prideful? (Yes, vs. 1 says that Moses knew that they wouldn't even listen to him.)
What did God have to do to make them listen to Moses? (He had to do miracles, vs. 2-4)
What did Moses say to God that showed he was not prideful? (Vs. 10 Lord, O my Lord, I am not eloquent, neither heretofore, nor since thou hast spoken unto thy servant; but I am slow of speech, and of a slow tongue.)
Did he know his weaknesses? (It seems to appear so from this scripture.)

Why did God get angry with Moses? (He did not trust God enough to know that He could speak for Him.)

How can we learn from Moses? (That in our humbleness we need to depend on God to be our strength and trust Him. Moses depended on Aaron, a man, rather than fully trusting God to be with his mouth and teach for him.)

Lesson Twenty-Two
FAITH
Loyal Subjects ... Listening!

PARENT: We have been learning so many new things about FAITH! We learned that we are to believe, to be loyal to God, to trust God, and to give our allegiance to God. This is all part of FAITH! Today we are going to talk about being DUTIFUL. What is the difference between HEARING the Word of God and DOING the Word of God?

READ: Romans 10:16-17

PARENT: We must first HEAR the Word of God, for FAITH comes by HEARING! After hearing the Word of God, you BELIEVE!

READ: John 5:24
        Acts 18:8

PARENT: It is very important that we have a character that LISTENS! This act of listening is a very important part of entering into the Kingdom of God, for your FAITH comes by hearing! As you grow up and you live different experiences in the life of a BELIEVER, you will find that there are those who do NOT have ears to hear. This is a very sad thing. The Bible also talks about these types of souls.

READ: Matthew 13:13-15
        Luke 8:10
        Acts 28:27-27

PARENT: Isn't this a sad thing? The saddest thing about it is that the people Jesus and Paul are talking about are people that think they KNOW God. They are the leaders of the religious system of that time.

Remember reading Romans 10:2 that says: "For I bear them record that they have a zeal of God, but not according to knowledge. For they being ignorant of God's righteousness, and going about to establish their own righteousness, have not submitted themselves unto the righteousness of God."

It again comes down to HEARING God's Word and then becoming a DOER of His Word.

We need to look to our own selves that we stick to the Word of God! As you children grow up, the world will be becoming worse and worse, the Bible says, so you must become stronger and stronger in following God and His Word.

READ: Matthew 13:1-23

QUESTIONS

What happens when a person hears the Word of the Kingdom, but doesn't understand it? (Vs. 19, The wicked one comes and catches away what was sown in his heart.)

How does the person that received the seed in stony places react towards the Word? (Vs. 20, He HEARS the Word, and receives it with joy!)

What happens to the person in stony places? (Vs. 21, When tribulation or persecution comes because of God's Word, he falls away or becomes apostate, which is the Greek definition for offended.)

Why does this happen? (Because he has no root in himself.)

Does the seed among thorns receive the Word? (He HEARS it. Vs. 22)
But what happens to this person? (The world and riches choke the Word they have heard, and they become unfruitful or BARREN, vs. 22)
How did the world choke the Word? (The person cared for the world more than the Word they received.)
How did riches choke the Word? (Riches are deceitful, making one lust or desire worldly things. It's easier for a camel to go through the eye of a needle than for a rich man to enter into the Kingdom of Heaven.)
What happened to the seed that fell on good ground? (He HEARD the Word and UNDERSTOOD it!)
What does it mean to bear fruit?
Which seed do you want to be?
How can you try to become that?
What do you need to watch out for? (The perils that the other seeds found themselves in.)

Lesson Twenty-Three
FAITH
Allegiance ... Doing the Will of the Father

PARENT: What did we learn in the last lesson? ... We need to LISTEN to the Word of God. It is like the relationship with your parents. You need to listen to your parents so they can train you up in the way you should go. The next step is to DO what your parents say to do. This is the same with our Father, God! We need to listen to the Word of God and then we need to DO it. Today we are going to talk about being a DOER of the Word of God, not HEARERS only! This is the next step for being Loyal Subjects.

READ: Matthew 12:48-50
Mark 3:33-35
Luke 6:46-49
Luke 8:19-21

QUESTIONS

Who does Jesus call His family? (Those who DO the will of His Father.)
There are three steps in Luke 6:47? (1. You come to Jesus; 2. Hear His sayings; 3. Do what He says.)
What is a person likened to that does these three things? (Vs. 48; He built the foundation of his house on rock!)
What does Jesus say the second man does? (He hears but does not!)
What does Jesus liken this person to? (A man without a foundation built on dirt.)
What happened to the house this man built? (When the stream came against it, it IMMEDIATELY fell!)
How ruined was that house? (GREAT! Vs. 49.)

READ: John 9:31
John 12:24-26
Ephesians 6:6-8
1 John 3:22-24

QUESTIONS

If a man serves Jesus what is he suppose to do? (Follow Him!)
In 1 Jn 3, why do we receive of Him whatsoever we ask? (Vs. 22; because we keep His commandments.)
What else? (Because we DO those things that are pleasing in His sight.)
What is His commandment? (That we should BELIEVE on the name of Jesus and love one another.)
Who is the person that dwells in God and He in him? (Vs. 24 The person that keeps His commandments.)

READ: 1 John 5:1-5

QUESTIONS

How do we know that we love the children of God? (1Jn. 5:2; When we love God, and keep His commandments.)

Are God's commandments grievous? (Grievous means causing grief, pain, or anguish. The Word says NO, they are not.)

If we are born of God what do we overcome? (1Jn.5:4; the world.)

What is the victory that overcomes the world? (Vs. 5; our faith!!)

So our faith is the victory that overcomes the world?

Is FAITH a very important characteristic of a believer? (It is what decides between heaven and hell.)

Is it what we DO that gets us into heaven? (NO! It is our faith! If you have faith in God you will LOVE Him and want to do what He says.)

READ:	James 1:19-25

QUESTIONS

What are we to be swift to do? (Swift to hear.)
What things are we to be slow in doing? (Slow to speak, and slow to get angry; vs. 19.)
Why are we to be slow to anger or wrath? (Vs. 20; for man's anger works not the righteousness of God.)
What are we to lay apart or aside from us? (Vs.21)
If we were hearers only, what would we be doing to ourselves? (Vs.22; Deceiving our-selves.)
What example does the Word give? (Vs.23- 24 says he is a man looking into a mirror and when he walks away he forgets what type of a man he is.)
What are we NOT to be? (Vs.25; a forgetful hearer!)
What shall a DOER be? (Vs.25; Blessed in his DEED or in what he DOES!)

ACTIVITIES

Have each child give a practical example of DOING the Word of God, not HEARING it only.

Lesson Twenty-Four
FAITH
Conviction

PARENT: We are learning that FAITH is much more than simple head knowledge. It is loving the Lord our God with ALL our hearts, ALL our souls, and ALL our minds. We are to BELIEVE in God with our HEARTS. When we do this, the Lord will lead us into following Him as we live out the Kingdom of God! The Kingdom of God is within us, as WE are His subjects. What we need to learn is to be LOYAL SUBJECTS! Today we are going to study what CONVICTION means? Are you familiar with this word? ...

DICTIONARY: Conviction

(1. The act or process of finding or proving guilty. 2. The state of being convicted or so proved. 3. The act or process of convincing. 4. The state of being persuaded. 5. A fixed or strong belief. 6. Certainty.)

READ:	John 8:1-11

PARENT: According to this scripture, who was convicted? ... Let's look up in the Strong's what the meaning is in this context.

STRONG'S: Convicted

(Greek #1651; (This is the same Greek word used as the word CONVINCED!) To confute;

admonish; convict, convince, tell a fault; rebuke; reprove.)

PARENT: Back in the second lesson we learned that the Strong's definition of FAITH was ... ? Persuasion, credence; conviction; reliance upon Christ; Constancy; assurance; belief; fidelity. We need to know how this pertains to FAITH! The word, convicted, and its root are only mentioned in the Bible one time so let's find scriptures that have the word CONVINCED ...

READ: 1 Corinthians 14:24
             James 2:9
             Titus 1:9
             Jude 15

QUESTIONS

What is this word, convinced, used for? (It is to convince sinners of their ungodliness and need for salvation.)
So, before you are convinced you need a Savior, what must you be convinced of ? (Your sin and that you are guilty!)
So, first you must be convinced that you are guilty and then what do you do? (You have FAITH in Jesus to save you from your sins. You have been convicted or proven guilty!)

READ: 1 Corinthians 10:1-11

PARENT: According to the Strong's Concordance, the word convicted also means to admonish. It says in this scripture that the writings about Moses and the children of Israel are for our ADMONITION! To convict us if we are guilty of doing the same things they have done. They are examples for us to look at and learn what NOT to do and what to DO!

It talks about the children of Israel in vs. 5 being OVERTHROWN. Overthrown means to bring about the downfall or destruction of. The Word of God is written for our ADMONITION so that we can learn how to please our Father.

QUESTIONS

Was God pleased with many of the children of Israel? (Vs. 5; No.)
Why was He not pleased? (Because they were overthrown in the wilderness.)
Why were these scriptures our examples? (Vs.6; so that we should not lust after evil things as they lusted.)
What else were some of them? (Vs. 7; Some were idolaters: As it is written, "The people sat down to eat and drink, and rose up to play.)
What else did they do for us to learn from? (Vs. 8, Some committed fornication and the downfall in one day was 23,000 people.)
What did they do to Jesus? (Vs. 9; some of them tempted Jesus and were destroyed by serpents.)
Why were they destroyed by the destroyer? (Vs. 10; for murmuring!)
Why were all these things written? (Vs. 11.)

ACTIVITIES

READ: Numbers 14;25:1-9
             Exodus 32;
             Deuteronomy 32

❖❖❖❖❖❖

Lesson Twenty-Five
FAITH
Being Fully Persuaded ... Not Doubting!

PARENT: According to the Word of God we are to be convicted or admonished of our sins! When we BELIEVE in Jesus and confess our sins, He is faithful and just to FORGIVE us our sins and to cleanse us from all unrighteousness! We must be humble to admit to God when we make mistakes and sin! If we do not admit that we are wrong and have sinned, we had better look inside ourselves to see if we have an attitude of pride.

When we have faith in God, we will not DOUBT Him! Today we are going to read scriptures and find out what God says about DOUBTING. The opposite of FAITH is to DOUBT! If one does not have FAITH in God, He DOUBTS God or the belief in God. We must learn to be STEADFAST in our belief in God and be Loyal Subjects. A Loyal Subject does not doubt His King, but follows Him blindly, trusting Him.

READ: Matthew 8:23-26

QUESTIONS

What happened to the ship that Jesus and His disciples were in? (Vs.24; A great storm arose and the ship was covered with the waves.)
What did Jesus call His disciples? (Vs. 26; Ye of little faith.)
Why did He call them that? (Could it be because they doubted the Messiah? If they had really believed WHO He was, they wouldn't have been afraid.)
What did His disciples marvel at? (Vs.27; That the winds and the sea obeyed him.)
If they truly KNEW who He was and BELIEVED, would they have marveled?

READ: Matthew 14:22-33

QUESTIONS

What did Jesus tell His disciples to do? (Vs.22; to get into a ship and go ahead of Him to the other side while He sent the multitudes away.)
What did Jesus do that no one else had done before? (Vs.25; He walked on the sea when it had waves!)
What did the disciples think when they saw Him? (Vs.26; That it was a SPIRIT!)
How did they react? (Vs.26; They were afraid.)
How do you think YOU would react if you saw this?
What did Jesus do to try to calm them? (Vs.27; He told them that it was He; To be of good cheer; and not to be afraid.)
What did Peter say to test Him? (Vs.28; If it be You, tell me to come to you on the water.)
What did Jesus say? (Come on!)
Did Peter walk on the water to go to Jesus? (Vs.29; Yes!)
What happened to Peter? (Vs.30; He saw that the wind was strong and he became afraid.)
What happened when he became afraid? (He started to SINK!)
What did Peter do? (He cried unto the Lord saying, "LORD! SAVE ME!")
How did Jesus rescue him? (Vs.31; Jesus IMMEDIATELY stretched forth His hand and caught Him.)
How did Jesus ADMONISH Him? (Vs.31; O you of little faith, why did you doubt?)
When you doubt, do you have a lot of FAITH? (No, you have little faith.)

PARENT: We need to not doubt Jesus. It is very important that we learn to BELIEVE IN Him, and to BELIEVE what He says! We need to develop in our hearts a love and belief in God. We need to know that EVERYTHING and EVERYONE on earth might not always tell the truth, but you can ALWAYS trust God's Word. He has written in His Book all that He wants us to know and we need to read it to find out what that is. You can trust Him to fulfill His Word. If God tells us something, He will do it. God does not Lie, and we can TRUST Him! We can have FAITH in God because He is TRUTH! We need to learn to TRUST and have FAITH in Jesus and our Father God, through His Holy Spirit.

This is the last lesson on Faith. By God's grace, through FAITH, we can be SAVED. We must BELIEVE in our hearts; and then our hearts will want to learn to have characters of faithful, LOYAL subjects of the Kingdom of God. Remember we are serving a King! We are to be ruled by that King. We will trust Him, rely on Him, put our confidence in Him, put our hope in Him, give our allegiance to Him, and learn to become obedient, LOYAL subjects!

❖❖❖❖❖❖❖

Lesson Twenty-Six
FAITH
REVIEW

PARENT: We have finished with the lessons on FAITH. Today we are going to review some of the things we have learned. I am going to ask you questions, see if you can remember what we have talked about and if you can answer them.

QUESTIONS

What does BARREN mean? (Not producing offspring; unproductive; fruitless; unprofitable.)
What are we suppose to learn and if we don't learn this we will be barren? (2 Peter 1:4-8)
What is faith? (Confident belief in the truth, value, or trustworthiness of a person, idea, or thing. Loyalty to a person or thing; allegiance; religious conviction; etc.)
What are some characteristics of faith? (Belief, loyalty, trust, allegiance, conviction.)
Tell me some things you know about God ...
What is God? (He is a King ...)
If God is a King what does He do? (He reigns and rules.)
Where is the Kingdom of God?
How do you enter the Kingdom of God? (By believing in the only begotten Son of God.)
What do we need to learn to be when we enter God's Kingdom? (Loyal Subjects.)
How much are we to love our King? (With ALL our hearts, ALL our minds and ALL our souls.)
What does it mean to be steadfast? (Firmly loyal or constant; unswerving! Fixed or unchanging.)
Is God steadfast?

In the story of the sheep and the goats which were rewarded? (The sheep.)
Why were they rewarded? (Because they were faithful in their characters. They were not faithful because they would get something for being faithful.)

Who are some people in the Bible who trusted God?
How did they trust God?
Who is our confidence in? (God)
Are we to be confident in ourselves? (No!)

What does it mean to give our allegiance to something?
When you give your allegiance to God, what do you pledge? (Your obedience.)
Are we to obey God? (Yes, the Bible says to.)

What does God think of pride? (It is an abomination to Him.)
What should we develop? (Humility; Humble spirits.)
If we are prideful is it easy to obey God?
What do we need to learn to be? (Humble servants.)

What is the difference between being a DOER of the Word of God and a HEARER only?
In the parable of the house built on a foundation, which house stood? (That which had a FIRM foundation on ROCK.)
What did this man do? (He came to Jesus; heard His sayings; and did what He said to do.)
What did the other man build his house on? (Dirt or sand.)
What happens to him? (His house FELL!)
Why did it fall? (Because he hears but does not.)

How do we LOVE the children of God? (by obeying God's commands.)
What does CONVICTION mean? (It means to prove guilty and also to BELIEVE something STRONGLY.)
What is the opposite of FAITH? (Doubt.)
What must we do? (Have FAITH!)

Faith

There was once a country that claimed to be inhabited by the most intelligent people in all the world. The people of this land prided themselves in the knowledge that they sought out. They believed that the most important thing a person could find was knowledge.

They saw the stars in the sky and made telescopes so they could see them and study them and found out many things about the stars.

They saw the mountains and wanted to know why they were there so they studied the earth and how it shifted and moved over time, and discovered how the mountains were formed.

They saw the miracle of birth and wanted to know how babies were created, so they made instruments that could see the stages of development of a child in its mother's womb.

One day, an old man came to tell them that they also had something they couldn't see or study with their minds. They wouldn't be able to look at it through a microscope or record it on film. They wouldn't be able to dissect it or have it for an exhibit.

"You each have a spirit!" he told them.

They scratched their heads, thinking, could this possibly be true? But if you can't see it, touch it, or study it, could it be real?

But the man went on, "You each have a spirit and when you die you will be judged for all the wrong you have done by a great King, who is also a spirit. But, this Mighty King sent a Son to Die for your wrong and all you have to do is believe in that Son and you can live forever!"

The intelligent people knew for sure that there was absolutely no way to prove that after one was dead you would be judged by a King you couldn't see... And then, you were suppose to believe in His Son, who also couldn't be seen, to live forever!!! ... which everyone knew was an impossibility!!!

Many shook their heads in disbelief and demanded, "Give us some proof!"

And the man shook his head. "No, you must only believe."

The most intelligent turned their backs on the man and went back to their laboratories to study their newest research that they could see, touch and study!

The man continued talking to those who remained, "All you have to do is believe in your hearts and say that you believe in the King's Son and you will live forever!"

There were many who thought that they had heard enough from the old man, and just so they would stop being bothered said "There might be a king," and walked away. They were so used to thinking with their heads that they just couldn't bring themselves to believe in their hearts.

The minute they walked away, they started doubting. After all, they couldn't see, touch or study any of what the old man said, so they couldn't prove this was true.

After they were gone, the man looked down to see who was remaining. There, sitting quietly at his feet, was a little child.

"I believe!!" the little child joyfullly stated. "I believe that there is a king, and I believe in His Son!! I believe that I have a spirit and when I die my spirit wil live forever!! I believe!"

The old man laid his hand tenderly on theboy's shoulder and asked, "My son, have you started school yet?"

The little boy shook his head.

The old man reached into a worn leather bag and handed him an old, used, black book that contained the Words of the King and said, "Here is your education. This is all you will need to ever know. You can see it, you can touch it, and best of all, you can study it."

The little child took the book, and with his faith, went on to become the most intelligent in all the land.

Lesson One
VIRTUE

PARENT: The next characteristic we are to develop in 2 Peter 1:4-8 is VIRTUE. Do any of you know what VIRTUE is?

DICTIONARY: Virtue

(1. The quality of moral excellence, righteousness, and responsibility; probity; goodness. 2. Conformity to standard morality or mores. 3. Effective force or power; efficacy. 4. Manly courage; valor.)

PARENT: What we are going to study are the characteristics of virtue and hopefully, we can develop virtue ourselves, with the help of the Holy Spirit! We are going to study moral excellence, righteousness; goodness; power; and courage!

STRONG'S: Virtue (In 2 Peter)

(Greek #703; manliness; VALOR; excellence; praise; virtue.)

STRONG'S: Virtue (In Mark 5:30)

(Greek #1411; force; miraculous power, mighty deed; worker of miracles; power, strength, mighty work.)

STRONG'S: Virtuous (In Prov. 12:4)

(Hebrews #2428; a force, army, wealth, virtue, valor, strength, able.)

READ: Ruth 3:11
        Proverbs 12:4

QUESTIONS

What does the scripture say Ruth was? (Vs. 11 says she was a virtuous woman.)
How many people knew Ruth to be a virtuous woman? (All the city of Boaz' people knew this.)
According to Proverbs 12:4, what is a virtuous woman to her husband? (She is a crown to her husband.)
What does it say the opposite of being a virtuous wife is in this scripture? (One who makes her husband ashamed.)

READ: Mark 5:30
        Luke 6:19
        Luke 8:46

QUESTIONS

What did Jesus know had gone out of Him? (Virtue.)
In Luke 6, what went out of Jesus and healed the whole multitude that sought to touch Him? (Virtue.)
Does this sound like the same virtue that is talked about in Ruth and Proverbs? (No, it is a totally different thing. The same word, but two different meanings.)
What is this virtue talking about? (This virtue is talking about miraculous power!)

READ: Philippians 4:8
        2 Peter 1:3

What does virtue contain in Philippians 4:8? (Truth, honesty, justness, purity, loveliness, good reports.)
According to 2 Peter 1:3, what are we called to? (Glory and VIRTUE.)
What is Strong's definition of this VIRTUE in 2 Peter 1:3? (Greek #703; manliness; valor; excellence; praise; virtue.)

PARENT: According to the Bible, virtue has quite a few different meanings. Since we are required to develop virtue, we are going to study what the Bible has to say about most of the characteristics of virtue. Virtue has been defined as VALOR. Do you know what VALOR is?

DICTIONARY: Valor

(1. Courage and boldness. 2. Bravery. 3. To be strong.)

PARENT: Isn't this another interesting aspect of VIRTUE? It also means to be bold, brave or courageous. Do you think we are all these things? We might not be yet, but we can sure try to learn to develop these things with God's help. Tomorrow we are going to learn what made a virtuous woman virtuous. We are going to study the Proverbs 31 woman and see what qualities she had. This will be good for the girls to learn to grow into virtuous women and for the boys to know what characteristics to look for in a future bride.

Lesson Two
VIRTUE
The Virtuous Woman

PARENT: This is one of the most important chapters that a young girl can learn. In today's society we have been trained that there is no difference between men and women. We need to get back to the Word of God and find out what the Bible says women are to be. Girls need to be studying all Scripture that pertains to women, and the boys need to be seeing what Godly men are to be doing. It is important for boys to know what virtuous women are, so they will be able to find godly wives.

READ: Proverbs 31:10-15

QUESTIONS

How much is a virtuous woman worth? (Vs. 10; her worth is far above rubies.)
According to vs. 11, how does her husband feel about her? (He TRUSTS her! In fact he can SAFELY trust in her.)
How does this woman treat her husband? (Vs. 12; She does him GOOD all the days of her life. She does not do EVIL to him. She does GOOD.)
Is this woman making things with her hands? (According to vs. 13, she spins and knits.)
Does she feed her family? (Yes, vs. 14 says she brings her food from afar.)
Does this woman love to sleep in? (No, she rises while it is still dark out to get food ready for everyone to eat.)

READ: Proverbs 31:16-20

QUESTIONS

Does the virtuous woman grow food? (Vs. 16 says she buys the land and then plants a vineyard.)
Does it sound like this woman is weak and lazy? (No! Vs.17.)
According to vs.18 is she careful with what she buys? (Yes, she sees that what she buys is good. She does not buy cheap oil that burns quickly and would leave the family in darkness at night.)
What proves that she is busy making cloth? (Vs. 19; a spindle is a notched stick for spinning fibers into thread by hand. It is also used for holding a bobbin upon which yarn is wound on a spinning wheel. A distaff is a staff that holds on its cleft end the unspun flax, wool or tow from which thread is drawn in spinning by hand.)
Besides the needs of her own family, who does this woman take time for? (Vs. 20, the poor and needy.)

READ: Proverbs 31:21-25

QUESTIONS

Is the virtuous woman afraid for the cold weather and snow to come? (No.)
Why not? (Because they are all clothed with scarlet or double garments. The original

Hebrew uses the word shenayim, which means DOUBLE garments.)
Does she make her own clothing? (Yes.)
Is her husband in a place of respect? (Yes, he sits amongst the elders of the land.)
Is he a man of bad reputation? (No, he is known in the gates as an elder.)

READ: Proverbs 31:26-31

QUESTIONS

When this woman speaks what comes out? (Vs. 26, wisdom.)
What is in her tongue? (The law of kindness, vs. 26.)
Is she self-centered? (No, she looks WELL to the ways of her household, vs. 27.)
Does she ever have NOTHING to do? (No, she is not IDLE.)
What is idleness? (Being inactive, avoiding work, lazy, to pass time avoiding work.)
What do her children call her? (Blessed.)
What does her husband have to say about her? (He has praises to say about her.)
What is favour? (It is deceitful, favour being here objective beauty or finding favour.)
What is beauty? (It is vain! Meaning lacking substance or worth. Hollow, shallow. No use or purpose for.)
Who should be praised, a woman that is favoured or beautiful? (No! A woman that FEARS THE LORD.)

PARENT: Can you think of some characteristics that make up this virtuous woman? ... She does good, she gives of herself to others, she fears the Lord, speaks wisdom and kindness, she takes care of her family. These are just a few of the things that make this woman virtuous. We need to all learn to be virtuous in these ways, even the boys!

ACTIVITIES

Have all the children draw a picture of the virtuous woman.

Lesson Three
VIRTUE
Ruth ... Known for her VIRTUE!

PARENT: We learned yesterday many things that the Bible has to say about a virtuous woman. Another virtuous woman mentioned in the Bible is Ruth. We read that she was known throughout the city as a virtuous woman. What did she do that she was known for such a reputation? Let's read the Book of Ruth and find out!

READ: Ruth 1:1-22

QUESTIONS

When Ruth's husband died where did her mother-in-law want her to go? (Vs. 8; to her mother's house.)
What did Orpah do? (She kissed her mother-in-law and left.)
What did Ruth do? (Ruth clave unto her.)
How was Ruth faithful to her mother-in-law?
What characteristic does vs. 18 call Ruth? (Steadfast.)
What happened when Ruth and Naomi reached Bethlehem? (The people came and recognized Naomi.)

READ: Ruth 2:1-23

QUESTIONS

Does Ruth seem slothful and idle? (No! Vs. 2 says Ruth suggested that she go and glean corn in Boaz' fields.)
Why did Boaz react so generously to Ruth? (Vs. 11, because he had heard how she had left everything that was familiar to her to faithfully remain with Naomi.)
What makes us know that Ruth had come to serve God? (Vs. 12 says the Lord recompense thy work, and a full reward be given thee of the Lord God of Israel, under whose wings thou art come to trust.)
What type of man was Boaz? (He was of the

Lord, vs. 20, and was kind.)
How was Ruth obedient? (Vs. 21-23.)

READ: Ruth 3:1-4

QUESTIONS

What did Naomi want Ruth to do? (Go in and keep Boaz' FEET warm.)
Was Ruth obedient to Naomi? (Yes.)
What did Boaz call Ruth? (Vs. 10, kind and virtuous.)
What did Boaz do to reward Ruth for her kindness? (He received her as family and gave her a family's share of barley.)

READ: Ruth 4:1-22

QUESTIONS

Was Boaz sitting amongst the elders of the city as was the husband of the virtuous woman? (Yes, vs. 1, 2.)
Did he act faithfully according to the laws of inheritance among kinspeople?
What happened to Ruth? (She married Boaz and had a beautiful baby boy!)
How was Ruth praised? (Vs. 15, that she was better to Naomi than seven sons!)
How was Naomi blessed? (She became nurse to Ruth's baby.)
What was the name of this baby? (Obed.)
Who was he? (The GRANDFATHER of DAVID the king!)
Who was Ruth? (She was the great-grandmother of DAVID!)

PARENT: Do you see some similarities between Ruth and the description of the virtuous woman? We need to be good, kind, faithful, trustworthy, obedient ... can you think of some other characteristics shown?

❦❦❦❦❦❦❦

Lesson Four
VIRTUE
Righteousness ... God's

PARENT: As we start to talk about righteousness, it is very important to remember that no one is GOOD except God. If we were all GOOD our Father would not have had to send His only Son to die for us. We cannot be saved by our own righteousness, but through God's gift of grace through FAITH ... What we need to find out is what this part of VIRTUE is. We read that an attribute of VIRTUE was RIGHTEOUSNESS. We need to know what the Bible says we need to develop in ourselves in this area. First, we are going to study about God's righteousness. We have learned many things about God and what an AWESOME, powerful King He is. Let's find out more about His righteousness ...

READ: Psalms 119:7
        Psalms 119:62
        Psalms 119:106
        Psalms 119:160
        Psalms 119:164
        2 Thessalonians 1:5
        2 Timothy 4:8
        Revelation 16:7
        Revelation 19:2

QUESTIONS

In Psalms 119, what does the author say he has learned? (God's righteous judgments.)
Should we also learn God's righteous judgments?
What are we to do according to Psalms 119:62? (Give thanks for His righteous judgments.)
According to 2 Timothy, what will God as the righteous judge give to those who love His appearing? (A crown of righteousness!)
According to Rev. 16:7, besides being righteous, what else are God's judgments? (TRUE!)

PARENT: If we love God, we will want to please Him. The following scriptures are those which tell us that God loves righteousness.

READ: Psalms 11:7
Psalms 5:12
Psalms 58:11
Psalms 146:8
Hebrews 1:8-9

PARENT: Now we know that God is righteous, everything He does is righteous, and He LOVES righteousness! If our Father loves us to do something we should be studying HOW to please Him. If God wants us to have VIRTUE, and a part of VIRTUE is RIGHTEOUSNESS, we had better continue on in finding out what the Word has to say about this...

❈❈❈❈❈❈

Lesson Five
VIRTUE
Righteousness ... God's Righteous Ones

PARENT: We are learning to follow the King of ALL and we are finding out many different things about Him. What did we learn about God in the last lesson? ... God is a RIGHTEOUS God and everything that He does is RIGHTEOUS. Did you know that in the Bible God calls certain people RIGHTEOUS? I sure want to find out more about these people, don't you?

READ: Psalms 1:5,6
Psalms 32:11
Psalms 34:15-21
Psalms 97:12

QUESTIONS

According to the first scripture, what is the opposite of righteous? (The ungodly.)
According to Psalms 32:11, what else are the righteous called? (Those who are upright in heart.)
What are the righteous to do? (Be glad in the Lord, and rejoice, shout for joy!)
In Psalms 34, what do the eyes of the Lord look upon? (The righteous.)
What does He hear? (Vs. 15, His ears are open to their cry.)
According to vs. 18, who is the Lord near to? (He is near to them of a broken heart.)
Who will He save? (Those of a contrite spirit.)
What is a contrite spirit? (Contrite means humbled by guilt and repentant for one's sins.)
What will the Lord redeem? (Vs. 22, the soul of His servants.)
What will happen to them that trust in God? (They will not be desolate, vs. 22.)

STRONGS: Righteous

(Hebrew #6662, 6663; to be right, in a moral sense, to do justice, lawful, cleanse, clear self.)

PARENT: Can we say that a righteous person tries to do what is right? ... A righteous person would do the Word, not just HEAR it, don't you think? Do you think a righteous person then is someone who does right according to God?

READ: Romans 3:10-31

QUESTIONS

Is there a righteous person? (The Bible says NO! not one.)
Who is the Word talking about then when it calls some RIGHTEOUS? (Those who BELIEVE.)
Are there any people that do good on their own? (NO!)

Why was the law of God given? (To show all the world that it is GUILTY before God.)
What is the law for? (Vs. 20, by the law is the knowledge of sin.)
What is the righteousness of God? (Vs. 22 says: Even the righteousness of God which is by faith of Jesus Christ unto all and upon all them that believe; for there is no difference.)
How are men justified or made righteous? (Freely! by His grace through the redemption that is in Christ Jesus. All we have to do is BELIEVE and we are the RIGHTEOUS!)
What did Jesus do for us? (Vs. 25, God set forth Jesus to be an offering THROUGH FAITH in His blood, to declare HIS righteousness for the passing over of our sins that are past. In simple terms, BELIEVING in Jesus cleanses us and makes us RIGHTEOUS!)
Are we righteous by what we do? (No! By faith!)
Do we not obey His Word then? (Vs. 31, no, we need to find out what God wants us to do and do it with ALL our hearts!)

PARENT: So the righteous are not righteous by what they DO, but rather by what they BELIEVE! We also need to remember that those who BELIEVE would not want to throw out the scriptures and just do whatever THEY want to do. Those who believe will NOT just HEAR the Word of God, but DO the Word of God. They would not love the Lord their God with PART of their hearts, PART of their souls, and PART of their minds, would they? No, they would love the Lord their God with ALL their hearts, ALL their souls, and ALL their minds. They will want to read His precious Words and find out what He wills as KING!

ACTIVITIES
Review with the children the attributes of FAITH.

❈❈❈❈❈❈❈

Lesson Six
VIRTUE

Righteousness ... What the Righteous DO

PARENT: Are the righteous, righteous because of what they DO? ... Remember in the last lesson we learned that what makes a person righteous is because they BELIEVE in our Lord! But once they BELIEVE they become RIGHTEOUS through Jesus Christ, the RIGHTEOUS! So, a person becomes RIGHTEOUS through BELIEVING or FAITH. But once a person becomes righteous, WHAT does that righteous person DO?

READ: Proverbs 10:11
            Proverbs 10:21
            Proverbs 10:32

QUESTIONS

What comes out of a righteous man's mouth? (Pr. 10:11 says the mouth of a righteous man is a WELL of LIFE.)
What else does Pr. 10 have to say about his speech? (Vs. 21 says that it FEEDS many.)
In the same verse, why do fools die? (For want of wisdom.)
In vs. 32, how else do the righteous know how to speak? (They know what is acceptable.)
Should we learn to speak acceptable things that give LIFE and FEED?

READ: Proverbs 12:7
            Proverbs 12:10
            Proverbs 12:12
            Proverbs 12:26
            Proverbs 12:28

QUESTIONS

In vs. 7, who will be overthrown? (The wicked.)
What will happen to the house of the righteous? (It will stand.)

How does a righteous man treat his livestock or animals? (He takes care of them, vs. 10.)
What do the wicked do to theirs? (They are cruel to them.)
We are learning not to be BARREN, what does vs. 12 say the righteous do? (They yield fruit!)
What do the righteous need to be careful of? (Vs. 26 says that the way of the wicked can seduce.)
What is in the way of righteousness? (Vs. 28 says LIFE.)
Does this go along with Proverbs 10 where it says the righteous speak LIFE?

READ: Proverbs 13:5
       Proverbs 13:9
       Proverbs 13:21
       Proverbs 13:25

QUESTIONS

What does a righteous man HATE? (Vs. 5 says he hates lying.)
What pursues (chases) sinners? (Evil.)
Do we sin? (Yes, but a righteous man does not LOVE to sin. It makes a person who loves God sad when he does sin, and he asks God for forgiveness with a repentant heart.)
What makes us righteous? (Believing in Jesus.)
Shall the righteous starve? (No. Remember that man does not live by bread alone, but by the Word of God.)

READ: Proverbs 14:9
       Proverbs 15:6
       Proverbs 15:19
       Proverbs 15:28
       Proverbs 15:29

QUESTIONS

What do fools do? (They mock, meaning to imitate, sin.)
Do the righteous?
Does the house of the righteous have treasure? (Pr. 15:6)
If a virtuous woman's worth is far above rubies, does this necessarily mean earthly treasure? (No, for wisdom of God is worth far more than gold or silver, the Bible says.)
Is a righteous man slothful or lazy? (No, vs. 19 says he is not. A lazy man is too lazy to even weed his path, but the righteous' way is made plain.)
Does the righteous speak quickly without thought? (No, vs. 28 says he thinks before he answers. Remember the vs. we learned that said to be quick to hear, slow to speak and slow to anger, James 1:19.)
Is the Lord near to the wicked? (Vs. 29 says He is far from the wicked.)
Whose prayers does He hear? (The prayers of the righteous.)
What MAKES a person righteous? (What they believe, not what they do.)

PARENT: When we BELIEVE in Jesus we become righteous only through Him. But after we BELIEVE we have the honour of having the title of RIGHTEOUS. What we need to do next is find out more of what God says the RIGHTEOUS DO. We must try to do these things. The way we find out what God wants us to do is by reading His Word. The more we read it, the more we will know it and then we know what to DO!

※※※※※※

Lesson Seven
VIRTUE
Righteousness ... More of What the Righteous Do

PARENT: We are learning about what those who BELIEVE in our Lord Jesus are to do. The Book of Proverbs has many things to say about the righteous. It also tells us what the righteous do and what they don't do. In the last lesson we found many things that were similar in the lesson about the virtuous women we read about. They spoke kindness and wisdom, they were not lazy ... can you think of some other similarities? ...

Today we are going to read more scriptures in Proverbs that refer to the righteous. First, it is very important that we know where OUR righteousness comes from.

READ: Isaiah 45:24

PARENT: Remember, it is in the Lord that we have righteousness, right?

READ: Proverbs 21:12
         Proverbs 21:21
         Proverbs 21:25-26

QUESTIONS

In vs. 12 is the righteous man wise? (It says he considers WISELY the house of the wicked.)

What will the person who follows after righteousness and mercy find? (Vs. 21 says that he will find life, righteousness and honour.)

According to vs. 26, are the righteous greedy? (No, they give.)

Do they give grudgingly? (No, they give and they spare not.)

Are we to do the same?

Do you know of a scripture in the New Testament that says the same thing? (Jesus told us in Luke 6:30, Give to every man that asketh of thee; and of him that taketh away thy goods ask them not again.)

READ: Proverbs 28:1
         Proverbs 28:10
         Proverbs 28:12
         Proverbs 28:28

QUESTIONS

Are the righteous cowards? (Vs. 1 says that they are BOLD as lions!)

According to vs. 10 can a righteous man go astray? (Yes, Remember the scripture that says to be careful of the wicked man's ways? Pr. 12:26.)

Can a righteous man that goes astray be forgiven? (Yes, all he has to do is to repent to his Father, God.)

What happens when the righteous rejoice? (There is great glory.)

Why do you think men hide themselves when the wicked rise to power?

READ: Proverbs 29:2
         Proverbs 29:6-7
         Proverbs 29:16

QUESTIONS

What happens when the righteous are in authority? (Vs. 2 says the people rejoice.)

Why do you think the people mourn when the wicked rule?)

What do the righteous do in vs. 6? (They sing and rejoice.)

Do the righteous people sound sad?

What do the righteous do towards the poor? (They consider the cause of the poor.)

What do the wicked do? (They do not even THINK about them nor want to think about them.)

As believers, should we be thinking of the poor and how to help them?

What happens when there are many wicked people? (Vs. 16 says sin increases.)

What shall the righteous see happen to the wicked? (The righteous shall see the wicked fall.)

Should we be happy when they fall? (We are not to rejoice in our enemies' decline.)

PARENT: We are learning many things about what our hearts should be thinking on. We need to learn to be bold, to think how to help the poor, to watch out for the ways of the wicked lest we are enticed and go their ways, plus many more. As we read the Bible, we will be getting into our hearts more and more knowledge of God's ways, and less and less knowledge of humanism, or the way of men. This is very pleasing to God, and hopefully, we will all BEAR fruit!

ACTIVITIES

Have the children tell you without prompting them some of the things the righteous (those who believe) do. Reinforce that what makes you righteous is your believing. What you DO results from what you BELIEVE.

Lesson Eight
VIRTUE
Righteousness ... Purity

PARENT: According to God's Word, there is a difference between being one who is RIGHTEOUS, and doing what is RIGHT. Through faith we become righteous, not because of anything we DO. But doing righteousness is in the heart of one who has faith, and this person wants to DO what is right, or pleasing to God.

READ: 1 John 1:8-10

QUESTIONS

Do we sin? (Yes.)
How are we cleansed from unrighteousness? (If we confess our sins, He is faithful and just to forgive them and CLEANSE us.)
What if we say we have no sin? (We deceive ourselves.)
Is the truth in us?
What if we say we have NOT sinned? (We make Jesus a liar.)
Is His Word in us if we say this? (No.)

READ: 1 John 3:1-3

QUESTIONS

For those who believe, what are they called? (The sons of God.)
How much does God love us?
Does the world know us? (No.)
Does it know God? (No.)
Who is the world? (The world's inhabitants.)
Do we know what we shall be when Jesus comes? (No. We know that we shall be like Him, though.)
How do you feel about seeing Jesus?
Do you hope to see Him soon?
What are those who have this hope to do? (Vs. 3 says that we are to purify ourselves as He is pure.)

READ: 1 John 3:4-10

QUESTIONS

Who was sent to take away our sins? (Jesus.)
What are we not to be deceived in? (Vs. 7 says, "let no man deceive you. The truth is that he that does righteousness is righteous even as Jesus is righteous".)
Do these scriptures go along with the idea that we ought to not walk as the world walks, and that we are to purify ourselves from the world and its ways?
Why was Jesus sent? (Vs. 8 says Jesus was sent so He might destroy the works of the devil.)
Are these scriptures hard sayings?
Should we throw them out if we do not understand them?
Can we obey this by ourselves? (No! Only with the Lord's help and His giving us understanding.)

READ: 1 John 3:11-24

QUESTIONS

What is the message we have heard from the

beginning? (That we love one another.)
Why did Cain kill his brother? (Vs. 12, because his own works were evil, and his brother's righteous.)
What are we not to be surprised at? (Vs. 13, if the world HATES us.)
What does hate mean? (It means to detest and persecute.)
Did Cain hate Abel? (Yes, for righteousness sake. He KILLED him!)
How do we know we have passed from death into life? (Because we love the brethren.)
If we do not love those who BELIEVE what do we live in? (Vs. 14, death.)
If we hate our brothers what does the Bible say we are? (Murderers.)
Will murderers enter into eternal life? (No, Rev. 21:8 says: But the fearful, and unbelieving, and the abominable, and murderers, and whoremongers, and sorcerers, and idolaters, and all liars, shall have their part in the lake which burns with fire and brimstone; which is the second death.)
How much did God love us? (He laid down His own life for us.)
What should we do for our brethren? (Lay down our lives for them, vs. 16.)
If you see a brother that has a NEED, not a want, but a NEED, and you do not help him, do you love him? (No. The Bible also says that a person like this does not love God either, vs. 17.)
How are we to love God, by our words and mouth? (No! By our deeds and in truth, vs. 18.)
What are we to do? (Vs. 22, those things that are pleasing in His sight.)
How do we love one another? By telling someone you love them, or watching for their needs and meeting those needs?

ACTIVITIES

Discuss with the children any brethren that you know that have needs and how you can meet them.

❦❦❦❦❦❦

Lesson Nine
VIRTUE

Righteousness ... What the Righteous Should Follow After

PARENT: The Word of God has been teaching us many things on righteousness, which is a characteristic of VIRTUE. Can you tell me some of the things you have learned? Today we are going to read more scriptures on living righteously.

READ: 1 Timothy 6:9-16

QUESTIONS

What will happen to those that strive after being rich? (Vs.9 says that they will fall into temptation and a snare, and into many foolish and hurtful lusts.)
What do these lusts do? (They drown men in destruction and perdition.)
What is perdition? (Perdition is eternal damnation or the loss of your soul.)
What is the love of money? (Vs. 10, the root of all evil.)
What happened to some of those that coveted after money? (They erred from the faith, and pierced themselves with many sorrows.)
What is a man of God to do? (Vs. 11, but YOU, O man of God, FLEE THESE THINGS!)
What is a man of God to follow? (Righteousness, godliness, faith, love, patience, meekness.)
If the Word of God tells us to follow these things, what do you think we should do?
We are studying righteousness, what should a righteous person (One who BELIEVES in the Son of God) follow after? (These attributes.)

READ: 2 Timothy 2:19-26

What does the Lord know? (Vs. 19, He knows every one who are His.)
What do we want to be, a vessel unto honour

or a vessel unto dishonour?
If we are a vessel unto honour who will we be used by? (We will be ready for the Master to use us and prepared for every good work.)
What are we to flee? (Vs. 22, we are to flee youthful lusts, desires, WANTS.)
What are we to follow? (Righteousness, faith, charity, peace.)
Who are we to follow with? (Other believers that call on the Lord out of a pure heart.)
What must a servant of the Lord NOT do? (Vs. 24, He must not strive, meaning to struggle or fight.)
What is a servant of the Lord to BE? (Be gentle unto all men, apt to teach, patient, in meekness instructing those that oppose themselves.)

READ: 1 Peter 3:8-18

QUESTIONS

What are we to refrain from speaking? (Vs. 10, we are to not speak evil or guile; guile meaning being deceptive.)
What are we to do? (Vs. 11, do good, seek peace and ensue it.)
Are the eyes of the Lord on us? (Yes! And He hears the prayers of those who love Him.)
If we suffer for being righteous what should we be? (Vs. 14 says we should be happy.)
Are we to be afraid of what the wicked may do to us? (Vs. 14 says not to be afraid of their terror (their ways to hurt us) nor to be troubled by it.)
What are we to do instead of being afraid or troubled? (We are to sanctify the Lord God in our hearts.)
What are we always to be ready for? (To give an answer of the hope we have in Jesus with a meek and reverent attitude.)

READ: Revelation 22:11-14

QUESTIONS

What does the Word say about the unjust? (Let them be unjust still.)
What does it say about the filthy? (Let them be filthy still.)
What about the RIGHTEOUS? (Let them be righteous still.)
And the holy? (Let them be holy still.)
Out of these four things, which do you want to be?
How can you be righteous? By what you do? (No, you believe and are the righteous.)
Then, what does the Bible mean when it says to follow after righteousness? (It means that those who BELIEVE will have a heart to want to hear the Word of God and then DO it. The righteous will want to do what is right according to the will of God.)
Is Jesus coming quickly? (Vs. 12 says He is.)
What will Jesus be bringing with Him? (He will bring a reward to give every man according as his work shall be.)
What is your precious hope? (That the Lord is returning!!!)
Who does Jesus say are blessed? (Those that DO His commandments.)
What will they have right to? (They will have the right to the tree of life.)
What else? (Vs. 14, they may enter in through the gates into the city.)
Do YOU want to do His commandments?

Lesson Ten
VIRTUE
Righteousness ... Righteous Lot

PARENT: We have been reading in the Bible that God wants us to walk an upright life. This means that we, as those who BELIEVE, are to be different than the world. We are also not to conform ourselves after the WORLD, but after the WORD. Today we are going to read what the Bible has to teach us about Lot...

READ: 2 Peter 2:4-9

QUESTIONS

What was Noah called? (Vs. 5, a preacher of RIGHTEOUSNESS.)
Why was Sodom and Gomorrah turned into ashes? (It was an example for all people of what God thinks of the ungodly.)
What did God deliver Lot from? (The filthy conversation of the wicked.)
Was Lot righteous? (It says in vs. 8 that he was.)
What happened to his soul? (It was vexed.)
What does vexed mean? (It means to be terribly annoyed or agitated.)
What vexed his soul? (Seeing and hearing the wicked's unlawful deeds day after day.)
What happened to Lot? (God delivered him out of the wicked city.)

READ: Genesis 18:16-19

QUESTIONS

What did God know about Abraham? (Vs. 19, that he would command his children and his household after him and they would KEEP THE WAY OF THE LORD.)
When you grow up, how are you going to command your children?

READ: Genesis 18:20-33

QUESTIONS

Why did God come to see Sodom and Gomorrah? (Because their sin is very grievous.)
What did Abraham ask the Lord? (Vs. 23, "Will you destroy the righteous with the wicked.")
How many righteous people did God say He would have to find in the city to not destroy it? (Ten.)

READ: Genesis 19:1-11

QUESTIONS

What did the angels do to Lot when the people of the city tried to get them? (Vs. 10, they pulled Lot into the house to them, and shut the door.)
What did they do to the men outside? (They blinded everyone so they couldn't find the door!)

READ: Genesis 19:12-26

QUESTIONS

What did Lot's sons-in-law do? (They mocked Lot.)
What happened to them? (They were destroyed.)
What happened to Lot and his family? (Vs. 16, the angels put their hands on them and brought them out of the city.)
Was the Lord merciful to righteous Lot? (Yes, vs. 16 says that the Lord was merciful unto him.)
According to these scriptures, Lot was not perfect, and even argued with the Lord, but why was He righteous? (Because he BELIEVED in the Lord.)
Did Lot's wife obey the Lord? (No.)
What happened to her because of her disobedience? (She was turned into a pillar of salt.)

FACT

Did you know that when you go to Israel, to the place where Sodom and Gomorrah use to be, that all that is left is SALTY ground and the Dead Sea. There is so much salt in the sea that it forms salt formations that stick up out of the water. The land is so desolated that nothing will grow anywhere near it. The land is uninhabited and BARREN.

PARENT: This is the last lesson on righteousness. A righteous man is not a righteous man because of what he does, but because of what he BELIEVES. But a man that truly believes in God as his King will do the RIGHT things that his King would have him do. It all comes back to the fact that once we enter into the Kingdom of Heaven by BELIEVING, we then become subjects of the KING. Like a scripture we recently read, we can become LOYAL subjects or DISLOYAL subjects, vessels unto dishonor or vessels unto honour. There is a scripture that says CHOOSE TODAY WHO YOU WILL SERVE!

ACTIVITIES

Review with the children certain characteristics we have read about that the righteous and virtuous people had.

Lesson Eleven
VIRTUE
Moral Excellence

PARENT: One of the definitions of VIRTUE was MORAL EXCELLENCE. Before we can be excellent in being moral, we need to find out what MORAL means...

DICTIONARY: Moral

(1. Concerned with the judgment of the goodness or badness of human action and character. 2. Pertaining to the discernment of good and evil. 3. Designed to teach goodness or correctness of character and behavior. 4. Instructive of what is good and bad. 5. Acting in accordance with what is good. 6. Integrity.)

PARENT: So what does moral mean? It has to do with knowing good and bad. It means to be able to judge and discern good and evil. We are going to study in the next few lessons discernment, integrity, being upright and DOING what is good. We want to be morally excellent!

READ: Genesis 2:9-17

QUESTIONS

What two trees were in the middle of the garden of Eden? (Vs. 9, the tree of life and the tree of knowledge of good and evil.)
What tree did God say that Adam could not eat? (Vs. 17, the tree of the knowledge of good and evil.)
What would happen if Adam ate it? (Vs. 17, the day that he ate of it he would die.)

READ: Genesis 3:1-7

QUESTIONS

Did the serpent call God a liar? (Not in those words, but he said totally the opposite of what

God said. God said, "You will die." And the serpent said, "You will not die.")
What did Adam and Eve do? (They ate the fruit.)

READ: Genesis 3:8-21

QUESTIONS

What did Adam and Eve bring about? (Death.)
What would be like if Adam and Eve had obeyed God? (Righteousness would dwell on earth, now.)

READ: Genesis 3:22-24

QUESTIONS

What did God say that man had become like? (Vs. 22, like Father God, Jesus, His Son, and the Holy Spirit, that knew good and evil.)
Why did God drive Adam and Eve out of the garden? (To keep them away from the tree of life.)
Why did God want them way from the tree of life? (So they would not eat it, because if they did, they would live forever.)

PARENT: Now we know the history of where the knowledge of good and evil came from. Being loyal subjects of the King of Heaven, we are to now pursue righteousness, godliness, faith, love, patience, meekness. We are also told to add to our FAITH, VIRTUE. We need to find in the Bible how it instructs us to be morally excellent. Adam is also talked about in the New Testament. Let's read what it has to say.

READ: 1 Corinthians 15:20-28

QUESTIONS

What brought death? (Vs. 21, says by man came death.)
Because of WHO do all die? (Vs. 22, because of Adam all die.)
But who shall make us alive? (Jesus!)
Did Adam bring death because of his disobedience? (According to these scriptures, yes.)
But who is the WAY, the TRUTH and the LIFE? (Jesus! Through Him we may LIVE!)
What will Jesus do as He reigns? (Vs. 25 He will put all enemies under His feet and they will be trampled.)
What is Jesus' last enemy that He will destroy? (Vs. 26, DEATH!!!)
We now have the knowledge of good and evil because of Adam, but what awful enemy came with this? (Death.)
Who will destroy this enemy? (JESUS!!)
What is it to be MORAL? (To judge and discern between good and bad and then choosing to do good!)
How can we know what is good? (If we read God's Word it will instruct us what is good in God's eyes. The Bible teaches us that every thing in a man's own eyes seems good to him, but we are to find out what God would determine is good.)
Is there any man that is RIGHTEOUS in himself? (No, nor is there any man good, save God.)

❦❦❦❦❦❦

Lesson Twelve
VIRTUE
Moral Excellence ... Discernment

PARENT: Do you remember where the knowledge of good and evil came from? ... We are learning about moral excellence. What does this mean? ... It means to judge and discern between good and evil and then choose to do good. What does it mean to discern?

DICTIONARY: Discern

(1. To perceive something obscure. 2. To detect something. 3. To perceive differences. 4. To make distinctions. To distinguish between.)

PARENT: What things are we to tell the difference between? ... That of good and evil. Let's see more of what God's Word has to tell us about this.

READ: Hebrews 5:12-14

QUESTIONS

What is a person like that is compared to using milk? (Vs. 13, this is a person unskillful in the Word of righteousness.)
What is he called? (A babe.)
What is strong meat for? (Vs. 14, those who are of full age or mature in the Word.)
What is a MATURE christian according to these scriptures? (Vs. 14, those who by reason of use have their sense exercised to discern both good and evil.)
Is a Christian of full age, one who discerns both good and evil?
If a babe is unskilled in the Word of God, what is a person of full age? (Skilled in the Word of God.)
What are you to be doing? (Becoming skilled in the Word of God.)
Then what will you be able to do when you are grown up? (Be able to discern, through being skilled in the Word of God, good and evil.)

PARENT: Many people might tell you that a mature Christian is someone who has been a Christian a long time. According to this scripture, there are some people who SHOULD be teachers if they have been a dedicated BELIEVER, but because they are unskilled in the Word of God, they are only babes and can't seem to even understand the very FIRST things a believer ought to know. We as Christians need to know that we are to OBEY and FOLLOW the Word of God? We need to be sure that we do not fall into the error of disobeying God's Word, and learn the GOOD things that the Lord says to do.

READ: 2 Samuel 14:17
          1 Kings 3:9-12
          Job 6:28-30

QUESTIONS

Again, what is discernment for? (To discern between what is good and what is evil.)
What happens when you discern between good and evil? (You make a judgment, vs. 11.)
What did Job say that he could discern? (Vs. 30, those things which were perverse or evil.)
When he discerned did he have to make a judgment? (Yes. Between that which was good and that which was evil.)

PARENT: We are going to be talking in the next lesson on judgment. There may come a time that you may hear people telling you not to judge. But if we are to discern good and evil, we are to judge. The Bible says that we are not to be hypocrites and judge others when we ourselves are doing evil. But we need to judge ourselves! We do not want to become self righteous people, thinking that we are better than others and then fall into the abomination of pride. We are to discern good and evil so that WE, each person for himself, can stay away from things that are evil and not pleasing to God and choose to follow after the good and perfect will of God!

READ: Ecclesiastes 8:5-6

QUESTIONS

What does a wise man's heart discern? (Both time and judgment.)
What happens to a person that tries to keep God's Word? (They will feel no evil thing.)

Lesson Thirteen
VIRTUE
Moral Excellence ... Judging Vs. Condemnation

PARENT: The Bible has been teaching us about discernment. What is a MATURE Christian? ... One who is able to discern, through being skilled in the Word of God, good and evil. It is very important that we learn the difference between judging and condemnation, so that we never fall into the sin of the latter.

READ: Matthew 7:13-14

QUESTIONS

What gate are we to enter into? (The strait gate.)
Which is the wide gate? (Wide is the gate to destruction.)
How big is the way to destruction? (Broad is the way, broad means LIBERAL and tolerating many things; spacious.)
What is the number of people that follow this road? (Many.)
What is the gate like that leads to life? (Strait.)
What does strait mean? (Here the word means as thin as a needle, from Greek #2476.)
How narrow then is the way?
How many enter into the strait gate? (Few...)
How many is few? (The Greek #3641 word means puny, briefly.)
What do we need to do? (Be one of the few.)

An Analogy

There is a narrow path in the middle of a huge area of land. There is a wide expanse to the left of the narrow way. On this left side are those who say that they believe but they do not obey the Word of God and throw it away. These are those who have believed only with their head, and not their heart. They rationalize the Word of God away with their traditions and do not obey it.

To the right of the narrow way are those who try to follow the Word of God, but add to it in making laws and obligations in practicing the Word. These are those who start making up their own traditions from the Word of God and end up having the Word of God plus many more rules and regulations that exceed the Word of God.

In the middle is the narrow way, by which only those who follow the Lord in Spirit and in Truth will follow through obedience to the Word of God, neither adding to it, nor taking away from it.

PARENT: We are going to be learning the difference between judging and condemning. We are to follow the NARROW WAY and the only way we can do this is if we discern between good and evil through the Holy Spirit, and then choose to do good. In this we must make judgments for ourselves of what WE will DO. Since the narrow way is not a wide way, we can judge around us of what we will follow and do. We are not to judge others in a condemning manner. We are only to judge in accordance to what we will do.

DICTIONARY: Judgment

(1. The ability to perceive and distinguish relationships or alternatives; discernment. 2. The capacity to make reasonable decisions towards goodness.)

DICTIONARY: Condemn

(1. To express disapproval of; censure; criticize. 2. To sentence; to doom. 3. To convict. 4. To declare to be unfit for use.)

PARENT: We need to be very careful of what we say. Did you know that we will have to give an account to God for every word we utter? We need to never condemn ANYONE. It is God who will pass sentence on people. We are not in the position to ever do so. It is God who searches and tries the hearts of men. We need to look to make sure WE are right with God and not pass SENTENCE on others.

READ: Matthew 7:1-5

STRONG'S: Judge (Here in Mt. 7) (Greek #2919; to try; to CONDEMN; to punish; damn, decree, decide sentence.)

PARENT: We need to know the difference between condemning and judging. Judging is only for good. Condemning is passing sentence as if we were God. This is God's job.

※※※※※※

Lesson Fourteen
VIRTUE
Moral Excellence ... Judging Between Good and Evil

PARENT: Do you remember the difference between judging and condemning? ... Judging is distinguishing what is good or evil. Condemning is to punish, decide someone's sentence or to condemn them. Remember the scripture in Matthew 7 that used the word JUDGE which in the Greek means CONDEMN? We are not ever to CONDEMN another person. This would not show an attitude of humility, would it? What we are to do is to know the Word of God well enough to line things up in our lives and follow the Bible in every situation we encounter. Remember, judgment means to DISCERN.

READ: 1 Corinthians 2:9-16

QUESTIONS

What has God been doing for those who love Him? (Vs. 9, He has been preparing things for those who love Him, that eyes have not seen nor ears ever heard, nor can we even think of what these things are they are so wonderful.)
Will He reveal these things to us? (Vs. 10 says God has revealed them to us by His Spirit.)
Do we speak things that the world thinks is wise? (No.)
Can the natural man understand things of the Spirit of God? (No.)
Why? (Vs. 14, because they are spiritually discerned or judged.)
What does a person that is spiritual do? (Vs. 15, he judges or discerns ALL things.)
How can we know the mind of the Lord? (By having the mind of Christ by BELIEVING in Him.)

READ: 1 Corinthians 11:28-32

QUESTIONS

What are we to do in vs. 28? (We are to examine ourselves.)
What does this mean? (The Greek word #3985 means to test ourselves or scrutinize, to see if we line up with God's Word in what we do and say.)
What are we to do in vs. 31? (We are to judge ourselves.)
What is this judgment for? (To be chastened by the Lord so we will not be condemned with the world.)
Is this judgment good for us? (We need to judge ourselves with hearts that just want to be right with God. We need to be constantly looking within to see if anything that is unpleasant to our Father has sprung up. Such as: pride, envy, lust, idolatry, ... and if something has sprung up we need to repent and the

Lord is just to forgive us our sins and cleanse us from unrighteousness.)

What happens when we judge ourselves? (We see if we are walking in the Word, which is good, or if we are walking in the ways of the world, which is evil.)

READ: Psalms 32:5

PARENT: Isn't this wonderful that the same Truth about confessing our sins is in the Old Testament AND the New? When we judge ourselves and see sin, our hearts repent and we confess our sins, and God forgives us. Isn't He a wonderful Father that we are serving? Another word for judge or discern is to perceive. Here are some scriptures that refer to perceive.

READ: 1 Samuel 12:17
2 Kings 4:9
Proverbs 1:2
Proverbs 14:7

In 1 Samuel, did he discern between good and evil? (Yes, Samuel perceived or saw that he was wicked.)
Did the woman discern between good and evil in regards to Elisha? (Yes, she discerned that he was a HOLY man of God.)

STRONG'S: Perceived (In these scriptures) (Hebrew #3045; discern...)

PARENT: Again, the most important thing is to know the Word of God so that we will be able to discern or judge between good and evil choices we will have to make in our lives. God has given us His Word, and in order to become MATURE Christians we need to remember Hebrews 5:14, "But strong meat belongeth to them that are full age, even those who by reason of use have their senses exercised to discern both good and evil."

Lesson Fifteen
VIRTUE
Moral Excellence ... Being Upright

PARENT: We are studying the characteristics of being VIRTUOUS. What are the two main aspects of virtue we have been studying? ... (Righteousness and moral excellence.) A righteous person is one who believes in God and it is a part of his belief that leads him to do what is right, according to the Bible. Moral excellence is learning to discern what is good and what is evil according to the scriptures and then choosing to do what God would have you do. Another name for having moral excellence is to be UPRIGHT. Let's read the Word of God to find out what it says about being UPRIGHT.

READ: Psalms 7:10
Psalms 32:11
Psalms 36:10
Psalms 64:10
Psalms 94:15
Psalms 97:11

QUESTIONS

Who is the defense of the upright of heart? (God.)
Who are the upright of heart to be glad in? (The Lord.)
What will God continue in towards the upright of heart? (Psa. 36, His loving kindness and His righteousness.)
In Psa. 64, what shall all the upright do? (They shall glory!)
In all these scriptures, where are these people upright? (In their hearts!)

STRONG'S: Upright (Hebrew #3477; straight, convenient, equity, just, righteous, upright.)

DICTIONARY: Upright

(1. Morally respectable. 2. Honorable.)

READ: Proverbs 11:3, 6
Proverbs 11:11, 20

QUESTIONS

What shall guide the upright? (Their integrity.)
So are we to try to have integrity? (Yes.)
What shall deliver the upright? (Their righteousness or their BELIEF, which leads them to follow God and serve Him in the good things He wants us to do.)
How is a city exalted? (By the upright being there and THEM being blessed by trying to follow God.)
What is God's delight? (The upright of heart.)
Where are we to be upright? (In our hearts.)
Who can see and judge our hearts? (Only God.)

READ: Proverbs 2:7, 21

QUESTIONS

What is God to those who walk uprightly? (He is a buckler.)
What is a buckler? (A buckler is a shield or protector.)
What is God to the upright of heart? (He is a shield or protector of them.)
Who will dwell in the land? (God will have the upright dwell in the land.)

READ: Proverbs 28:6, 10, 18

QUESTIONS

Which is it better to be, rich and perverse or poor and upright? (Poor and upright.)
What will happen to a person that causes the upright to go astray? (He will fall into a deep pit.)
Do we need to keep a watch for people that might lead us away from the Truth of God? (Yes. Jesus warned us again and again to beware of falseness.)
What will the upright have? (Good things in possession.)
Does this necessarily mean riches as in gold and silver? (No, this could mean knowledge of God which is the most valuable thing on earth.)
Who shall be saved? (He that walks uprightly.)
Where are we upright? (In our hearts.)
Where are we saved? (In our hearts.)
How are we saved? (By believing in Jesus the Messiah in our hearts.)

READ: Proverbs 29:10, 27

QUESTIONS

Who will hate the upright? (The bloodthirsty.)
Who else does the scriptures say will hate those who believe in Jesus? (The world.)
Are we to fear men? (No, only God.)
What does God think of an unjust man? (He is an abomination to Him.)
What is an abomination to the wicked? (The upright!)
What is an abomination? (Abomination means something disgusting, an abhorrence.)

❊❊❊❊❊❊

Lesson Sixteen
VIRTUE
Valor

PARENT: Do you remember what VALOR was when we looked up the definition under VIRTUE? It means courage and boldness. Bravery. Did you know that a person who has valor is called valiant?

DICTIONARY: Valiant

(1. Possessing or acting with valor. 2. Brave. 3. Courageous. 4. Stouthearted.)

READ: Psalms 60:12
            Psalms 108:13
            Psalms 118:15-16

QUESTIONS

How shall WE do valiantly? (Through God.)
Shall WE tread down our enemies? (No, we are to love our enemies. God will render punishment, not us.)
Which hand of God does valiantly? (His right hand.)
Is God valiant, then? (Yes.)
Was Jesus valiant? (Yes, He was courage in itself when He layed down His own life for us instead of calling His angels to save His flesh. He CONQUERED death, as a valiant KING!)

PARENT: Valiant means to be brave and have courage. It is important to realize that our courage comes not from our own selves. If a person BELIEVES in something with all his heart, soul, and mind, he will face any obstacle that might come against it. If we believe in God, we will stand against anything that comes in the way of TRUTH, even to the very point that men might hurt our flesh to make us deny the TRUTH. But even if it comes to the point of death, death would be preferable rather than not standing for the TRUTH of what one BELIEVES in. This is VALOR. Valor comes from truly BELIEVING. If one truly BELIEVES, nothing can stop him from standing for the TRUTH. What is the opposite of VALOR? It is being FEARFUL. Let's see what God thinks of people being fearful...

READ: Revelation 21:8

QUESTIONS

Who shall have their part in the lake of fire and brimstone? (The FEARFUL, the unbelieving, the abominable, murderers, whoremongers, sorcerer, idolaters, and all liars.)
What is the opposite of VALOR? (Being fearful.)
What is this lake also called? (The second death.)
What is the first death? (When your flesh dies.)
What is the second death? (When you are thrown into the lake of fire and brimstone for being these things.)
What is an unbeliever? (One who does not BELIEVE in Jesus the Messiah.)
Is this right of God? (Yes, because His judgments are just and True and righteous. He alone is RIGHTEOUS and He judges RIGHTEOUSLY.)

STRONG'S: Fearful (In Rev. 21:8)

(Greek #1169; means dread, timid, faithless; fearful.)

PARENT: We are not to dread anything but to stand for God's Word. The Bible says that in the last days, God's people might have to lose their fleshly body in order to stand for the Testimony of Jesus, and for the Word of God. If we truly BELIEVE in God, we will never be fearful of what men may do to us, but will LOVE God even more than our own bodies. Did you know that most of the disciples stood for the Word of God, even to the point of death? They didn't try to be courageous. They just BELIEVED so much in God, that it was the RIGHT thing to do in the face of ERROR. They could have stopped speaking truth in order to save their own skins, but instead kept preaching Truth past the point of death. Isn't this MARVELOUS faith? This is true VALOR!!

READ: Acts 7 (The story of Stephen)

QUESTIONS

Was Stephen fearful? (No! He was bold as a lion.)
Did Stephen bother the religious leaders? (Vs. 54, they were cut to the heart.)
Did Stephen worry about what they would do to him?
Should we worry about what men will do to us in the face of speaking truth?

Lesson Seventeen
VIRTUE
Valor ... Fearing God

PARENT: We need to learn the difference between fearing God and fearing men. Valor, or courage, is the opposite of being fearful. The Bible says that the fearful will have their part in the lake of fire and brimstone. This fearful means those who are faithless and are fearful of men, not God. We are commanded all through the Word of God to FEAR him, not men!

READ: Proverbs 1:7

PARENT: This is one of the most important verses we can ever learn. The fear of the Lord is the beginning of knowledge. The opposite of this is being a fool. Fools despise wisdom and instruction. Do you remember that God will teach us the fear of Him? Let's look up what this FEAR means in the Strong's.

STRONG'S: Fear (In Proverbs 1:7) (Hebrew #3374; fearing, REVERENCE.)

DICTIONARY: Reverence

(1. A feeling of profound awe and respect and often love. 2. An act of showing respect, especially obeisance, meaning deference or homage.)

PARENT: We are to reverence God or FEAR Him! This is the beginning of knowledge.

READ: Acts 9:31
Acts 13:16
Romans 3:13-18

QUESTIONS

In Acts 9, what were the believers walking in? (In the fear of the Lord.)
What happened as they were walking in this? (They were multiplied.)
How did Paul address the people? (Men of Israel, and those that FEAR God.)
In Romans 3, was it a good thing or bad thing that men did not have a fear of God? (A bad thing!)

READ: 2 Corinthians 7:1-4

QUESTIONS

What are we to cleanse ourselves from? (Vs. 1, all filthiness of the flesh and spirit.)
What are we to try to perfect? (Vs. 1, Holiness in the FEAR OF GOD.)
In Vs. 4, how did Paul speak to the Corinthians? (Boldly.)

READ: Ephesians 5:20-21
Hebrews 12:28-29

QUESTIONS

What are we to always give thanks for? (Everything!)
How are we to submit to one another? (In the FEAR OF GOD.)
According to Hebrews, how are we to serve God? (Acceptably, with reverence and GODLY FEAR.)
What does the Word say God is? (Vs. 29, Our God is a consuming fire.)

Can the Kingdom of God be moved? (No!) What are we to have in order to serve God? (Grace.)

READ: 1 Peter 2:17
        1 Peter 3:15

QUESTIONS

What are all four commands in Vs. 17? (1. Honour all men (Humble ourselves.). 2. Love the brotherhood. 3. FEAR GOD. 4. Honour the king.)
In 1 Peter 3, what are we to do in our hearts? (Sanctify God in our hearts.)
What are we always to be ready for? (To give an answer to every man that asks you the reason for the hope that is in you.)
How are you to give this answer? (With meekness and FEAR.)
What does this fear mean here? (With reverence, not the fear of men.)

READ: Revelation 14:7
        Revelation 15:4
        Revelation 19:4-5

PARENT: What is the opposite of VALOR? It is being fearful. There is a big difference of being FEARFUL of men and being FEARFUL of God. Today we have been learning what the Bible says about having a healthy FEAR of God. This fear means to hold God in AWE and reverence. We are to FEAR God. What is this the beginning of? It is the beginning of KNOWLEDGE!!! In the next lesson we are going to learn what the Bible has to say about having a FEAR of men, rather than a FEAR of God. This is the type of FEAR we are NOT suppose to have. We are never to be afraid of what men will do to us for the sake of TRUTH and RIGHTEOUSNESS! We can be of great use to God when we never fear anything but Him!!!

Lesson Eighteen
VIRTUE
Valor ... We are Not to Fear Men

PARENT: It is very important to know that if you BELIEVE in something you will STAND for it when opposition comes. If a person does not stand, then he must not really believe, or he might only believe in his head, not his heart. We, on the other hand, are going to BELIEVE with everything in our being. We are going to learn to NOT fear men, but to fear only God more than anything else. We have some wonderful examples in the Word of people who TRUSTED and FEARED God more than the situations they were in. We need to look to them as our examples and be instructed by them.

READ: Matthew 10:16-39

QUESTIONS

What did Jesus liken his disciples to? (Sheep in the midst of wolves.)
What are we to be? (Vs. 16, wise as serpents, and harmless as doves.)
In Vs. 22, how many men will hate Jesus' disciples?
Who shall be saved? (He that endures to the end.)
What were the disciples told to do when they were persecuted? (To flee to another city.)
Must we be FEARFUL of men? (No! The gospel will be spread this way.)
What did Jesus forewarn his followers? (In vs. 25, He told them ahead of time if HE, the Lord, was called Beelzebub, how much more would they call his followers!)
What is our response to be to these people who might hate us and want to hurt us? (Vs. 26 says FEAR them NOT therefore.)
Are we to be ashamed of Jesus' teachings? (Vs. 27 says no! What Jesus tells us in darkness we are to speak in light, and what we hear in the ear, we are to preach from the housetops!)

Who are we not to FEAR? (Vs. 28 says to fear not them which kill the body, but are not able to kill the soul.)
Who ARE we to FEAR? (Fear Him which is able to destroy both soul and body in hell.)
How much does God know about us? (Vs. 29 says not one sparrow falls to the ground without our Father knowing. Vs. 30 says the very hairs on our head are COUNTED!)
Why are we not to fear? (Fear not, vs. 31, for we are of more value than MANY sparrows.)
What is the sword of Jesus? (The Sword of the Spirit is the WORD OF GOD.)
If you love your mother and father more than God are you worthy of Jesus? (No.)
If a parent loves their children more than Jesus are they worthy of Him? (No.)
What will happen to those that lose their lives for Jesus' sake? (They will find their life.)
If we pick up the cross and follow Him, is this a cowardly thing to do, or valiant?
To follow Jesus, what will enable us to stand anything that may come against us? (Our faith in Him!!! or our BELIEF!!!)

READ: Luke 12:5
        2 Timothy 1:7
        Hebrews 2:14-15

QUESTIONS

According to Hebrews 2:15., what did man live in fear of before Christ? (The fear of death.)
What was this fear? (Bondage!)
Do we need to fear this any more? (No, Jesus conquered death.)

READ: Hebrews 13:5-6

QUESTIONS

What is our conversation to be like? (Without covetousness.)
What are we to be? (Content with exactly what we have.)
What did Jesus say to us? (That I will never leave you or forsake you.)
What are we to boldly say? (That the Lord is my helper.)
What else? (I will not fear what man shall do to me!)
Why can we boldly say these things? (Because Jesus told us He would NEVER leave us or forsake us. We are to take heart in this fact when men will persecute us.)

READ: Revelation 2:10

PARENT: Here in America we have the freedom to worship God and obey Him, but right now in other countries there is great persecution going on. There are people sitting in prisons ONLY because they believe in Jesus, the Son of God. Jesus tells us to never fear things that might happen to us. We need to have confidence in Him that He is with us through EVERYTHING, and we must always, ALWAYS be faithful first to God.

Lesson Nineteen
VIRTUE
Valor ... The Courage of David Part 1

PARENT: We have learned that we are to have the FEAR of God but not the FEAR of man. Being valiant is something you do not TRY to be, you just are, because of what you believe. If you believe something, you will lay down your life for that cause, just like the disciples did. Remember Jesus' words that told us that we must pick up our cross and follow Him, and those that find their life will lose it, and those that lose their life will find it? This is Valor ... This is Courage ... To BELIEVE at any cost!

We are going to read about David. David believed that God could defeat the Philistine giant, and with that belief, went after Goliath with a sling shot and SLEW HIM! David did not have the courage himself, it was his faith in the Lord that made him valiant. Our faith in God will also make us valiant. This is all a part of walking in the belief of God!

READ: 1 Samuel 17:1-11

QUESTIONS

Who were the Israelites fighting? (The Philistines.)
What was Goliath called? (Vs. 4, a champion.)
What did Goliath have on? (A brass helmet, a metal coat made out of 5,000 shekels of brass, brass leggings, and a brass breastplate. The total weight in American pounds was 318 lbs. of armor he carried.)
What did Goliath say to the Israelites? (Give me a man to fight!)
What did this do to the Israelites? (Vs. 11, says they were dismayed and greatly afraid.)

READ: 1 Samuel 17:12-19

QUESTIONS

Who was David's father? (Jesse.)
Do you remember who his great grandparents were? (Boaz and Ruth.)
How many brothers did David have? (Seven.)
Who was the youngest son? (David.)
What did David do for his family? (He took care of the sheep.)
What was David instructed to do? (He was to take food to his brothers that were camped against the Philistine army.)

READ: 1 Samuel 17:20-27

QUESTIONS

As David was talking to his brothers, what happened? (Vs. 23, Goliath came out begging for the Israelites to send someone to fight him.)
What happened? (Vs. 24, ALL the men of Israel were sore afraid!)
What did David hear the men of Israel say? (That the person that could kill Goliath would get riches, one of the king's daughters, and make his father's house free in Israel.)
What was David's response? (WHO is this uncircumcised Philistine, that he should defy the armies of the LIVING GOD!)

READ: 1 Samuel 17:28-37

QUESTIONS

Why was David's brother angry with him? (Because he thought David was simply boasting plus neglecting his duty with the sheep.)
What was David's response? (Vs. 29, he said that there was a CAUSE to say what he said, then he turned to the other warriors of Israel and said the same thing again!)
What did the warriors he said these things to do? (Vs. 31, they went and told King Saul, and he summoned David to him.)
Was David fearful of seeing the king? (No, he went in and told the king that he wanted to fight Goliath!)
What was Saul's response? (He took one look at David and saw his age and said that it couldn't be done.)
What had God prepared David with? (God sent a lion and a bear as training.)
Why did David want to kill Goliath? (Because he defied the armies of the living God.)
What did David say that showed his BELIEF? (Vs. 37, THE LORD delivered me out of the paw of the lion, and out of the paw of the bear, HE WILL DELIVER me out of the hand of this Philistine.)
What did the king do? (Vs. 37, he let David go and said, "The LORD be with thee.")
Was David prideful, like his brother thought?

(No, he truly believed that no one should defy the armies of the living God and be successful.)
Was David valiant? (Yes.)
On his own? (No, it was only his belief in God that made him valiant.)

ACTIVITIES

Have the children draw a picture of what they think Goliath looked like.

❦❦❦❦❦❦❦

Lesson Twenty
VIRTUE
Valor ... The Courage of David Part 2

PARENT: In the last lesson, we learned that Goliath was a Philistine that had all the armies of Israel quaking. A little shepherd boy named David thought it was TERRIBLE that this Philistine would DREAM of defying the GOD of Israel's armies and set out to fight against him, even though the King told him he was only a youth, and he was setting out against a giant of war! The place where David's courage lay was with the Lord. Let's find out more about the courage of David...

READ: 1 Samuel 17:38-42

QUESTIONS

What did Saul do for David? (Vs. 38, he put his own armour on David.)
What did David say to Saul about that? (I cannot wear these things because I have not PROVED them.)
What does PROVED mean? (According to Strong's proved means to test or try it.)
So what did David do? (He took off the armour and took his shepherd's staff and five smooth stones which he put in his shepherd's bag, and had sling in hand and went to the Philistine.)
What did the Philistine do when he saw David? (He disdained him, because he saw this young BOY coming to fight him.)

READ: 1 Samuel 17:43-48

QUESTIONS

What did the Philistine say when he saw David? (Am I a dog that you come to me with staves?)
What are staves? (A stave is a thin branch or rod that you use to spank children with.)
How did Goliath threaten David? (He said he'd feed his flesh to the birds and beasts.)
What are the mighty words David spoke to Goliath? (Vs. 45, "YOU come to me with a sword, and a spear, and a shield, but I come to you in the NAME of the LORD OF HOSTS, the GOD of the armies of Israel, whom you have DEFIED!!!")
Did David say "I" will kill you? (No! He said, "God will deliver you into my hand and then I will smite you.")
Why did David want to do this and know God would do this? (So ALL the earth would know that there is a God in Israel.)
Why did David not bring a spear and sword? (Vs. 47, says that all this assembly would know that the Lord does NOT save with sword and spear, for the battle is the Lord's.)
Did David want to kill Goliath so he would become "someone" or because he wanted the king's reward? (No, David was still upset that this Philistine would defy the Lord God of Israel and had such faith in God that he just wanted God to be glorified.)
Did David back up when the Philistine started towards him? (No! He RAN to meet him.)

READ: 1 Samuel 17:49-58

QUESTIONS

How many stones did it take of the five David had to kill the Philistine? (Vs. 49, THE VERY FIRST ONE!)

What happened when the Philistine army saw their champion dead? (Vs. 51, they fled!!)

What did David do? (He took Goliath's head and armour to Jerusalem.)

Did the king then take notice of David? (Yes.)

Was this why David went and slew Goliath? (No, he only did it because of his FAITH in the Lord.)

What gave David his courage? (It came from what he BELIEVED.)

If we believe, will we have this courage or VALOR? (YES!)

PARENT: It is very important for you to know that 2 Peter's list of character traits is exactly in order! It says to add to your FAITH - VIRTUE. You have to have FAITH or you must BELIEVE in something FIRST, in order to have VIRTUE. You must BELIEVE that the Bible says to obey it, and then you will walk in righteousness. In order to have VALOR or COURAGE, you do not merely just have it! You only have VALOR when you are standing in the BELIEF of something, up against the UNBELIEF of that thing. It is so important that we are truly grounded in the Word of God and BELIEVE ALL that it says! Then we can all have the FAITH and then the VIRTUE of David!

The next thing we are going to talk about is being BOLD. Not in the sense of being loud-mouthed, but in a sense of never being ashamed of the gospel. This is also a part of VIRTUE. We need to boldly speak the truth in LOVE. But if you have faith, how could you not?

❦❦❦❦❦❦

Lesson Twenty-One
VIRTUE
Boldness

PARENT: We have been learning a part of VIRTUE, which is VALOR. Another aspect of virtue that goes right along with valor is being BOLD, or not being afraid to speak the Truth. All through the Bible we can see the characteristic of boldness. Can you tell me some instances of boldness that we have already read about? ... We are going to read some more scriptures about being BOLD, but first, let's find out exactly what it means.

DICTIONARY: Bold

(1. Fearless and daring. 2. Courageous. 3. Clear and distinct. 4. Unduly forward or brazen.)

READ: Proverbs 28:1

PARENT: We have read this scripture before. Lions are very bold creatures. They are called the King of the Jungle because of their boldness. Jesus is also called the Lion of Judah. He is very bold also and has much VALOR! He is sinless, yet he stood and DIED for us.!

STRONG'S: Bold

(Hebrew #982; to be bold, confident, secure, sure, careless, confidence, hope and trust.)

READ: Acts 3:2-9
Acts 4:1-14

QUESTIONS

In this scripture, in Vs. 13, what did the religious leaders see that Peter and John had? (They saw the BOLDNESS of Peter and John.)

Was it in what they did or what they said? (In

what they said.)

READ: Acts 4:15-22

QUESTIONS

What did the leaders then do to Peter and John? (They commanded them to not speak at all nor teach in the name of Jesus.)
What was Peter and John's reply to this? (They said, "You tell us whether it is better to listen to YOU than to GOD!")
What about us, is it better to listen to men or to God?
If someone is threatening us, are we going to still be BOLD because we BELIEVE? Will we still listen and follow God?
What happened to the disciples after they spoke in vs. 21? (They were threatened more.)

PARENT: The way we have BOLDNESS is in speaking what we truly believe in. We are not going to be sure of speaking in something we do not know much about. The more we know about the Word of God, the more confident we will become in the Lord. The more confident we are in the Lord, the more BOLD we will become. But the most important thing to remember is that BOLDNESS comes from GOD! The believers in the Word prayed to our Father for boldness to speak His Word! We need to do this also!

✯✯✯✯✯✯✯

Lesson Twenty-Two
VIRTUE
Boldness ... Waxing Bold

PARENT: We read yesterday how the believers prayed to our Lord for boldness and that he granted it for speaking the Word of God. We are going to read some more instances of where Paul and Barnabas WAXED Bold. What does waxed mean?

STRONG'S: Waxed

(Greek #3955; to be frank in utterance, or confident in spirit and demeanor; be bold, preach or speak boldly!)

READ: Acts 13:44-52

QUESTIONS

Did the people come to hear Paul and Barnabas? (Vs. 44 says they came to hear the Word of God.)
What did the Religious Jews do when they saw the WHOLE city come to hear the Word of God? (They were envious, and spoke against what Paul and Barnabas said.)
What did Paul and Barnabas do then? (THEY WAXED BOLD.)
What were they bold to say in front of the Jewish Religious Leaders? (They were bold to tell them that salvation has come to also the Gentiles. At this time, the religious people thought that Gentiles were infidels and would never be able to come to salvation because it was something you were BORN into. You were BORN a Jew. Now it was what you BELIEVED!)
How did the Gentiles respond? (Vs. 48.)
Because of the Gentiles believing, what happened? (The Word of the Lord was published throughout all the region.)
What did the Jewish leaders do? (They

stirred up persecution against Paul and Barnabas.)
Who did they stir up? (The devout and honourable women, and the chief men of the city.)
What did these people do to Paul and Barnabas? (They were kicked out of their land.)
What did Paul and Barnabas do? (Vs. 51, they shook off the dust of their feet against them and came to Iconium.)
What were the disciples filled with? (Joy and the Holy Spirit!)

READ: Acts 14:1-7

QUESTIONS

What did Paul and Barnabas do in Iconium? (They went into the synagogue of the Jews and spoke.)
What happened when they spoke? (A great number of Jews and Greeks believed.)
What did the ones that DIDN'T believe do? (They stirred up the Gentiles and made their minds evil against the brethren.)
Did this stop Paul and Barnabas? (No!)
Did they speak BOLDLY of themselves? (No, Vs. 3 says they spoke BOLDLY in the LORD.)
Who gave them testimony? (It says the Lord did.)
So from where did the thoughts and POWER to speak Truth that caused people to believe come from, Paul and Barnabas? (No, it came from the Lord.)
Was it from their own thoughts? (No, it was through the grace of the Lord.)
Did they do miracles because THEY had the power to do so? (No, it was GRANTED them to do so by God, vs. 3.)
What happened to this city because of the Words Paul and Barnabas spoke? (The city was divided.)
What did the ones who DIDN'T believe do? (They were going to stone them.)
Where did Paul and Barnabas go then? (They went to Lystra and Debre, and the cities of Lycaonia, and all around there.)
Did Paul and Barnabas become scared of what men would do to them if they spoke the Word of God? (No! They PREACHED THE GOSPEL!)

PARENT: We need to see that no matter what opposition Paul and Barnabas came against, they still continued to preach the Word of God. They were BOLD! We need to remember that if we are going to follow after the Lord, we are also going to have opposition from those who do NOT believe. Jesus told us over and over that we will be hated by the WORLD, or those who do not follow after Him. The ones who were most ZEALOUS against the believers and stirred up the Gentiles, or Pagans, were those who thought they had God already, but refused to follow His Word. If the Jews had loved and obeyed the Word of God, they would have known that Jesus was the long-awaited Messiah of Israel. We need to learn to NOT be afraid of what men may say or do to us, but to be solidly FOUNDED in the Word of God and care what IT says rather than men. If we do this, we can never go wrong!

❦❦❦❦❦❦

Lesson Twenty-Three
VIRTUE
Boldness ... In Word

PARENT: Being bold is saying the Truth regardless of what people think or do to us. It is BELIEVING that something is TRUE and so you react accordingly. For example, if your name is Dan, and someone comes to you and tells you that you are wrong, your name is Tom, you would know this wasn't right, and no matter what, stick to the FACT that your name was Dan! This is the TRUTH, your name is Dan! It is the same with the Word of God. If there is something being said that is not the Word of God, and you know that this is TRUE, how could you NOT stand up for the TRUTH and say what the Truth is? As we get closer to the return of our King, we know that many things will be contrary to the Word of God. We need to BELIEVE in the Truth enough to oppose FALSENESS, which is anything that is contrary to the Word of God. Today we are going to read more of the Bible that tells us to be BOLD...

READ: 2 Corinthians 7:4
Ephesians 6:19, 20

QUESTIONS

According to these scriptures, what are the disciples BOLD in? (In speaking the Gospel.) What should WE be bold in?

READ: 1 Thessalonians 2:1-9

QUESTIONS

How were the disciples treated before they came to the Thessalonians? (They suffered and were shamefully treated, vs. 2.)
With what did they speak the gospel of God? (With much contention.)
How did they speak? (Vs. 3, without deceit, uncleanness or guile.)
Did they speak trying to please men or as men pleasers? (Vs. 4, says no! They spoke as God pleasers.)
Did they flatter the people? (No! Vs. 5 says they spoke not using flattering words and not with a cloke of covetousness.)
Were they seeking the glory of men? (No!)
In there boldness were they harsh? (Vs. 7 says they were gentle, even as gentle as a nurse who cherishes her children.)
How much did the disciples love the believers? (Vs. 8 says they were not only willing to impart the gospel of God, but also their own souls.)

READ: 1 Thessalonians 2:10-13

QUESTIONS

How did the disciples behave? (Vs. 10, they were holy, just, and unblameable. They comforted, exhorted and charged the believers as a father does his children.)

PARENT: This scripture gives us a very clear idea of how we are to behave towards those who we are speaking the TRUTH to.
We are not to condemn others and speak to them in a harsh manner. We are to have gentle spirits. Men and women. Titus talks very clearly to women that they are to ornament themselves with a quiet and gentle spirit. But according to this scripture our BOLD apostles were also gentle. As gentle as a woman with her babies. We need to learn from the apostles and cultivate these traits. In our boldness we are to be gentle.

ACTIVITIES

Make a list of the HOW we are to speak the Word of God and hang it in your schooling area.

When we BOLDLY speak the Word of God we are to:

1. Never be deceitful, which means to stray from the Truth.
2. Never talk uncleanly or in a lewd manner.
3. Never speak in guile or in a wily, crafty way.
4. Not use flattering words to make people like you or listen better.
5. Nor with a cloke of covetousness or with the thought of getting money. Not being eager for gain, either of power or of money.

6. Never seeking our own glory or with the thought of becoming a well-known name.
7. Speaking gently to everyone.
8. Loving those who you are speaking to.
9. ...

❦❦❦❦❦❦❦

Lesson Twenty-Four
VIRTUE
Boldness ... Even in Bonds

PARENT: The Bible teaches us that the apostles spent an awful lot of time in jail. This is a very sobering thought. When they spoke the Gospel, they knew that they would probably be taking the chance that they would offend those who did not believe and so spend some time behind bars. The Bible also tells us that we are NOT to suffer as evil doers. This means, if we are put into jail because we have STOLEN, or have done something illegal or wrong, this is very, very bad and gives the name of Jesus a bad reputation if that person is calling himself a Christian. But, if we are suffering and put into jail because of righteousness sake which is because of speaking the truth or preaching the gospel, then we are to REJOICE! Today we are going to read about Paul. He spent much time in jail because of preaching the Gospel. This is important to know, because even in his bonds, he continued to speak the TRUTH. This is being BOLD!

READ: Colossians 4:2-6
         2 Timothy 2:9-10

QUESTIONS

Why was Paul in bonds? (For what he spoke.)
Even though he was in jail because of speaking the gospel, what did he want the believers to pray for? (That God would open doors for them to speak MORE!!!)
Did they care that they were in jail? (No! They wanted more opportunities to speak the Gospel even though this would mean more opportunities for being in chains!)
In 2 Timothy, was Paul an evil doer? (No! He was suffering as IF he was an evildoer. He was being treated as an evildoer for only speaking the TRUTH.)
Why did Paul endure these sufferings? (For the elect's sake.)

READ: Philemon 9-22
         Hebrews 10:32-39
         Hebrews 11:35-36
         Hebrews 13:3

QUESTIONS

According to Phil. 22, how did Paul hope to get out of jail? (Through the believer's prayers.)
Through all these times of being in prison, did Paul ever give up hope? (No! His hope was in the Lord.)
Did he ever draw back into the world? (No! He kept having the hope that the Lord would return!)
Are we to have this hope?
According to Hebrews 11:35, why were others tortured, not accepting deliverance? (They wanted to obtain a better resurrection.)
If you BELIEVE, are you able to withstand ANYTHING? (If you believe something is the TRUTH, you cannot accept anything less and it is a matter of INTEGRITY, or PRINCIPLE that makes you stand in that BELIEF. If you KNOW something is TRUE you will WANT to endure anything! God is the one who makes a heart know TRUTH, and with HIM we will be able to be BOLD as HE is our CONFIDENCE!!!)

PARENT: We need to remember that we need to BOLDLY speak the Truth even if it means that we might bodily be harmed. It is easy to speak the Truth or the Word of God when we know everyone agrees, but it is TRUE faith when you can speak the Word knowing your flesh might be in jeopardy. According to the scriptures on BOLDNESS, is being bold doing something? ... It is speaking in something without fear. Remember the scriptures that tell us how we are to speak. We are to be gentle when speaking the truth. If we are harsh, our attitude is not right and may get in the way of someone receiving the Word of God. Speaking the Truth in Love needs to be always in our mind.

Lesson Twenty-Five
VIRTUE
Goodness

PARENT: What did we learn about VIRTUE? What is virtue? ... Virtue is after you BELIEVE in Jesus, you then try to do what is RIGHT according to the Word of God. If you BELIEVE something is true, you will NATURALLY have VALOR because it is a BELIEF, and you will stand up for that belief. A person that does not stand up for something they say they believe, must not really believe in their heart. Sadly, they must only be giving lip service ... Lip service is only SAYING with your mouth, but nothing else in your life will show that you believe. It is being a HEARER only and it is a form of hypocrisy. Hypocrisy means you are pretending. Jesus had many things to say to the hypocrites of His day and we sure do not ever want Him saying these things to us! Today we are going to study GOODNESS. If you BELIEVE in Jesus and love Him you will want to do what He says. We are to try to follow His Words. A part of goodness is doing the will of our Father. The Bible says that no man is righteous! it also says that there is no man that is good, only our Father. But through our BELIEVING in Him, He will help us to do the GOOD things of the Word of God.

DICTIONARY: Goodness

(1. The state or quality of being good; excellence; merit; worth. 2. Virtuousness; moral rectitude. 3. Kindness, benevolence, generosity.)

DICTIONARY: Good

(1. Having positive or desirable qualities. 2. Serviceable. 3. Of moral excellence; virtuous; upright. 4. Benevolent, kind. 5. Loyal. 6. Obedient. 7. Competent; skilled. 8. Being sound or whole.)

READ: Acts 10:37-38
           Romans 2:8-11
           Romans 11:22
           Romans 15:14

QUESTIONS

What did Jesus do in Acts 10? (He went about doing GOOD.)
Do you think we should try to imitate our Lord? (Yes, through His Holy Spirit.)
Does God want us to have hearts that want to do good? (Yes.)
Do we have goodness of our own? (No, Ro. 11:22 says that we are to continue in HIS goodness. It is just the same as righteousness. We ourselves, are not RIGHTEOUS, it is what you BELIEVE that makes you righteous. But those who BELIEVE will have hearts that want to do good and will walk in HIS goodness.)
What are we to be filled with? (Full of goodness and filled with all knowledge.)
What is the sequence of what we are to have? (We are to have FAITH, and add VIRTUE and next is KNOWLEDGE!)

READ: Galations 5:22

Galations 6:10
Ephesians 5:9
Ephesians 6:8

QUESTIONS

What are the fruits of the Spirit? (Love, joy, peace, longsuffering, gentleness, GOODNESS, faith, meekness, temperance.)
Who are we to do good to? (ALL men, especially of the household of faith, or those who BELIEVE.)
According to Ephesians 5:9, what is the Fruit of the Spirit in? (It is in ALL goodness, righteousness and truth!)
Does goodness go along with righteousness?

READ: 1 Timothy 6:17-19
Titus 2:4-5
Hebrews 13:16
James 4:17
1 Peter 3:10-13
3 John 11

QUESTIONS

What is SIN according to James 4:17? (Sin is if you know to do good, but you do not do it.)
How are we to live our lives? (1 Peter 3, says we are not to speak evil or guile, run from evil, do GOOD, and pursue peace.)
What does the Bible say NOT to follow? (Evil.)
What are we TO follow? (Good.)
Who are we from if we do GOOD? (God.)
Does the Bible teach us to do Good?
Should we try to follow the Bible?
What happens if our hearts LOVE to follow evil? (We are not of God.)
Will we sin? (Yes, but our hearts do not LOVE to do evil. This is why Jesus died for us. He died for our sins.)

Lesson Twenty-Six
VIRTUE
Goodness ... Being Competent or Serviceable

PARENT: The Bible tells us that we are to do good, and stay away from evil. This is a part of being VIRTUOUS. One of the definitions of goodness was being serviceable, competent or skilled. The Bible talks about us being in the service of our King. Let's see what else the Bible has to say about this.

READ: Ephesians 6:5-8

QUESTIONS

If a man works at a job, is he a type of servant? (Yes, a paid servant.)
How are we suppose to serve our employers? (Vs. 5, with obedience in our HEARTS!)
Who are we to be doing the work for in our hearts? (We are to do all that we do as if we were doing it for JESUS.)
Will the Lord reward men for the good that they do? (Vs. 8 says yes! But this is not why we are to want to do good. We are not doing things for a reward, only for the LOVE of Christ.)

READ: Philippians 2:12-18

QUESTIONS

Who is working in us? (God.)
How are we to do ALL things? (Without murmuring and arguing.)
What are we to be? (Vs. 15 says that we are to be blameless, and harmless, and without rebuke.)
What is the world? (Vs. 15, says crooked and perverse.)
What are we to be? (Lights in the world.)

(This next portion is the story of Joseph. In the first part of this story it uses the term "to lie with". Each parent will have to determine if they want to read this or go on to the next part of the Bible in Genesis 41:1-46.)

READ: Genesis 39:1-23

QUESTIONS

Did Joseph serve his master, the Egyptian, well? (Yes.)
What did the Lord do for Joseph? (The Lord made all that Joseph did prosper.)
What does Vs. 6 say Joseph was? (And Joseph was a GOODLY person, and well favoured.)
Did Joseph dishonour his master? (No!)
Who does Joseph say he would sin against, his master? (No, vs. 9 says he would sin against God.)
When we sin, who do we sin against? (God.)
What happened to Joseph? (He was wrongly put into prison.)

READ: Genesis 41:1-46

QUESTIONS

What was Joseph able to do? (He was able to interpret Pharaoh's dream.)
Did HE do this? (No, it was the Lord.)
What was Joseph's interpretation of the dream called? (Vs. 37, says, "And the thing was GOOD in the eyes of Pharaoh, and in the eyes of all his servants.")
What did Pharaoh know about Joseph? (Vs. 38, that the Spirit of the Lord was in Joseph.)
According to the Bible, Joseph was known as a "goodly person". Should we too be known as "goodly persons"?
Did Joseph prove to be a good servant?
How should we behave in all that we do?

READ: Proverbs 22:1
            Ecclesiastes 7:1

QUESTIONS

What is better than great riches? (A good name.)
What does it mean to have a good name? (This means to have a reputation of doing good, rather than a reputation of one who is in trouble or follows evil.)
What else is a good name better than? (It is better than precious ointment that costs lots and lots of money.)
Should we work to keep our name from being mentioned as one who does evil?
Did Paul have a good reputation? (No, the believers were at first afraid of him because of his reputation for persecuting the believers.)
Did he always have a bad reputation? (No, he earned their trust and a good name for himself in the name of the Lord.)

PARENT: *We need to learn to be like Joseph. He was known as a goodly man and this is what we want to be known as. We are to learn to do what is good and turn away from evil. This is what pleases our Lord, the King of All. Remember, we are to learn to be loyal subjects of God and a loyal subject is one who does GOOD towards the King, even when the King is not looking (or you don't THINK He's looking!).*

Lesson Twenty-Seven
VIRTUE
Goodness ... Being Sound and Whole

PARENT: What did you learn in the last lesson? ... Are we to have a reputation of being GOOD, or of being evil? ... We learned that Joseph was known for being a good man. We need to also have the reputation for being good. Do you remember the dictionary definition for GOOD? ... It said, having desirable qualities; being serviceable; of moral excellence, virtuous, upright; being sound or whole. Today we are going to see what the Bible has to say about this. First, let's find out what it means to be SOUND.

DICTIONARY: Sound

(1. Free from defect. 2. Having a firm basis; solid; unshakable. 3. Correct. 4. Complete. 5. Free from moral defect; upright; honorable. 6. Trustworthy.)

READ: Psalms 119:80

QUESTIONS

What are our hearts to be sound in? (In God's statutes, or in other words, in God's Word.)
What will happen if we are sound in God's Word? (We will not be ashamed before Him.)
Do we care if we are ashamed before men? (We shouldn't care. If we do, then we would be men pleasers and we sure do not want to be that ... We want to be GOD pleasers.)

READ: Proverbs 2:7
Proverbs 3:21
Proverbs 14:30

QUESTIONS

What type of wisdom does God lay up for the righteous? (SOUND wisdom.)
Does this mean wisdom of the WORLD? (No, God's wisdom which is not of this world.)
What are we to keep? (Sound wisdom and discretion.)
What is the life of the flesh? (A sound heart.)
What does envy do to our bodies? (It rots our bones.)

READ: 1 Timothy 1:9-10
2 Timothy 1:7-13
2 Timothy 4:1-3

QUESTIONS

According to 1 Timothy 1, what are things that are opposite of SOUND doctrine? (Lawlessness, disobedience, ungodliness, sin, being unholy or profane, murdering, defilers, menstealers, liars, perjurers... to name just a few.)
Can you think of some things not listed here?
What has God not given us? (Vs. 7, a spirit of fear.)
What has He given us? (A spirit of power, love and sound mind.)
What does this SPIRIT mean here? (It means mental disposition.)
Why has He given this to us? (Vs. 8, So we will not be ashamed of the testimony of our Lord, and so we will be able to be partakers of the afflictions of the gospel according to the power of God.)
In Vs. 13, we are to hold fast. What are to hold fast onto? (SOUND words.)
What are the five things we are to do? (1. Preach the Word. 2. Be instant, meaning to stand firmly in the Word, in season and out of season. 3. Reprove. 4. Rebuke. 5. Exhort.)
How are we to exhort one another? (With all long-suffering and doctrine, or with the Word of God!)
What time did Paul say would come? (When people will not endure sound doctrine.)
What types of teachings will they have? (Teachings that will be after their own lusts and they will just listen to fables or CONCEPTS of men, rather than to the Word of

God.)
What will we listen to? (Sound doctrine!)

STRONG'S: Sound (In this text.)

(Greek # 5198; to be well; to be uncorrupted or TRUE in doctrine.)

READ: Titus 1:9-13
Titus 2:1-8

QUESTIONS

What are we to hold TIGHT to ? (Ti. 1:9; to the faithful Word.)
Why? (So we will be able to exhort and convince gainsayers.)

PARENT: We need to know Titus 2 very well. If we follow this scripture it will help us to live lives that will be pleasing to the Lord. It gives a list to older men, younger men, older women, and younger women ... This covers what you, as children, are to grow into!

✿✿✿✿✿✿✿

Lesson Twenty-Eight
VIRTUE
Goodness ... Being Kind

PARENT: We are learning about GOODNESS which is a characteristic of VIRTUE. A quality of goodness is KINDNESS. We need to develop spirits that show kindness to those within the body of Christ and also to those without. Did you know God is KIND? The Bible tells us that the only one who is truly GOOD is God. God is full of loving kindness! Isn't it wonderful to know that we serve a KING who is good, kind and loving?

READ: Nehemiah 9:16-17
Isaiah 54:8
Joel 2:13

What does Nehemiah say about the children of Israel? Did they do good? (No, they hardened their necks and were rebellious.)
What does it say God is, even though they were hard and rebellious? (It says God is ready to pardon, gracious and merciful, slow to anger and of GREAT kindness, and forsook them not.)
If we make mistakes, what do you think God's attitude will be towards us? (The very same.)
Should we sin because of God's loving kindness? (No! That would not be having a heart that wants to please our King.)
What kind of kindness does God have? (Isaiah 54:8, everlasting kindness.)

PARENT: God is full of everlasting kindness. God's kindness far surpasses any kindness that we might ever have, but He wouldn't tell us to develop these characteristics if it were impossible to do so. If God tells us to be good and to be kind and to be virtuous, then through HIS HOLY SPIRIT, we CAN develop these things! Otherwise He wouldn't tell us to DO these things!

READ: Acts 4:31-37

What did the believers do here that showed kindness towards one another? (They had all things in common, they shared. They sold belongings and gave the money to whoever had need.)

READ: Romans 12:9-21

QUESTIONS

How affectioned are we to be to one another? (Kindly.)
In these scriptures can you name some things you DO to be kind to one another?
Does being KIND mean just a nice look on your face and a friendly tone of voice? (No.)
What are other ways of being kind? (By doing
kind things.)
What are we to have an ATTITUDE of? (Kindness.)

READ: Ephesians 4:31-32

QUESTIONS

Many times brothers and sisters fight, is this having an attitude of kindness?
What are some things we are to put away? (Bitterness, wrath, anger, fighting, evil speaking, and malice.)
When you fight with others, have you put these things away? (No.)
What are we to be to one another? (KIND, tenderhearted, forgiving.)
Where is the best place to start doing these things? (Right in your very own home, with your family. If you develop these attributes with your own family, it becomes a REALITY.

READ: Colossians 3:12-16

QUESTIONS

What are we to put on? (Vs. 12, bowels of mercies, kindness, humbleness of mind, meekness, long-suffering, forbearing one another, forgiving one another, charity.)

PARENT: The Word of God tells us to do these things and through Christ, we can put these on! If we do these things we will have added VIRTUE to our FAITH!

ACTIVITIES

Make a list of things you are to put away in Ephesians 4:31 and hang it on your refridge. One idea is that the next time an argument starts in your home, let the children read it.

Lesson Twenty-Nine
VIRTUE
Review

What is VIRTUE? (Virtue is moral excellence, righteousness, goodness, and valor.)
What is a good scripture for young girls to read? (Proverbs 31.)
How much is a virtuous woman worth?
Should we follow these scriptures also?
What are some things that a virtuous woman does?

Who is RIGHTEOUS? (God.)
How will God judge? (Righteously.)
What makes us righteous? (Believing in Jesus.)
If we are righteous by BELIEVING, why do we have to DO anything righteous? (A righteous person will want to DO the Word of God, not hear it only.)
How much are we to love God? (With ALL of us!)

How does a righteous person speak? (They speak acceptable things that give life and feeds others.)
How does a righteous man treat his livestock? (He takes care of them with kindness.)
What do the righteous need to be careful of? (The way of the wicked.)
Is a righteous person lazy? (No, he does not eat the bread of idleness.)
How bold are the righteous? (As bold as a lion.)
How do the righteous treat the poor? (They consider their cause.)
Do they help them grudgingly? (No, they give and spare not.)

What are the people who BELIEVE called? (The sons of God.)
Does the world know us? (No.)
Does the world know God? (No.)
Did it know Jesus? (No.)
Will it love us? (No.)

Are we to be like the world?
If the world is doing something should we fashion ourselves after it?

How are we to treat other believers?
If you see a brother in need and do not give to him what are you? (The Bible says that a person like this does not love God.)
How do we love God?

Are we to be a vessel unto honour or a vessel unto dishonour?
Why does Jesus liken us to a vessel? (Because we are to be used, like a vessel is used.)
What are we to follow after? (Righteousness, faith, charity, peace ...)
What must a servant of the Lord NOT do? (Strive.)
How are we to speak? (Gently, and not with evil or guile, which means to be deceptive.)

How are we to be if we suffer for righteousness sake? (We are to be happy and to rejoice.)
Are we to be afraid of what the wicked will do to us? (No!)
Who is our shield and our protector? (God!)
What are we to ALWAYS be ready for? (To give an answer of the hope we have in Jesus.)
In what manner do we speak this? (With a meek and reverent attitude.)

What does it mean to be morally excellent? (It means to have discernment of what is good and what is evil, having integrity, being upright and DOING what is good.)
What is the difference between judging and condemnation? (Judgment is to discern what is good and what is evil. To condemn is to pass sentence.)
Are we to condemn? (NO! Only God can do this.)
How will we know what is good and what is evil? (By knowing the Word of God.)

Where are we upright? (In our hearts.)
So is it believing that makes us upright?

(Yes.)
What will an upright person WANT to do? (They will want to do what is pleasing in the sight of the Lord.)
What is VALOR? (It is being brave, courageous, and stouthearted.)
Who are we to fear? (God.)
What does this FEAR mean? (To reverence God.)
Who are we NOT to fear? (Men.)
What does it mean to be bold? (To not be afraid, to not be afraid to speak what we truly believe.)
What did the believers pray for? (Boldness.)
What are we to be bold in? (Speaking the Gospel and speaking TRUTH.)

❦❦❦❦❦❦

Virtue

There was once a young orphan boy that lived in a land that was known for the superior intelligence of its inhabitants. One day, an old man had come to his village and proclaimed the message that there was a mighty King that had made man and that He would judge each man according to His deeds, and if you believed in this King's Son you could be found guiltless at this judgment and live forever with the King!

The young boy was the only one who had believed the old man's message and so the elder had given the boy a book that contained all the Truth about the great King. It was an instructional book and the youth hungrily read every single page, gleaning and growing, in the love of his King.

One day, as the child was reading the Book on the bank of a quiet, running stream, he came upon a passage that startled him! He read it again... And then he read it again!... He sat up with a great shout of joy!!! The King was coming! The King was returning for those who believed!!!

The boy quickly got up, grabbed his book, and rushed back to the village. He saw some young boys that he knew and told them excitedly, "The King is coming! The great King of all the Kings is coming here!!!"

The boys looked at him with scorn and one said, "Are you still going on with that nonsense? Why don't you start living in the real world. Your mind is so much on things you can't see that you aren't any fun any more!"

They grabbed their school books, turned their backs on him, and walked away.

The boy looked after them with a determined look in his eyes and glanced down at the worn black book in his hands. "This is true!" he thought. "How can they call this nonsense?!"

He went back to his reading place near the stream and read more about the wonderful Kingdom that he would be going to once the King returned.

A few weeks later he saw some of the children that he played with, calling him to come play. He went to his playmates and listened to what they wanted to do.

"Let's go over to old Mrs. Peabody's and see if we can steal some of her cherries from her tree!"

The boy looked at his friends in horror. "We can't do that to that poor old widow! Those trees belong to her and we shouldn't steal!!"

His friends turned to glare at him. "What's got into you? You used to steal cherries from Mrs. Peabody's trees all the time! You and your stupid King! Your imaginary friend has ruined you and now you are ruining our fun! If you don't come with us and get some cherries, we are not going to play with you any more!"

The boy stood straight and tall. "Ok. If that's the way it must be... I will not go with you. I know that my King is returning and in His book He tells us that it's wrong to steal. I must do what He tells me to do!" The boy boldly stood up to them, then turned and walked away.

From that time on, the boy had many encounters with everyone telling him how stupid it was that he would believe in something he couldn't see. Everyone in the village decided that for his own good, they were going to have to put a stop to this. He was taking this King thing a little bit too far. It was fine when he kept it to himself, but when that was all he talked about, all he thought about, the concerned people knew this showed he was becoming obsessed! The only humane thing to do was to save him from his illusions.

The people of the village brought the boy to the center of town and stood him up for all the people to look at.

The mayor told him, "Young man, the people of this village are very concerned for your welfare. We want to make you see that there is no way to prove that your King exists, and it is very unhealthy for you to live in this make believe world you have been living in. For your own good, we are going to lock you in your room at the orphanage so you will have plenty of time to realize that there is no such thing as this King! You may come out when you can face this fact!"

The boy looked at the mayor then glanced around at all the faces of the village people. "You may not see the King, yet. But my King has written a book about all that He is and will be, and He is coming soon! You can lock me in my room, Your Honor, but I believe in Him and Know he is King! I can't help but believe!"

The townspeople felt terribly sad at the dementia of the child and locked him in his room. Days went by and still the young boy refused to give up his belief in his King. The people decided that more drastic measures were called for. This young child was becoming dangerous, for because of his firm stand that there was a King, he was causing many more of the people in the village to start questioning if there really was something to all he was saying!

The village people decided to scare the child into giving up his hallucinations! They brought the boy before the people again, and told him to reconsider. The boy firmly said, "There is nothing to reconsider. It is the Truth! There is a King, and He is coming soon!"

The mayor said, "Young man, we have an abandoned well that we are going to put you in. It is dark, cold and very scary down there, with many sorts of creepy crawlies. Are you sure you do not want to reconsider now, or do you need more time in there to think it over?"

The boy valiantly stood tall, with his chin up. "How can I reconsider Truth? If I deny this, I will be lying, for there is a King and He is coming soon! It is so important for You to believe in the King too! He will be judging everyone, and if you do not recognize Him as King, there will be great peril for you!"

This speech only further enraged the crowd.

The townspeople all followed as they took him to the opening of the well. The boy looked down and saw a dark, endless hole of black, scary nothing! What sort of creatures would be in there? ... Especially at night?!!

He talked to his King inside his heart, knowing that He was such a great King, that He could hear him anywhere. He asked the King to please help him not be afraid.

Suddenly, there was the sound of a trumpet and the gallop of many horses hooves! There, rushing towards them, was the King that the young boy had been talking about!! The boy's face was alit with exceeding Joy! The townspeople's faces were terrified.

"I knew you were coming soon!" the boy exclaimed as he bowed low before His awesome Majesty.

The King picked up the boy and put him behind Him on the back of His horse. He turned towards the rest of the people. "I'll see you at the judgment."

Then He left them with these words ringing in their ears, "All you had to do was believe."

Knowledge

Lesson One
KNOWLEDGE

PARENT: What are the first two topics we have been studying? ... We have learned FAITH, and have added VIRTUE. The next thing we are to add is KNOWLEDGE. There is a difference between the knowledge that the world has and knowledge that God has. Many people go to college and learn many things, but this is not true knowledge. Today we are going to find out what GOD has to say about KNOWLEDGE. What do you think KNOWLEDGE is? ...

DICTIONARY: Knowledge

(1. The state of knowing. 2. Familiarity, awareness, or understanding gained through experience or study. 3. That which is known; the sum or range of what has been perceived, discovered, or inferred. 4. Learning. 5. Enlightenment.)

READ: Proverbs 1:7

STRONG'S: Knowledge

(Hebrew #998; from 995, to separate mentally or distinguish; understand; attend, consider, diligently, inform, instruct, understanding; knowledge, wisdom.)

PARENT: The Word of God tells us that the beginning of knowledge is the fear of the Lord. We have learned that this fear is to reverence God and to bow to Him and Him alone. The first thing we need to do is to FEAR God. If you do not fear God then you will not be able to have knowledge.

READ: Proverbs 9:10

QUESTIONS

What else is the fear of the Lord? (It is the beginning of wisdom.)
What are we to have knowledge of? (Knowledge of the HOLY.)
What do you think this HOLY is?

STRONG'S: Holy

(Hebrew #6918; sacred, God, sanctuary.)

PARENT: We are to have knowledge of God and what He has to say. Where do we go to find out what He says to us? ... The Bible is our handbook. If we read the Word of God, we will have knowledge. There is nothing else on earth that can give us this knowledge, but His Holy Word. If we are to have knowledge of what is Holy, then we are to have knowledge of the Word of God. We should know it better than we know anything else, better than any other book, better than ANY other thing on this earth! For in God's Word is our INSTRUCTION for living life!

READ: Proverbs 2:3-6
Proverbs 2:10-12

QUESTIONS

What are we to CRY after? (Knowledge.)
Do you remember how we shall understand the fear of the Lord? (1. Cry after knowledge. 2. Lift up your voice for understanding. 3. Seek knowledge as if it were silver. 4. Search for knowledge as for hidden treasures. THEN shall you understand the fear of the Lord.)
What else will you find if you do these things? (Vs. 5, you will find the knowledge of God.)
Where does knowledge come from? (Out of the Lord's mouth, vs. 6)
What will happen to us when knowledge is pleasant to us? (Vs. 11 & 12; 1. Discretion shall preserve you. 2. Understanding will keep you. 3. To deliver you from the way of the evil man. 4. To deliver you from the man that speaks froward things.)

READ: Proverbs 5:2
        Proverbs 8:8-13

QUESTIONS

What does a person understand? (God's wisdom.)
What are the Words of God to a person with knowledge? (He will know they are RIGHT.)
What should we want more than gold? (Knowledge.)
Do you remember what the fear of the Lord is? (It is to hate evil.)

PARENT: We are learning that the beginning of knowledge is the fear of the Lord. What is the fear of the Lord? It is to hate what is evil.

ೞೞೞೞೞೞ

Lesson Two
KNOWLEDGE
Knowing God's Word

PARENT: We learned in the last lesson that we are to seek the knowledge of God.
To have the FEAR of God is what? ... It is the beginning of having knowledge. Do you remember what the fear of the Lord is? ... It is to hate evil. Doesn't this go along with what being a mature Christian is? The Word of God tells us in Hebrews 5:14: But strong meat belongeth to them that are of full age, even those who by reason of use have their senses exercised to discern both good and evil. This is a mature Christian. We need to know that this is something we grow into. It comes from knowing God's Word which tells us what is pleasing to God and what is evil.
Knowledge is to KNOW.

READ: Isaiah 28:9-12

QUESTIONS

At what age do you start teaching a child the knowledge of the Word of God? (Vs. 9 says as soon as a child is weaned from his mother.)
How do you teach a child? (Precept upon precept.)
What is a precept? (In this scripture it means God's commandments.)
So how are you suppose to learn? (One commandment at a time.)
What would happen if you tried to learn everything in one day? (You wouldn't be able to remember it all.)
What is the knowledge of the Lord to those that find it? (A rest.)
What else? (It is refreshing to those who hear.)

READ: Proverbs 22:12
        Proverbs 22:17-18

QUESTIONS

What do God's eyes do? (They preserve knowledge.)
What does it mean to preserve knowledge? (Preserve means to guard or protect)
If we are to seek knowledge as if it were more precious than gold or treasure, then does it make sense that God would guard and protect this knowledge?
What are we to apply our heart to? (Vs. 17, says that we are to apply our hearts to knowing the knowledge of God.)
What is it to us if we do this? (It is a pleasant thing.)

READ: Proverbs 22:19-21

QUESTIONS

What are we to know according to vs. 21? (We are to know the CERTAINTY, or TRUTH in Hebrew, of the Word of God.)
What are we to speak to people? (Words of Truth.)

READ: Proverbs 23:12

QUESTIONS

What does God's Word tell us over and over again to do? (To apply ourselves to instruction and to knowledge.)
How do we get God's knowledge? (From the Word of God, the BIBLE!!)

PARENT: According to God's Word, it is a wonderful thing to learn about God and His ways. The Bible says that it is a pleasant thing, that it is refreshing to us and is a rest to us. To learn of God is to obtain knowledge that is GOOD for us. Remember, when Jesus said in Matthew 4:4, "Man shall not live by bread alone, but by every word that proceedeth out of the mouth of God". We cannot truly LIVE without God's Words and His Words are in the Bible!

READ: Ecclesiastes 1:18

QUESTIONS

Why do you think the Bible would say something like this?
What does the Bible say we will enter the Kingdom of heaven through? (Acts 14:22 says: "Confirming the souls of the disciples, and exhorting them to continue in the faith, and that we must through much tribulation enter into the kingdom of God.")
But what are we be JOYFUL in? (2 Corinthians 7:4 says... I am exceeding joyful in all our tribulation.)

STRONG'S: Sorrow (In Ec. 1:18)

(Hebrew #4341; anguish or affliction.)

PARENT: This sorrow is the same meaning as tribulation! Through much tribulation we will enter into the Kingdom of heaven... We are to be JOYFUL when tribulation comes!!!!!

❦❦❦❦❦❦

Lesson Three
KNOWLEDGE
Enlightenment

PARENT: The Bible tells us that we are to go after knowledge of Him, as if it were more precious than gold or treasure. Later we are going to read about what the Lord thinks about VAIN knowledge or WORLDLY knowledge. He does not want us to be ruined by vain philosophies that the world teaches. God wants us to be a people separate for Him. In order to become this way we must search for knowledge! We do this through reading His Word. We looked up the definition of KNOWLEDGE. One of the aspects of knowledge was being ENLIGHTENED. Did you know that this is mentioned in God's Word?

READ: Psalms 18:28
Psalms 19:8

QUESTIONS

Who will enlighten us? (The Lord our God.)
What does this darkness mean? (It means ignorance.)
What do God's statutes do? (They rejoice our heart!)
What are the commandments of the Lord? (They are PURE.)
What do God's commandments do according to Psalms 19:8? (They enlighten our eyes.)
Do you remember what the Bible said about God's eyes and knowledge? (His eyes protect and guard knowledge. He is watching over it!)

STRONG'S: Enlighten

(Hebrew #5050; means to illuminate; to glitter; enlighten)

DICTIONARY: Enlighten

(1. To give knowledge or truth to. 2. To endow with spiritual understanding. 3. To

edify. 4. To instruct.)

READ: Ephesians 1:17-23

QUESTIONS

According to vs. 17, what are we to have knowledge of? (Knowledge of Him!)
Who will give us the spirit of wisdom and revelation in the knowledge of Him? (The God of our Lord Jesus Christ, the Father of Glory.)
What will be enlightened? (The eyes of our understanding!)
When we are enlightened, what will we know? (Vs. 18, we will know what is the hope of His calling.)
What else? (And what is the riches of the glory of his inheritance in the saints.)
What is the inheritance of the saints? (Eternal life!)
What did God's power do? (He raised Christ from the dead and set Him at the right hand of the Father.)
What else did God's power do in vs. 22? (It put ALL THINGS under His feet and gave Him to be the head over all things to the Church!)
Who is the head of us as the Church? (Jesus.)

READ: Hebrew 6:1-9

STRONG'S: Enlightened (In Heb.6:4)

(Greek #5461; means to make see; to shed rays; to brighten up.)

QUESTIONS

According to these scriptures what does the word ENLIGHTENED here mean to you?
Do you think it means those who have knowledge of Jesus or the Gospel?
So is it fair to say that when a person comes to know the Lord that person becomes enlightened?

PARENT: Isn't it interesting that when one comes to understand the knowledge of the Lord he is ENLIGHTENED! This means that the eyes of our understanding are opened. The Lord called many people BLIND in the Word...

READ: Matthew 23:16, 17, 24, 26
          Mark 8:18
          John 12:40

PARENT: Some people will have eyes to see the TRUTH and some people will not, they are blind. What do we want to do? ... We want to have eyes that see and ears that hear the Word of God.

ACTIVITIES

Put blindfolds on the children and make them walk around for a while. Then, take them off and discuss what it was like to be blind. Then talk about being blinded spiritually and stumbling and falling about!

❦❦❦❦❦❦

Lesson Four
KNOWLEDGE
Being Illuminated

PARENT: What did you learn about being ENLIGHTENED? ... Are there people who will see and people who are blind? ... Being enlightened and being illuminated are almost the same thing.

DICTIONARY: Illuminated

(1. To provide with light; focus light upon. 2. To make understandable; clarify. 3. To enable to understand; enlighten.)

READ: Hebrews 10:32

QUESTIONS

What does this scripture call salvation? (Being illuminated.)
What does this mean? (To have our eyes shown the light.)

PARENT: Do you ever recall seeing a comic picture of someone thinking and then a little picture of a light bulb that is illuminated? ... Or have you ever heard the expression, "I finally saw the light", that talks about finally understanding something. Another saying is, "He brought this to light..." Which means to teach or give understanding to something. Can you think of some other sayings that we use to show light? ... We need to realize that it is our spirit which finally sees when it perceives TRUTH or knowledge of the Word of God.

READ: Proverbs 29:13

QUESTIONS

What does the Lord do to both the poor and the deceitful? (He lighteneth their eyes.)
What does this lighteneth mean? (It is the same Hebrew word as ENLIGHTEN! Or to give knowledge.)
Where does knowledge come from then? (From God.)

PARENT: It is very important to know that our eyes are to see the knowledge of God! The scriptures say so much about the eye.

READ: Luke 11:34

QUESTIONS

What is the light of the body? (The eye.)
What is your body when your eye is single, which means clear? (Your whole body is full of light.)
What happens when your eye is evil? (Your body is full of darkness.)

REFERENCE

Dake's Annotated Reference Bible says: "If the eye is single and sound morally and free from any lusts, the whole body will be free from sin and morally sound and perfect. Light and darkness are used to contrast spiritual KNOWLEDGE and spiritual BLINDNESS."

READ: Proverbs 4:23-27

QUESTIONS

In vs. 25 what are we to have our eyes look on? (We are to look RIGHT on.)
What does it mean to look straight before thee? (It means to look on what is UPRIGHT, not crooked or perverse.)
We are to ponder the path of our feet, what does this mean to you? (Ponder means to look ahead and weigh. To think about.)
So again, what are our eyes to see?

PARENT: Over and over again, our Lord Jesus talked about those who SAW or were enlightened and those who were blind and did not understand. In the last lesson we read some scriptures regarding this. Let's read some more about it!

READ: 2 Peter 1:9
          Revelation 3:17

PARENT: Did you know that there are other religions that claim to lead people to enlightenment? Hinduism, Buddhism and many others all say that they have true knowledge. But this is not true. Many things may seem wise to the world but any other knowledge other than God's knowledge is false! The Word of God says in 1 Corinthians 1:27 "But God hath chosen the foolish things of the world to confound the wise; and God hath chosen the weak things of the world to confound the things which are mighty; and base things of the world, and things which are despised, hath God chosen, yea, and things which are not to bring to nought things that are."

❦❦❦❦❦❦

Lesson Five
KNOWLEDGE
Understanding

PARENT: Do you know what it means to have knowledge? ... As a Christian or BELIEVER, it is to know of God and His Word and ways. We are to have knowledge of what God wants us to KNOW, not what the world would tell us that we need to know. If a person knows English, Math, Science, History, Spelling and Reading and do not know about God, are they smart? They might be smart according to the world, but according to God they are not. They know nothing. And all their worldly knowledge will not allow them to enter into the Kingdom of Heaven. We are going to learn about what it means to have understanding. Understanding is a part of knowledge.

READ: Proverbs 1:1-6

QUESTIONS

What are we to understand in these scriptures? (Vs.6, a proverb.)
What will a man of understanding do? (Vs. 5 says he will listen to wise counsels.)
What is a wise counsel? (Wise counsel would be listening to advice from someone who LIVES the Word of God.)
In the world today people go to psychologists and others who study the mind, for advice. If they do not counsel with God's Word, are we to listen to them?
What are we to know? (Wisdom.)
In this same scripture, what are we to perceive? (The words of understanding.)
What are the four things we are to be instructed in in vs. 3? (1. Wisdom. 2. Justice. 3. Judgment. 4. Equity.)
What are we to understand? (We are to understand a proverb and the interpretation; the words of the wise, and their dark sayings. This dark here in the Hebrew means hard questions.)

READ: Proverbs 2:1-9

QUESTIONS

What are we to hide in us? (God's commandments, God's Word.)
What are we to listen to? (Wisdom.)
What should we long for in our hearts? (Understanding.)
Do you remember what we are to do to understand the fear of the Lord?
Are we to do the same thing to know the knowledge of God? (Yes! Vs. 2-4.)
Where does knowledge and understanding come from? (Vs. 6, out of God's mouth.)
Do you think this is why knowledge that comes from God's mouth is called the WORD of God?

READ: Proverbs 8:5

QUESTIONS

If you are simple, what are you to do? (Understand wisdom.)
If you are a fool what should you do? (Be of an understanding heart.)
Are you to then understand with your mind or your heart? (Heart.)

Lesson Six
KNOWLEDGE
Understanding ...
We are to GET IT!

READ: Proverbs 19:25

QUESTIONS

What happens when you reprove one that has understanding in his heart? (He will understand knowledge.)
Should we not WANT to be corrected or reproved? (No!)
Why do we need to be corrected? (So we will know our error!)
Does God chastise us to teach us?

READ: Hebrews 12:5-11

QUESTIONS

Does chastise mean the same as reprove? (Yes, they both are a form of correction.)
To gain more understanding, do we need to be corrected when we are wrong? (Yes.)
Is it fun to be corrected? (No, no correction is fun at the time of correction, but afterwards it yields unto good fruit!)
Are we to despise being corrected? (No! When parents correct their children it is for the benefit of the children!)
Is God our parent? (Yes, He is our Father.)

PARENT: We need to learn that understanding starts in the heart. We need to be corrected when we are wrong, with the Word of God. If we are doing something that is opposite to what the Bible says, we NEED someone to come and point out scripture. This is where wise counsel comes in. We also need to be corrected. Just like your parents correct you, our loving Father, God, corrects us, too! He wants us to know TRUTH, not ERROR!

✿✿✿✿✿✿

PARENT: In our last lesson we learned that we are to understand God's Word. You can read the Word of God, you can memorize the Word of God, but if you do not understand it, it is all in vain. We need to have hearts that want to understand. If you love your King, our Father, God, you will WANT to understand all His ways! It is part of having FAITH in your hearts! The Word of God tells us to GET understanding ...

READ: Proverbs 4:5-7

QUESTIONS

What two things are we to GET? (1. Wisdom and 2. Understanding.)
Once we GET it what are we to do? (Vs. 5, NOT forget wisdom and understanding.)
What will understanding and wisdom do for you? (They will preserve you.)
If you love understanding what will she do? (She will KEEP you.)
With ALL your getting, what are you to GET? (Understanding.)
Does this sound as if it is very important?
Have you ever wanted something very, VERY badly?
Can you understand what it means to WANT understanding more than anything else?

READ: Proverbs 5:1-2

QUESTIONS

What are you to BOW your ear to? (Understanding God's Word.)
What are your lips to keep? (Knowledge.)
What should a TOP goal be for when you grow up? (To understand the Word of God.)
What is it to be a mature BELIEVER? (To discern good from evil through the Word of

God.)
Do you have to have understanding to do this? (Yes!)
How can you GET understanding? (Through seeking God through His Word and talking to Him.)

READ: Proverbs 9:4-6

QUESTIONS

What are we to forsake or stay away from? (The foolish.)
What are we to eat of? (Wisdom, which is called here bread and wine.)
Who also told us to come and eat bread? (Jesus did.)
Did Jesus have understanding of the Word of God? (Jesus WAS the Word of God!!!! Jn.1)
So if Jesus is the Word of God isn't it wonderful that also in Proverbs we are commanded to eat the bread and drink the wine of WISDOM, which is the Word of God?!!!
What way are we to go? (In the way of understanding.)
What is it to go in the way of the foolish? (Those that DO NOT have God or His Word. This is foolishness.)
Can you think of some things which are devoid of understanding and do not teach God's Word? (Public education, Public universities, etc.)
Are we to walk after these? ...
When you grow up, will you partake in things that do not teach God's Word?

READ: Proverbs 9:10

QUESTIONS

We read this scripture before..., what is UNDERSTANDING? (Knowledge of what is HOLY!)
What should we spend most of our time doing? (Gaining the knowledge of what is HOLY.)

READ: Proverbs 10:13,14

QUESTIONS

What do those who have understanding speak? (Wisdom.)
What is a rod for? (The back of those that do not have understanding.)
What do rich men store up? (Usually MONEY.)
What are WISE men to store up? (KNOWLEDGE.)
Any type of knowledge? (No!)

PARENT: God's Word is very clear as to what we as His children are to follow after and try to GET! We are to get understanding of what is Holy. This is what is meant by GETTING UNDERSTANDING.
When you grow up you are to have studied the Word of God. This is what is the most important thing in the WHOLE world. We are to GET it with ALL of our GETTING!

❦❦❦❦❦❦

Lesson Seven
KNOWLEDGE
Understanding ... Those Who are VOID of Understanding

PARENT: In our society today, there are many things that people want ... For example, some want fancy cars, some want new video games, some want fancy houses or clothes, and so with these wants in their hearts they work at jobs to GET them. We are to be different than this. We are to GET understanding of God's precious Holy Word. We should remind ourselves that this is more valuable and more important than anything else we spend our TIME or our MONEY on! God says that GETTING knowledge of His Word brings rest and refreshment to us. GETTING things of the world does not. It only feeds these WANTS or lusts, and makes us WANT more. Today we are going to learn what the Scriptures say about people who do NOT get understanding. We need to make sure that we are not appointed with those who do not seek after understanding of what is Holy.

READ: Hosea 4:6

QUESTIONS

Why are God's people destroyed? (For lack of knowledge.)
They didn't learn their Math?
What does it mean?
According to this scripture, did these people just not KNOW it? (No, they REJECTED it!)

READ: Hosea 4:12

QUESTIONS

What did God's people do that made Him angry? (They turned from Him, and were not FAITHFUL.)
Who did they get counsel from? (Their stocks.)
What are stocks? (They were idols made from wood.)
Did they get their counsel from wise people who WALKED the Word of God? (No!)
Do you think God is pleased when we take counsel from things that are not founded in His Word?

READ: Matthew 13:1-9

QUESTIONS

What vs. talks about understanding? (Vs. 9, He who has ears to UNDERSTAND, let him UNDERSTAND.)

READ: Matthew 13:9-17

QUESTIONS

Why did Jesus speak to the people in parables? (To some it is given to know and understand the mysteries of the Kingdom of Heaven, and to some it is not. Vs. 11)
Do all people today UNDERSTAND? (No.)
Why do some people not understand? (Vs. 15 says that these people's hearts wax gross or have hardened or thickened.)
What happened to their ears? (They became dull.)
What happened to their eyes? (They closed them to the truth.)
Where does one understand? (In one's heart.)

READ: Mark 4:21-23

QUESTIONS

What does Jesus say again regarding understanding? (If any man has ears to hear, let him hear.)

READ: John 8:39-47

QUESTIONS

Could the religious Pharisees understand

Jesus? (Vs. 43 says they could not understand His speech.)
Did they HEAR His Words? (Yes. They could HEAR Him speak.)
But did they HEAR, meaning understand? (No!)
Who HEARS God's Words? (Those that are of God, vs. 47.)
Why can't some HEAR God's Words? (Vs. 47, because they are not of God.)

STRONG'S: HEAR (In Jn.8)

(Greek #191; to hear, to be reported, UNDERSTAND.)

PARENT: We need to have ears to hear so we may HEAR! If we are of God we will understand His Words. But, remember, if we do not understand all of His Word right now, all we have to do is keep seeking understanding and knowledge and He will reveal it to us. The Word says that we are to learn ONE precept or commandment at a time. We are to build in knowledge. We could not learn the WHOLE Word of God in one day!

❦❦❦❦❦❦

Lesson Eight
KNOWLEDGE
Understanding ... Qualities of those With Understanding

PARENT: Will all people have understanding? ... We learned yesterday that there are people that have hardened their hearts to the TRUTH of God, and who's ears have dulled and who have also shut their eyes. We need to make sure that we NEVER do this. The most important treasure on earth is the KNOWLEDGE of what is Holy!

We need to search after this with everything in us. The Bible talks about people who have done this and what qualities they have. Let's read what the scriptures say about this ...

READ: Proverbs 11:12
Proverbs 13:15

QUESTIONS

How does a man that does not have understanding treat his neighbor? (He despises him.)
How does a man of understanding treat his neighbor? (He holds his peace.)
What does good understanding give? (It gives favour.)
Would YOU rather have favour with God or with men?

READ: Proverbs 14:29
Proverbs 15:14

QUESTIONS

What are we to be? (Slow to wrath.)
If you are slow to wrath, what do you have? (GREAT understanding.)
What happens if you are of a hasty spirit and not slow to wrath? (You will encounter FOLLY.)
What does the heart of the one who has understanding seek? (Knowledge.)
Is this the world's knowledge?
What type of knowledge?

READ: Psalms 119:144
Proverbs 17:27

QUESTIONS

How will we live? (With understanding.)
How does one with understanding speak? (Sparingly. Remember the scripture in James 1:19, "Be swift to hear, slow to speak and slow to wrath!")
What type of spirit does a man of understanding have? (An excellent spirit!)

READ: Proverbs 19:8
Proverbs 20:5

QUESTIONS

What shall a man that keeps understanding find? (He will find good.)
What will a man of understanding do with counsel? (He will draw it out of the hearts of wise men of God.)

READ: 1 Corinthians 14:20
Colossians 1:9-11

QUESTIONS

What are we to NOT be children in? (Understanding.)
What are we to be in understanding? (Men.)
What are we to be children in? (Malice.)
According to Colossians, what are we to desire to be filled with? (The knowledge of God's will in all wisdom and spiritual understanding.)
Does this mean to understand the things of the world?
What type of understanding? (The knowledge of the things of God.)
What will happen if we have this? (We will be able to walk worthy of the Lord in a pleasing manner, vs. 10.)
What is it to be pleasing? (Vs. 10, to be fruitful in every good work.)
What else? (To be INCREASING in the knowledge of God.)

READ: 2 Timothy 2:7
1 John 5:20

QUESTIONS

Who gives us understanding? (The Lord.)
Will He give us understanding in all things? (If we SEEK understanding.)
What are we to understand in 1 John? (That we may know Him that is true.)
Who are we in? (Jesus Christ.)

Lesson Nine
KNOWLEDGE
Wisdom

PARENT: As we have been reading many of the scriptures, we have seen the word WISDOM associated with understanding and with knowledge. Wisdom is a very important thing. God has all wisdom. He is wise in every single thing! Did you know that by WISDOM the earth was made? ... Let's first read what the word WISDOM means.

DICTIONARY: Wisdom

(1. Understanding of what is TRUE, RIGHT, or lasting! 2. Common sense; sagacity; good judgment.)

READ: Psalms 136:5
Proverbs 3:19
Psalms 104:24

QUESTIONS

What did God make in Psalms 136:5 by wisdom? (The heavens.)
What did God found the earth in? (Wisdom.)

PARENT: According to these scriptures God made EVERYTHING by wisdom. What is wisdom then? We know that it is understanding what is true, right or lasting, but are there some scriptures that tell us more?

READ: Proverbs 4:4-13

QUESTIONS

What does Vs. 7 say wisdom is? (Wisdom is the PRINCIPAL thing.)
What are we to get? (Wisdom and understanding.)
If you get wisdom what will happen to you? (Vs. 12 says when you go, your steps will not have to be straightened from crookedness, and when you run you will not stumble.)

READ: Proverbs 8:10-11
        Proverbs 17:24
        Ecclesiastes 7:12

QUESTIONS

What is wisdom in vs. 11? (It is better than rubies.)
What can you compare wisdom to? (Nothing. It is far above everything else that people desire.)
Where is wisdom? (Before those of understanding.)
What is wisdom? (It is a defense.)
What is a defense? (A defense is something that will defend you.)
Which does the Bible say is better, wisdom or money? (Wisdom.)
What does knowledge and wisdom give you that money won't? (They give you life.)

READ: Ecclesiastes 7:19
        Ecclesiastes 9:16-18

QUESTIONS

What does wisdom do to the wise? (It gives them strength!)
Is wisdom better than strength? (Yes!)
So, should we want to be strong or want to be wise?
What is a poor man's wisdom? (Despised.)
Who do you think would despise a poor man? (The world.)
In VIRTUE, what did we learn regarding the poor? How do the virtuous regard them? (They take care of the poor.)
Do you think a virtuous person would despise the poor? (No!)
What is wisdom better than? (Better than weapons of war.)
Why do you think this is?

READ: Ecclesiastes 10:10-12

QUESTIONS

What does vs. 10 say wisdom is?
What do you think this means? (One with wisdom can give advice.)
How does a wise man speak? (Graciously.)
Does a person with VIRTUE also speak graciously? (Yes!)

PARENT: We are learning what wisdom is. Wisdom is understanding what is TRUE, and RIGHT, and LASTING. Wisdom is knowing God's Word, which are all these things and more. God made everything by wisdom. If you look at how the birds are created, how the ocean is formed, how WE are made, it AWES us! God made all these things and He did it perfectly. Imagine making a living creature! Through wisdom God did ALL this.

Can you think of some of the other things we learned that wisdom is? ... Wisdom is the MAIN or PRINCIPAL thing we should GET; wisdom is better than rubies; it is a defense; it gives life; it gives strength; and a person with God's wisdom gives sound advice!

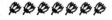

Lesson Ten
KNOWLEDGE
Wisdom ... Cry for It!

PARENT: We learned that wisdom is understanding what is TRUE, RIGHT and LASTING. We also learned a few other things of what wisdom is. Do you remember a few of these things? ... Today we are going to read what the Bible has to say to us about how we are to regard wisdom. It is just the same as knowledge and understanding. It is VERY important that we GET it! It is also very important that when you grow up and have children that you teach your children to GET these things too!

READ: Proverbs 1:1-9

QUESTIONS

According to vs. 3, what will wisdom give? (It will give a young man knowledge and discretion. It will give subtlety to the simple.)
Do you think it is important that a young man has wisdom?

READ: Proverbs 2:1-13

QUESTIONS

What are you to incline your ear to? (Wisdom.)
Who gives wisdom? (God, vs. 6.)
Who does God lay up wisdom for? (The righteous.)
Who are the righteous? (BELIEVERS!)
When wisdom enters your heart, what shall preserve you? (Discretion.)
What is discretion? (Discretion is being prudent, prudence means to be WISE.)

READ: Proverbs 3:13-20

QUESTIONS

What is the disposition of a man that finds wisdom? (Happy! vs. 13.)
Will a person that has wisdom have a long life? (It says length of days or long life is in her hands.)
Do we as BELIEVERS need to fear death? (No! God says that we who fear God and BELIEVE will have everlasting life! This sure is length of days, isn't it?)
What is the way of wisdom? (Vs. 17 says wisdom is pleasantness and peaceful.)

READ: Proverbs 3:21-24

QUESTIONS

What are we to KEEP? (Sound wisdom and discretion.)
Do you remember what SOUND means? (It means CORRECT, not false or error.)
If you walk in God's wisdom how does vs. 23 say we will walk? (We will walk safely, and we will not stumble.)
When you go to sleep at night, will a wise person be afraid? (No!)
How will a wise person sleep? (Sweetly.)
So when you say to a person that is seeking God's knowledge, wisdom and understanding, "Sweet dreams!" can they count on having a good night's sleep?
What should a person do that does not have sweet sleep? (He should try to get more of God's Word into him.)

READ: Proverbs 4:5-13

QUESTIONS

What are we to exalt? (We are to exalt wisdom.)
Does this mean to exalt universities and education? (No! It means to exalt the knowledge of God's Word and His ways.)
What goes along with wisdom? (Vs. 13, Instruction. All scripture is for edification for us to grow!)

READ: Proverbs 7:1-5

QUESTIONS

What does the Word of God say to lay up? (The commandments.)
What will wisdom keep young men from? (Strange women.)
What is a strange woman? (Someone who is not their legal wife. It is an adulteress.)
What are you to know through wisdom? (To stay away from such a woman.)
What type of woman is it **GOOD** to be?

ACTIVITIES

Make a list with the children of qualities you are learning from knowledge, wisdom, and understanding.

❦❦❦❦❦❦

Lesson Eleven
KNOWLEDGE
Wisdom ... God's Not Man's

PARENT: Are you getting the picture that we are to go after knowledge, wisdom and understanding of God's Word? This is what we are to want in our lives, not material things. God says that His wisdom will protect us. Why is this? ... If we are walking in the ways of God, we will not fear anything but Him. We will sleep peacefully at night and God will lead our paths!

READ: Proverbs 3:5-8

PARENT: This is one of the most important verses we could ever know. In this verse is how we should live our lives! We are not to be WISE in our own eyes. We are to walk in the wisdom of God, not of our own wisdom or concepts, but in the knowledge He gives us.
We are going to learn what the Bible has to say about worldly knowledge ...

READ: 1 Corinthians 1:17-21

QUESTIONS

What was Paul sent to do? (He was sent to preach the gospel.)
How was he to preach it? (Not with wisdom of words or speech.)
How does the world react to the preaching of the cross? (They think it is foolishness.)
Is it foolishness to us? (No, this is wisdom.)
What is the preaching of the cross to those who are saved? (It is the POWER of God.)
According to the Scriptures, does the world have wisdom? (Yes, in vs. 20 it says "the wisdom of this world".)
What does God call it? (He calls the wisdom of the world FOOLISH!)
Should we try to be wise according to the world's standard?
What does it say will happen if you have the world's wisdom? (Vs. 21, says that you will not know God.)
What pleases God? (Vs. 21, it pleased God by the foolishness of preaching to save them that believe.)
What will the wise of the world think of our following and knowing the Bible? (They will think it is foolishness.)
In our world today, is this true? (Yes!)

READ: 1 Corinthians 1:22-31

QUESTIONS

In vs. 22 it says that the Greeks seek after wisdom, do you think this is God's wisdom or the wisdom of the world? (They sought after the wisdom and philosophies of the world.)
What makes you KNOW it was the world's wisdom? (Vs. 23 says they preached Christ crucified, unto the Greeks FOOLISHNESS.)
How is preaching Christ perceived of those who are called? (Vs. 24 says it is the power of God and the WISDOM of God.)
Are there many people who are WISE and MIGHTY and NOBLE in the world who are called to Christ? (It says in vs. 26 that there

are NOT MANY of these types called or saved.)
How does God use preaching, then? (To confound the wise!)
How are we to have wisdom, righteousness, sanctification and redemption? (Through Jesus Christ!)

READ: 1 Corinthians 2:1-9

QUESTIONS

Are we to speak with wisdom of men? (No! Paul never did.)
Are we to speak the gospel with enticing words of man's wisdom? (No!)
What is our faith to be in, the wisdom of men, or in the power of God? (Vs. 5, in the power of God.)

READ: 2 Corinthians 1:12

QUESTIONS

Are we to have FLESHLY wisdom? (No, it clearly states in the Word we are not.)
What type of wisdom are we to have? (That of what is Holy.)
What is true knowledge? (Knowing what is HOLY.)

READ: James 3:13-18

QUESTIONS

What is a wise man to do that is a BELIEVER? (Vs. 13.)
Where does wisdom of the world come from? (Not above, from the devil, vs. 15.)
What is wisdom from above like? (Vs. 17 says it is first pure, then peaceable, gentle and easy to be entreated, fully of mercy and good fruits, without partiality, and without hypocrisy.)
Are we to have this wisdom? (YES!)

❦❦❦❦❦❦❦

Lesson Twelve
KNOWLEDGE
Wisdom ... Vain Philosophies

PARENT: Have you ever heard the term "A fool for Christ?" This is what we are all called to be. Many people today are more concerned with what other people think about them than what GOD thinks about them. We are not to be this way. If you see this in yourself, you need to examine this and confess this to our FATHER and "He is faithful and just to cleanse us from all unrighteousness." We are not to fashion ourselves after the world, but rather after the WORD.

READ: Ephesians 5:6-17

QUESTIONS

What are we to be careful of? (Vs. 6 says to let no man deceive you with vain words.)
What are VAIN words? (According to the Greek #2756; it means empty or vain. According to the dictionary VAIN means foolish!)
Are we to beware of foolish, worldly words and teachings?
What are we to do with people who only speak things of the world? (Vs. 7 says to not be partakers with them.)
How are we to walk? (According to vs. 15 we are to walk circumspectly, in wisdom.)
What is an important thing to remember? ('To redeem the time, for the days are evil.')
We are not to be unwise... What are we to be? (Vs. 17 says, to understand what the will of the Lord is.)

READ: Colossians 2:2-7

QUESTIONS

What are we to have assurance in? (Vs. 2 says the full assurance of understanding.)
What is hid in God? (Vs.3, All the TREASURES of wisdom and knowledge.)

If we find wisdom and knowledge will we find treasure? (Yes!)

Why do we need to be rooted, built up in Jesus, and established in the faith? (Vs. 4, so we do not be beguiled by any man with enticing words.)

How will we not be beguiled by such a man? (By KNOWING the Word of God and not being deceived by error.)

READ: Colossians 2:8-9

QUESTIONS

What are we to beware of? (Vs. 8, we are to BEWARE lest any man spoil us through philosophy.)

What is philosophy? (According to the dictionary philosophy is an inquiry into the nature of things based on logical reasoning.)

Vain philosophies would be what then? (Foolish reasonings ... not based on the Word of God but rather of concepts of men with their intellect.)

Are we to reason things out in our OWN minds? (No, we are to trust in the Lord with all our hearts and NOT lean on our own understanding!)

What else are we to beware of? (Vain deceit, and traditions of men which are after the world and NOT after Christ.)

PARENT: This is a very important scripture. The Bible tells us very clearly that we are NOT to do things according to traditions of men and walk in our own understanding, but rather we are to do ALL things according to scripture. The Word of God has an answer to EVERYTHING and all we have to do is to SEEK these answers and we will FIND them. We need to know that anything that does NOT line up with God's Word is merely a PHILOSOPHY, not TRUTH, and we are to beware of this!

READ: 1 Timothy 1:4-7

QUESTIONS

What is a fable? (It is a story or a concept that is not true.)

Are we to listen to fables, or concepts that are not based on the Word of God but rather traditions of men?

What does it say some people do? (They turn aside unto vain jangling, or foolish talking.)

Are we to do this? (No, we are to avoid this as this is not wisdom.)

PARENT: According to God's Word, we are to beware of philosophies that are not according to Him. Wisdom is to not entertain this type of idle chatter. Did you know that we will give an account for every idle word we have uttered? Matthew 12:36 says: "But I say unto you, that every idle word that men shall speak, they shall give account thereof in the day of judgment." We are to know that even our very words are very important. Words can do much harm or much good. Jesus is the WORD of God. He spoke TRUTH, and His Word is sharper than a two-edged sword. Our words can hurt or hinder. We need to speak things that give other people life. We need to only engage in words that are according to the Word of God.

❦❦❦❦❦❦

Lesson Thirteen
KNOWLEDGE
Being Void of Understanding

PARENT: What have we learned about knowledge? ... It is the most important thing to us. Did you know that God says that without knowledge His people perish? This knowledge that God is talking about is not the knowledge of the world but of Him! Did you know that the opposite of having knowledge is to be a FOOL? We are going to discover the attributes of a fool and foolishness and then learn to SHUN these things. First, let's look at the definition of FOOLISH, and FOOL ...

DICTIONARY: Foolish

(1. Lacking good sense or judgment; silly. 2. Resulting from stupidity or misinformation; ill-advised, UNWISE.)

DICTIONARY: Fool

(1. One who shows himself, by words or actions, to be deficient in judgment, sense, or understanding. 2. One who acts UN-WISELY.)

PARENT: A fool and his foolishness is a person who is not acting wisely. A fool is one who does not have any understanding or wisdom and cannot judge good from evil. In the Word of God, we are taught to not be foolish. We are also told not to be simple. We are going to read today what the Bible says about those who are VOID of understanding. That means they do not have any understanding. Let's first find out what simple means.

DICTIONARY: Simple

(1. Having little or no sense, silly. 2. A FOOL or a simpleton.)

READ: Proverbs 7:5-12

QUESTIONS

What does a young man void of understanding do? (He goes after women who do not love God.)
What would wisdom have done for him if he would have sought it? (It would have protected him from such a woman.)
What will a BELIEVING woman grow up to be? (A virtuous woman.)

READ: Proverbs 10:13

QUESTIONS

What do people of understanding speak? (They speak wisdom.)
What will help a person void of understanding? (The rod of correction.)
Do young children have understanding of what is Holy? (No, the Bible says they have foolishness.)
Do you think this is why God says to correct children with a rod (Prov. 22:15)?

READ: Proverbs 11:12

QUESTIONS

Do you remember how a man of understanding treats his neighbor? (He lives in peace with him.)
How does a man VOID of understanding treat his neighbor? (He despises him.)

READ: Proverbs 12:11

QUESTIONS

Are we to work to get food? (The Bible says to till your land and you will have bread.)
Are we to follow vain persons?
Do you remember what the last lesson had to say about following people who speak VAIN things? (Vain means empty and worthless,

things that are worldly, not Godly.)
If we go with people who are vain, what are we? (Void of understanding.)
What should we do then?

READ: Proverbs 24:30-34

QUESTIONS

What does a vineyard of a man void of understanding look like? (It is all overgrown with weeds and nettles. His wall is broken down.)
Is this man a hard worker? (No, he is slothful and lazy.)
If we have understanding, will we be lazy? (No, we will redeem the time, for the days are evil.)
What happens to a man like this? (He will not till their land and probably starve.)

ACTIVITIES

Have the children draw a picture of a vineyard of a man who has understanding and a man who does not.

❦❦❦❦❦❦

Lesson Fourteen
KNOWLEDGE
Foolishness

PARENT: In Lesson Thirteen we learned about a person being void of understanding. Today we are going to look up in the Bible and find what it says about foolishness. It will give us some examples of what NOT to do.

READ: Proverbs 12:23

QUESTIONS

What does this scripture mean to you?
What do fools speak? (Foolishness.)
Where does foolishness come from? (From the heart.)
What makes a fool a fool? (A fool is void of the knowledge of God.)
How can we not be a fool?

READ: Proverbs 14:24

QUESTIONS

What are the riches of the wise? (Their wisdom.)
What is the foolishness of fools? (It is folly.)
What is folly? (Folly is lacking understanding.)

READ: Proverbs 15:2
Proverbs 15:14

QUESTIONS

This scripture again talks about fools speaking. What do they speak? (Foolishness.)
How do the wise in God's knowledge speak? (They use their knowledge rightly.)
What keeps a fool going? (If you continue speaking foolishness to a fool, he feeds on this and it gives him fuel for his foolishness.)
If this is true, when we know that someone is speaking things that are NOT according to the

wisdom of God, do we argue with them? (No, this simply fuels their foolishness.)

READ:	Proverbs 19:3

QUESTIONS

What does the lack of God's knowledge do to man? (It makes the things a man does perverse.)
How has this happened in our world today? (There are evil things happening continuously in the news.)
Why are these things happening? (Because people do not want to know the wisdom of God.)
How does it say these people's hearts are towards God? (Their hearts FRET against Him.)
What does FRET mean? (Here it means get angry.)
So how are these people's hearts toward God? (They are angry towards Him.)
Do you think this could be why many BELIEVERS have been persecuted in the past?

READ:	Proverbs 22:15

QUESTIONS

Where is foolishness bound in children? (In their hearts.)
What is foolishness? (It is lack of knowledge of God.)
Why do you think children have foolishness in their hearts? (Because they do not know the Word of God, yet.)
Are we to correct children? (Yes.)
With what? (The rod of discipline.)

READ:	Proverbs 24:9

QUESTIONS

Is foolishness sin? (Yes.)
Is even the THOUGHT of foolishness sin? (Yes.)
So if we even THINK foolishness, is it sin? (It says here that it is. This is also what the scripture says; that if a man even think it, he has already done it.)
If we think something bad what do we need to do? (Tell God, and repent, and He will cleanse us.)

READ:	1 Corinthians 3:18-19

QUESTIONS

Are we to be wise according to the world? (No!)
If we ARE wise according to the world what are we to become? (Fools according to the world.)
What does God think of the world's wisdom? (He says it is FOOLISHNESS.)
So the wisdom of the world is foolishness to God and the wisdom of God is foolish to __?

PARENT: We need to know now that the wisdom of God will not be received by ANYONE who is not walking according to the ways of God. They will get angry with us and will think we are FOOLS. But, we are NOT to be FOOLS according to God! Remember that we are to be pleasing our King. We will be LOYAL SUBJECTS!

Lesson Fifteen
KNOWLEDGE
A Fool and His Folly

PARENT: We learned what the scriptures had to say about foolishness. What is foolishness? ... It is having knowledge that has nothing to do with God. It is concepts or ideas of men, and they are false. The lack of God's knowledge causes men to be perverse and do evil. Take a look at the world today and you can see that this is true. We are not to be like this. We are to saturate ourselves in the Word of God and then we will have TRUE knowledge. Today we are going to talk about FOOLS. In the New Testament we are told not to EVER call a believer a FOOL. A person who loves the Lord and His Word are not fools. They are learning the wisdom of God by reading Scripture. There are many people today who are fools. These are people who reject the Gospel of Jesus Christ.

READ: Psalms 14:1
            Psalms 53:1
            Psalms 92:6

QUESTIONS

What is an atheist? (It is a person who does not believe that there is a God.)
What are atheists according to Scripture? (They are fools.)
What else are they? (They are corrupt. They do abominable works. They do evil, not good.)
What does the scripture yoke together with a fool? (A brutish man.)
What is a brutish man? (Means a sensual, carnal or worldly man.)
Are we to be like this?

READ: Proverbs 17:7
            Proverbs 17:10
            Proverbs 17:12
            Proverbs 17:16

QUESTIONS

What can a fool not speak? (He cannot speak knowledge of God. This is what makes him a fool!)
Does a fool take correction? (No, it is very difficult for him to receive it.)
Can a wise man take reproof? (Yes, and he will be wiser from it.)
How are we to regard a fool in his folly? Are we to be around foolish, worldly people? (We are to be as cautious of him as we would a mother bear that had just had her cubs stolen.)
What is a mother bear like without her cubs? (DANGEROUS!)
Can a fool get wisdom? (Only if it becomes a desire of his heart; a fool is a fool because his heart loves earthly, worldly knowledge rather than Godly knowledge.)
Can God change a fool? (God can do ANYTHING!)

READ: Proverbs 17:21
            Proverbs 17:24
            Proverbs 17:28

QUESTIONS

Who can give a child Godly knowledge? (His parents.)
What if that parent does not do this? (They will bring up or beget a fool.)
In the world's society today, is the NORM to bring up a child in God's knowledge? (No, the NORM in public education is to bring up children SEPARATE from the knowledge of God.)
What type of knowledge is the world teaching then? (Worldly knowledge.)
What is this knowledge to God? (It is foolishness.)
What will the parents of fools not have? (They will have no JOY.)
What does it say a foolish son is to his father? (Vs. 25 says a foolish son is a grief to his father.)

What is a foolish son to his mother? (He is bitterness to his mother.)
What can even a fool be seen as if he is not a loud mouth? (Even a fool will be perceived as wise, if he is quiet.)
What are we to be? (Slow to speak, slow to anger, and QUICK to hear!)

PARENT: It is very important that you learn knowledge of God. If not, you will grow up to be fools. This is not pleasing to God and we sure do want to be LOYAL SUBJECTS!

❦❦❦❦❦❦

Lesson Sixteen
KNOWLEDGE
More Folly of a Fool

PARENT: We are learning that if parents do not bring their children up in the wisdom of God they will have great sorrow and grief. When you grow up and if you choose to marry, you must know that without God's wisdom, knowledge and understanding, your whole life is in VAIN. It is worthless. This is why it is so important that we learn to be pleasing to God in ALL ways. We are going to learn to walk in the WISDOM of God which is FOOLISHNESS to the world. We need to question if what we are doing is right if we are pleasing those of the world!

READ: Proverbs 10:8
        Proverbs 10:10
        Proverbs 10:18
        Proverbs 10:23

QUESTIONS

Will a fool receive commandments? (No.)
Will the wise in heart? (Yes, this is why they are wise.)
What will happen to fools? (They will fall.)
What is a prating fool? (To prate means to talk idly or endless babble about nothing worthwhile.)
Do we need to watch our mouths?
Are we to speak evil of others? (No!)
What does it mean to hate someone with lying lips and hide it? (To be kind and pretending friendship and then once they are gone to hate them.)
Are we to do these things? (No, only a fool would do this.)
What is fun to a fool? (A fool's fun is to do mischief.)
What is mischief? (To do evil, to do things that cause trouble, and to do things that are not pleasing to God.)
How will the wise walk? (According to the Word of God.)

READ: Proverbs 26:1
        Proverbs 26:4-6
        Proverbs 26:8
        Proverbs 26:10-12

QUESTIONS

Will fools have honour from God? (No, God regards a fool's knowledge as foolishness.)
Is it normal for snow to be in summer? (No.)
Is it good for rain to come in harvest? (No, your crops will ruin.)
Is it good for a fool to have honour? (No.)
Are we suppose to engage in foolish conversation with a fool? (No.)
Why? (He will think he is wise in his prating.)
If you answer a fool and engage in foolish conversation what will you do? (Become like the fool.)
Should you trust a fool to deliver messages? (No!)
Should you ever count on a fool to do what he says? (No.)
Do fools like folly? (Yes.)
What is WORSE than a fool? (A man WISE in his own eyes.)
What is there more hope for? (There is more hope for a fool than for a man wise in his own eyes. He is lower than a FOOL.)

READ: Proverbs 29:11
Proverbs 29:20

QUESTIONS

How does a fool control his mouth? (He doesn't.)
What does he do? (He speaks ALL that is on his mind.)
Is he speaking things of God? (No.)
Should we listen to things that are not from God? (No. This is foolishness.)
In this scripture what is WORSE than a fool? (A man HASTY in his words.)
What are we to be? (SLOW TO SPEAK, SLOW TO ANGER, and QUICK to hear!!!)

READ: Proverbs 12:15
Proverbs 14:16

QUESTIONS

Does a fool think he is foolish? (No, a fool thinks he is right.)
Does the world think it is right in its foolishness? (Yes, the ways of the Lord are foolishness to them!)
What does a fool do? (He rages!)
Are fools confident in their foolishness? (Yes.)
Do they know they do wrong? (No, for they are confident they are RIGHT.)
Why are they wrong? (Because their knowledge is without God's wisdom.)

PARENT: The thing that separates a fool from a wise man is knowledge. The fool piles up knowledge from the world and the more knowledge he gets the more foolish he is. A wise man saturates himself in the word of God and the more he does this the wiser he gets. The wise man and the fool can never meet nor fellowship for their knowledge will never meet.

❦❦❦❦❦❦❦

Lesson Seventeen
KNOWLEDGE
Discretion

PARENT: What do you know about discretion? We have been reading this over and over as we have been studying the scriptures on wisdom, knowledge and understanding. Discretion is a very good attribute to have. Do you know what it is?

DICTIONARY: Discretion

(1. Prudent or cautious reserve. 2. The freedom to act or judge on one's own.)

DICTIONARY: Discreet

(1. Having or showing a judicious reserve in one's speech or behavior. 2. Showing GOOD judgment.)

PARENT: Do you remember what we are supposed to be able to do as mature Christians? ... We are supposed to be able to discern what is good from what is evil. This is also showing GOOD judgment. A person with discretion ACTS according to good judgment. Let's read what the Word of God says about discretion.

READ: Psalms 112:5
Proverbs 1:4
Proverbs 3:21

QUESTIONS

How will a good (righteous) man guide his affairs? (With discretion.)
What does this mean? (It means he will be able to make good judgments in the choices he will have to make regarding his affairs.)
What else does a good man do? (He will show favour and lend!)
What other characteristic lends? (Virtue.)
What will wisdom give young men? (Discretion.)

How will this help a young man? (He will be able to make GOOD decisions regarding his life.)
What shall discretion or sound judgment do for a person of understanding? (It will preserve him.)

READ: Proverbs 5:1-2
        Proverbs 19:11

QUESTIONS

What is a person to learn? (Discretion. Judging from the Word of God what is good and what is evil and to DO what is good.)
What does a man's discretion do? (His sound judgment will defer his anger. He will remember what the Word of God says about being slow to wrath!)
What is a discreet man's glory? (It is his glory to pass up doing a sin!)
Can you give an example of knowing NOT to do something because it is against what GOD would have you do and NOT doing it even though you have a chance to?

READ: Jeremiah 10:10-12

How did God make EVERYTHING? (By His wisdom and discretion.)
Did God make the earth correctly? (Yes, by GOOD judgment!)

READ: Proverbs 11:22
        Titus 2:4-5

QUESTIONS

What is a woman without discretion likened to? (She is like a gold ring in a pig's snout!) Is this a good thing to be?
What should women learn to be, then? (Discreet.)
What are young women supposed to be learning? (To be sober, to love their husbands, to love their children, TO BE DISCREET, chaste, keepers at home, good, obedient to their own husbands.)
Does the world teach young women these things? (No, it teaches them the opposite. It is teaching them FOOLISHNESS, which is to walk in the wisdom of the world.)

PARENT: *According to the Word of God, we need to grow in discretion. Women and men alike are cautioned how important it is to develop this. But, discretion will only come with the knowledge of God's Word. The only way to obtain any of these characteristics is to read the Bible and then put it into action! Through Christ we can do ANYTHING.*

❧❧❧❧❧❧

Lesson Eighteen
KNOWLEDGE
Prudence

PARENT: *We learned that discretion is having good, sound judgment according to the Word of God. We need to remember to line up everything we hear, everything we say, and everything we DO with the Word of God. This is a discreet person. They will THINK before they act, according to God's TRUTH! We read that having discretion is to be PRUDENT. Do you know what PRUDENCE is?*

DICTIONARY: Prudent

(1. Exercising good judgment. 2. Careful about one's conduct; circumspect; discreet!)

DICTIONARY: Prudence

(1. The state, quality, or fact of being prudent; discretion.)

READ: Proverbs 8:12
              Proverbs 12:16,23
              Proverbs 13:16

QUESTIONS

What does wisdom come with? (Prudence.)
Does a prudent man speak ALL he knows? (No. He is slow to speak.)
What does a fool do? (He speaks quickly and speaks much foolishness.)
What do prudent men like to think about? (God's knowledge.)

READ: Proverbs 14:8, 15, 18
              Proverbs 15:5

QUESTIONS

What is the wisdom of the prudent? (To understand the CORRECT way.)
What is the way of fools? (To follow error and deceit.)
Do prudent people believe everything they hear? (No. They do not.)
Who does believe everything they hear? (The simple.)
What is the crown of the prudent? (Knowledge!)
Does a fool listen to his father's instruction? (No.)
Does a prudent man? (Yes.)
Why is this important? (By instruction wisdom comes, as long as this instruction is based on the Word of God, and not concepts of men.)

READ: Proverbs 16:21
              Proverbs 18:15
              Proverbs 19:14

QUESTIONS

What will the wise in heart be called? (Prudent.)
What increases learning? (Sweet, Godly, speech.)
Where does the prudent get knowledge? (In their HEART.)
How do the wise get knowledge? (Through listening.)
How are we to be? (Slow to speak, slow to anger, and quick to HEAR.)
Can a wife be prudent? (Yes!)
Who is a prudent wife from? (She is a gift from the Lord.)

READ: Proverbs 22:3
            Proverbs 27:12

QUESTIONS

What does a prudent man see? (He sees evil and hides himself from it.)
What does it mean to HIDE himself? (It means he will not participate in evil doings.)
What do the people that are NOT prudent do? (They go on and do the evil.)
What will happen to them? (They will be punished.)

READ: Ephesians 1:7-9

QUESTIONS

What has Jesus made abound towards us? (All wisdom and prudence.)
Does this mean we will have just a little wisdom and prudence? (No, it says that he has abounded toward us in ALL wisdom and prudence.)
How can we get wisdom and prudence? (Through seeking Him, and His knowledge.)
What has He made known to us? (Vs. 9, the wisdom of His WILL!)

PARENT: We have found that prudence, discretion, understanding and wisdom are all a part of KNOWLEDGE. We are NOT to learn the wisdom of this world, for it is counted as FOOLISHNESS to God. The Knowledge of

God is to know what is HOLY, which is His Word, His Ways, and HIM! If we have the knowledge of God we can walk through our lives making sound judgments in whatever we do and we will have discretion and wisdom to guide us. Many people are deceived thinking that happiness comes from doing whatever they WANT. True happiness comes by walking in the confidence of the Word of God.

Lesson Nineteen
KNOWLEDGE
Review

What is knowledge? (Knowledge is to know, instruct, understand and have wisdom.)
What two types of knowledge are there? (There is the knowledge of the world, and the knowledge of what is Holy.)
Which knowledge is the Word of God telling us to find? (That which is Holy.)
How hard are we to search after knowledge? (With everything in us. It is more precious than any treasure.)

How old is a child supposed to be to be trained in the teachings of God? (From the time that he is weaned from his mother.)
How old do you think that would be? (An article in the newspaper said that the worldwide average for weaning a child was at four years of age. Here in America, with most women leaving their children and working, the average is 6 months!)

What does it mean to be enlightened? (It means to understand.)
What are we to be enlightened to? (The Words of God.)
What is the opposite of being enlightened? (Being blind.)
Can Jesus make the blind to see? (Yes!)
Even the spiritually and physically blind?
Which would you rather see with? (It is better to have sight spiritually which leads to eternal life, than have sight physically to see earthly things.)

What is understanding? (It is to understand what the Word of God is saying.)
Does God correct His people? (Yes.)
Why?
What will understanding do for those who have it? (It will preserve them from evil.)
How does it do this? (By having the understanding of doing what is GOOD rather than evil.)
What are we to NOT be children in? (Understanding.)
What ARE we to be children in? (Malice.)
What does wisdom do for someone who is wise? (It is a defense.)
What did God make the universe in? (Wisdom and understanding.)
Does a wise man listen to advice from others? (Yes.)
From just anyone? (No, only from those who give SCRIPTURAL counsel.)
Where is wisdom when a man has it? (It is in his heart.)

What does the world think of God's wisdom? (The world thinks that it is foolishness.)
What does God think of the world's wisdom? (God thinks it is foolishness.)
Which do YOU want to please, the world or God? (God!)
So, what is the world going to think of you? (They are going to think you are foolish.)
What if the world loves you? (Then you are not walking in the knowledge and wisdom of God. The Bible says if you are a friend of the world, you are an enemy of God.)
How does God use preaching? (To confound the wise of the world.)
What do we need to be careful of? (Philosophies of men, and their VAIN words.)
Why? (Because they can spoil us, if we listen to them and do not know the Word of God.)
How can we not be spoiled? (By being rooted, built up in Jesus, established in the faith.)
What is a fable? (Anything that is not true.)
Are we to listen to fables? (No.)

What is a FOOL? (A fool is someone who walks in the wisdom of the world and lacks understanding of God. A fool is VOID of the knowledge of what is Holy.)
Are you to argue with fools? (No.)
Where is foolishness in children? (It is in their hearts.)
How do you get foolishness out of children?

(With correction and the Word of God.)
What is an atheist? (A person who does not believe in God.)
What are atheists? (They are fools.)
What does God say they do? (He says they are corrupt, that they do abominable works.)
Can you correct a fool? (No. They do not receive correction.)

How are we to be around fools? (Cautious.)
How cautious? (As if we were around a mother bear stolen of her cubs.)
Can we learn from fools? (Not knowledge. But we can learn NOT to be a fool.)
What happens when you argue with a fool? (You make him think he is right and encourage him in his foolishness.)

What separates a fool from a wise man? (Knowledge.)
Can ever the two have good fellowship? (What fellowship can LIGHT, understanding, have with darkness, ignorance?)
What does a fool do in regards to knowledge? (He piles up more and more foolishness.)
What does a wise man do regarding knowledge? (He saturates himself in the Word of God and gets wiser!)
What is discretion? (It is to be prudent or to make good judgment.)
How does a wise man judge? (Wisely! With discretion. He makes good judgment.)
How will this help him in life? (It will keep him from evil.)

What are women to be? (Discreet.)
What are men to have? (Discretion.)
What will they be like if they are these things? (They will have the knowledge of God.)
Do you have to have the knowledge of God to walk discretely? (Yes. Otherwise you would not know how to have good judgment.)
What is a woman without discretion likened to? (A gold ring in a pig's snout.)
Does the world teach women to be discreet? (No.)

What is the world teaching women today?
Is this the wisdom of God?
What are women to be learning? (To be sober, to love their husbands and children, to be DISCREET, chaste, keepers at home, good, obedient to their own husbands.)
Who is a prudent wife from? (The Lord.)

How does a prudent man speak? (Slowly and thoughtfully.)
What are the two things we are to be slow to? (Slow to speak, and slow to anger.)
What are we to be quick to do? (Quick to hear!)

KNOWLEDGE

There was once a mighty King who ruled over all the land as far as the eye could see. This King lived in a beautiful castle way up on the top of a high mountain where He could look out over all the land and watch His subjects. This mighty King had been King even before there were inhabitants in the land and He had written down in a book all the things that His Subjects would ever need to know so that they could live according to His commands. He called it the Book of Wisdom and promised that whoever studied this book would become the wisest people in all of the land. The King sat up in His castle and watched ...

There were certain people that claimed to be the wisest in all the land. They had spent much money in learning from the wisest people in the land. As years passed, many forgot all about their King and His Book of Wisdom. The King's Book was stashed away in the old and forgotten section of their libraries and they decided to expand their knowledge and find out where things really came from ...

They looked at animals and men and studied every sort of plant life and every sort of animal life and came up with the conclusion that the plant life had turned into animal life!!! "Oh," they said, "It had taken a long period of time for this to happen, but over a period of time a piece of algae had turned into a fish, a fish had turned into a turtle, a turtle had turned into a lizard, a lizard had turned into a raccoon, a raccoon had turned into a monkey, and a monkey had turned into a man!!!"

Then they decided to find out how the earth was made. They finally came to the conclusion that the earth was made from a giant explosion in the sky and from that explosion, all the stars and planets were made, including earth!

Knowledge became relative. This meant that anyone could believe anything they wanted to believe about whatever subject they chose to study. Truth became whatever you decided truth was. There were no absolutes! Why, over a period of time, everything changes, they said... Look at the monkeys! So, since no one could really say what men would be tomorrow, how could there be black and white opinions on anything? Everything evolves, they said, even truth!

The land continued in this from generation to generation ... waxing worse and worse.

One day, a woman was busy cleaning out her attic. As she was sorting through many old items she found a very old, dusty leather bound book. She looked at the title, "The King's Book of Wisdom".

"Hmmmm," she thought. "This is certainly an old book. I wonder what it's all about."

So she sat down and she read ... and she read ... and she read...

The first thing she read was that it mentioned a mighty King. Now she had heard from her grandmother that there was a King, but it was all just hearsay, she had thought at the time. But here was a whole book about this King's existence. Maybe there really was a King! And if there really was a King, it said in the Book that this King had made man! That would mean that men really didn't come from algae! It also said that this wonderful King had made the earth! In fact, He had made everything that there was to be made! The Book went on to say that there were absolutes! According to this Book there was nothing relative, as the wise men were saying, but there were things that were right, and there were things that were wrong! This Book was saying totally opposite of what the wise men were saying, on everything!

The woman took the book to her husband and he looked through the old Book. He read ... and he read ... and he read ...

He had been taught that there was a King from his grandfather, but had been told by the wise men that this was just fiction and make-believe. But maybe his grandfather had been right!!! What if this were true? What if, ... oh, how could this be, ... what if the wise men were wrong and there really was a King? The man decided to find out.

The man went to the wisest men of the land and asked them if it could be possible that there really was a King. They all looked at him as if he had lost his mind.

"Are you going to believe all that old-fashioned nonsense?!! We have the best researchers and scientists that the world has ever known and no one can prove that there is such a King. And if you can't prove that there is a King, then you just have to know that that Book of Wisdom is a bunch of fairy tale nonsense, not even fit for a child to read! It is foolishness! Why that fable passed away with my grandfather!"

The wise men laughed and clapped each other on the backs in pride for the wise counsel they had given the man.

The man continued reading the King's Book of Wisdom and read it diligently to his children. The rest of the land laughed at them as they started obeying its contents. They ridiculed, scoffed, and belittled them, but it didn't matter to the man. He continued his search for Wisdom in the Book and found so many treasures of the King's knowledge.

Life in the land became more difficult for the man and his family with each passing day. The wise men in the land became angry that this fool would hold to his antique ideas so firmly! They threw him out of his job because he was causing other people to doubt the wise men's wonderful expertise in knowledge.

Many of the other wise people in the land turned their backs on them and wouldn't sell them things they needed to live. Winter came, and there was not much food nor firewood for heat. They had read in the Book of Wisdom that the King knew all what they were enduring and trusted Him, knowing He wouldn't let them starve.

One day, when the man had had one terribly hard day of ridicule and there was absolutely no food left in the pantry, there was a knock at the door. The man hesitantly opened it. He cautiously peered through the opening, hoping it was not another person ready to give him more trouble for believing in the King. There before him was a messenger dressed in fine linen. With a broad smile on his face the servant handed him a sealed letter. The man opened it and read ...

To my Loyal Subject, I am requesting that you and your family come immediately to my castle. Leave everything and come in haste.
Your King.

The man looked at his family in astonishment. Then, he threw up his hands in joy!

"The King has sent this messenger to come and take us to Him! We are saved!!!" The family all rejoiced and danced with glee. They quickly put their coats on and followed after the messenger in their wagon, pulled by their faithful, old horse.

They traveled a long way, through many valleys, hills, and mountain passes. The closer they came to the King's castle the more they noticed a change in their surroundings. Even in the middle of winter, flowers were brightly blooming. There was lush green grass everywhere and birds were chirping brightly. As they came around a bend, they looked up and were astounded to see the most magnificent, the most beautiful sight they had ever beheld in all their humble lives. There before them, at the top of a huge mountain, was a castle all made out of luminescent pearl. A golden road paved the way up to the entrance. There was the sound of trumpets and they were greeted with great applause from all around the castle grounds. They were greatly surprised at the welcome!

After their ascent to the top, they alighted from their wagon and were ushered into the throne room! There, seated in all His Glory, was the King! The King stood and came forward to meet them. He warmly greeted the family with firm hugs and Kingly affection. The King glanced down tenderly and said, "I have been looking for those who would be Loyal Subjects. My children, I have waited eagerly for this time to fellowship with you. Come on in to your new home."

The family then followed the King into a resting area and they sat down in peaceful, awed conversation with their King. After a while, the man decided to ask His King something that had been bothering him for a long while. "Your Majesty, the people in your land do not even recognize you as King. Why don't you make yourself known? The wise men of the land are all saying you do not exist! How can you let this go on? Why don't you do something?!!!"

The King looked solemnly at the man and said, "I have done something. I have given them everything they ever need to know." The King walked over to a beautiful shelf carved in rubies and picked up a copy of the Book of Wisdom and held it up for the man to see. "And wise men will read it."

Temperance

Lesson One
TEMPERANCE

PARENT: Today we are going to study the next characteristic that we are to add to knowledge. What are the main characteristics we have studied so far? ... We have learned about FAITH, VIRTUE, and KNOWLEDGE. The next one on the list in 2 Peter is TEMPERANCE. What do you think TEMPERANCE is? Let's look it up in the dictionary.

DICTIONARY: Temperance

(1. The condition or quality of being temperate; moderation or self-restraint.)

DICTIONARY: Temperate

(1. Exercising moderation and self-restraint.
2. Moderate in degree or quality; tempered.)

PARENT: Can you put in simple words what having TEMPERANCE is? ... Temperance is controlling our fleshly body. This means we will not allow it to rule us in its lusts and desires, but we will rule it. When a person eats food NOT for nourishment, but for pleasure, and then this person becomes fat, have they controlled their flesh? ... When a person lets his body rule him instead of Christ, he does not yet have temperance. Temperance is doing things moderately, not doing things TOO much. This is the next important subject that we are to add to our knowledge. We need to learn to live certain things that we read in Word of God. The Bible tells us to be temperate so we need to ask Him to help us do this.

READ: Acts 24:24-25

QUESTIONS

According to the Word, what did Paul talk to Felix about? (Righteousness, temperance, and judgment to come.)
What was Felix's response to Paul? (He trembles and tells him to go away for a while.)
Should we be reasoning with others about righteousness, temperance and judgment to come? (Yes.)
If we are telling other people about these things, had we better be walking in righteousness and temperance? (Yes, or we will be hypocrites, saying one thing and doing another.)

READ: 1 Corinthians 9:24-27

QUESTIONS

What did Paul liken our lives to? (Running a race to win the prize.)
What are we to master? (We are to master our own bodies for Christ's sake.)
If we do not, is Jesus King over us? (No, our flesh has the control, not the Lord.)
What are we to do to our bodies? (We are to keep them under subjection.)
Why? (So that we are LIVING what we are preaching and that Jesus is Lord of our bodies, too!)

READ: Galations 5:22-24

QUESTIONS

What is a fruit of the Spirit? (It is something that a person produces when they are walking in obedience to God.)
Do you remember what Barren means? (It means unfruitful.)
So is temperance a fruit? (Yes.)
What have the people who are Christ's done to their flesh? (They have crucified the flesh with the affections and lusts.)

READ: Titus 2:1-2

QUESTIONS

What are we to speak? (Things that become

sound doctrine.)
What are the aged men to be? (Sober, grave, TEMPERATE, sound in faith, in charity, in patience.)
Are just the aged men to be this? (No, we are all to be temperate!)

READ: Philippians 4:5

QUESTIONS

What are all men to see? (Our moderation.)
What does moderation mean? (It means temperance.)

DICTIONARY: Moderation

(1. Not excessive or extreme.)

PARENT: We are ALL to learn to be temperate! This is a fruit of the Holy Spirit. If we do not have temperance all we need to do is ask God to help us and He will! It comes down to loving God MORE than we love anything on earth! And more than we love the pleasures that the world has to offer!

Lesson Two
TEMPERANCE
Controlling the Lusts of the Flesh

PARENT: God's Word is very clear on what it says about controlling our bodies. Temperance is the ability through the Spirit of God to not let our bodies have the things it lusts for. What does it mean to lust for something?

DICTIONARY: Lust

(1. Extreme, excessive or unrestrained cravings. 2. Pleasure; delight; relish.)

PARENT: Do you see what the Bible is trying to tell us? The world provides many pleasures for our fleshly bodies. Today, the norm in society is to be constantly entertained. We are not to be lead into the pleasing of the flesh, but we are to be pleasing to our Father! We are not to follow after the world and its uncontrollable appetites. We are to crucify our flesh and its lusts!

READ: Mark 4:1-20

What happened to the seeds that were sown among thorns? (The cares of this world and the deceitfulness of riches, and the lusts of other things entered in, and choked the Word, and it became unfruitful.)
What are some lusts that choke the Word? (Anything that robs you of obeying the Word. Pleasures ...)
What happens to us if we follow after the lusts of other things? (We will become unfruitful.)

READ: 1 Corinthians 10:1-7

QUESTIONS

Why were we told about the trials of the children of Israel? (Vs. 6, They were our examples so that WE should NOT lust after evil things as they did!)
In Vs. 7, how were they idolaters? (Vs. 7 says that the people sat down to eat and drink, and rose up to play.)
Can eating and drinking and playing make us idolaters? (It says here that that was the substance of their idolatry.)
Do we need to be careful that we do not OVER-do these things? (Yes.)
What are we to be? (Temperate, and moderate in all things.)

READ: 2 Timothy 2:21-22
        Titus 2:11-12

QUESTIONS

What are we to flee? (Youthful lusts.)
What are we to follow? (Righteousness, faith, charity, and peace.)
What does God's grace teach us in Titus? (To deny ungodliness and worldly lusts.)
Can you think of some things the world lusts after? (Money, power, positions, material objects, food, drink, drugs, etc.)
Are we to be partakers in these things? (No.)
How are we to live? (Soberly, righteously, and godly, in this present world.)
So are we to live in this world? (Yes.)
Are we to be partakers of its lusts? (No!)
Is it going to be hard to live like this? (Only if you have lust in your heart.)
What do you do if you have lust in your heart? (You repent, and Jesus will cleanse us from our unrighteousness.)

READ: James 1:12-15

QUESTIONS

How are we blessed? (We are blessed if we endure temptations.)
If we endure it, meaning to not give in, what will we receive? (A crown of life.)
What are we tempted by? (Our own lusts.)

READ: 1 Peter 4:1-2

QUESTIONS

How are we to live once we BELIEVE in Jesus? (We are to live the rest of our life to the WILL of GOD!)
How are we NOT to live? (We are not any longer to live according to the lusts of our flesh.)
How are we to arm ourselves? (Knowing we will suffer in our flesh.)
What is this for? (Vs. 1 says that he that has suffered in the flesh has ceased from sin.)

Lesson Three
TEMPERANCE
Lasciviousness

PARENT: The Bible tells us that we are not to be conformed to the ways of the world. This is a very difficult thing to do if you still WANT the things of the world. If a person doesn't care any more about anything but Christ, he will be able to temper his body. This means he will be able to control it from giving in to the lusts of the flesh. The Bible talks very clearly about certain lusts. One of the lusts of the flesh is LASCIVIOUSNESS. Do you know what this is?

STRONG'S: Lasciviousness

(Greek #766; incontinent, licentiousness, having VICES, filthy, wantonness.)

DICTIONARY: Lasciviousness

(1. Of or characterized by lust. Licentiousness.)

DICTIONARY: Licentiousness

(1. Lacking moral discipline.)

DICTIONARY: Incontinent

(1. Not self restrained or moderate.)

READ: Mark 7:20-23

QUESTIONS

Where does lasciviousness come from? (From out of the hearts of men.)
What does it do to people? (It defiles them.)
What does defile mean? (To be unclean.)
By whom are we clean? (Jesus.)

READ: Galations 5:17-21

QUESTIONS

What is against the Spirit? (Our flesh.)
Are they contrary to one another?
What does the flesh want to do? (Live after its own lusts.)
What are some of the works of the flesh? (Vs. 19-21.)
What happens to people who live in these things? (Vs. 21, They which do such things shall not inherit the Kingdom of God.)
Do we need to be temperate and bring our flesh under control of the Spirit? (Yes.)

READ: Ephesians 4:17-24

QUESTIONS

How does the world live and walk? (Vs. 17, in the VANITY of their mind.)
Do they have understanding of God? (No, their understanding is darkened.)
Can they have fellowship with God? (Vs. 17 says they are ALIENATED from the life of God.)
Why? (Vs. 17, through the IGNORANCE that is in them.)
Why is the ignorance in them? (Because of the blindness of their heart!)
What are they past? (They are past FEELING.)
What are they given over to? (They are given over to lasciviousness with GREEDINESS.)
So what goes along with lasciviousness? (Being GREEDY.)
What about BELIEVERS? (Vs. 20, We have not so learned Christ.)
What are WE to do? (Put off the former lifestyle of the OLD MAN, which is corrupt according to the deceitful lusts.)
How? (By being renewed in the spirit of our minds.)
What ARE we to walk in? (We are to live as a NEW man; which is after God, created in righteousness and true holiness.)

READ: Jude 4

QUESTIONS

What do ungodly men do? (Turn the grace of God into lasciviousness.)
What does this mean? (They say that because we have GRACE we can SIN.)
Why do ungodly men do this? (Because they want to have the lusts of the flesh and a form of godliness also. These ungodly people do not want to give up the world but love the things of the world. The Bible says if we are friends with the world we are at enmity with Him.)
What does the Bible teach us? (To deny the fleshly lusts and WANTS and to live according to the Spirit of God.)

READ: Jude 10-13

QUESTIONS

Are these people feasting with the believers in Jude? (Yes, vs. 12.)
How have they ran after the error of Balaam for REWARD? (It says GREEDILY!)
So we need to watch out for what? (Ungodly men that are following after God turning the grace of God into LASCIVIOUSNESS, who are doing it out of GREED for the rewards of money, just like Balaam!)
How can we be careful? (By watching our own souls so they do not ever ERR in this manner.)

Lesson Four
TEMPERANCE
Concupiscence and Gluttony

PARENT: This is a very interesting lesson. We are going to learn what the Word of God says about OVER- doing ANYTHING! Do you know what CONCUPISCENCE is?

STRONG'S: Concupiscence

(Greek #1939; A longing for what is forbidden. Desire, lust after.)

PARENT: The Bible is very clear that this is a sin. Did you know that over-eating is also a sin? This is a person that is a GLUTTON. And so is over drinking! This is a person that is a WINEBIBBER. Anything that the FLESH has control over rather than the Spirit, is SIN!

READ: Romans 7:8
            Colossians 3:1-10

QUESTIONS

What does sin bring us to? (All manner of concupiscence.)
What are we to seek? (Those things which are above, heavenly things.)
What are we to set our affections or mind on? (Not things of earth, but of God.)
What are we? (We are dead, vs. 3.)
Who are we alive in? (We are alive in Christ, He is our LIFE!)
What are we to do to our bodies? (Mortify them.)
What does MORTIFY mean? (Mortify means to discipline one's body and appetites by self-denial and austerity. It also means to cause to die.)
What are we to put to death? (Our earthly lusts and appetites.)
How do we do this? (By putting on the NEW MAN.)
How? (Vs. 10 says this new man is renewed in KNOWLEDGE of GOD! The more we know about God, the more we can be a new man!)

READ: 1 Thessalonians 4:1-5

QUESTIONS

How are we to walk? (By the Spirit, living our lives thinking of HEAVENLY things, not earthly. We are to walk in the KNOWLEDGE OF GOD!)
Who do we live to please, God, ourselves, or other men? (God!)
In this Scripture, what is the WILL of God? (That you should abstain from fornication.)
What else is the WILL of God? (Vs.4, that every one of us should know how to possess his vessel in sanctification and honour.)

STRONG'S: Fornication

(Greek #4203; harlot, indulge in unlawful lust; or PRACTICE IDOLATRY!!!! Ed. It doesn't mean only the sin of indulging with a harlot, fornication was another word for IDOLATRY!)

READ: Proverbs 23:1-3
            Proverbs 23:20-21

QUESTIONS

If we are given to APPETITE, or that means let our appetite rule us to where we LIVE to eat, not EAT to live, what should we do? (In Pr. 23:2 it says to put a knife to your throat!)
Do you think it is a BAD thing to be given to appetite? (Yes. It is idolatry.)
In vs. 21, what will the glutton and the winebibber come to? (It says they will come to poverty.)
Who are we not to be among? (Winebibbers and riotous eaters of flesh.)
Do you think a winebibber and a riotous eater of flesh have temperance? (NO!)

READ: 1 Peter 4:3-5

QUESTIONS

What did we do in our PAST life, before Christ? (Vs. 3, we walked in lasciviousness, lusts, excess of wine, revelings, banquetings, and abominable idolatries.)
Which of these had to do with food? (Banquetings.)
Can you tell me some ways that the world BANQUETS today?
What will the world think of us? (Vs. 4, they will think it strange that we do not do this! They will speak evil of us.)
Who do we want to please, ourselves or GOD? (God!)
By over-doing anything are we pleasing our King? (No, we are not being loyal subjects but are being TRAITORS to Him, with our own selves!)

PARENT: What are we to live for? ... We are to live for Christ, in all that we do, all that we eat, all that we say, and all that we think! We are to die to ourselves and LIVE in Christ. This is being a BELIEVER. God RULES!

Lesson Five
TEMPERANCE
Pleasures

PARENT: In the society that we live in, men often go seeking for things that give them pleasures. Many go to movies, go to amusement parks, go to bars, and many other things that people do to have fun. One of the most popular sayings children and adults say is "I'm BORED!" There are so many things that we can be doing as God's people that we should never have time to be bored.

God's Word in Ecclesiastes says that it is fine to enjoy the fruit of our labors. When you have taken time to plant blueberries, cultivate the blueberries, pick the blueberries and then bake a blueberry pie, there is nothing wrong with having a piece of the fruit of your labors. But there is something wrong with a person who continuously seeks to find ways to entertain himself with worldly pleasures. A person that is a NEW MAN in Christ Jesus will turn from these things. They will not WANT to go after things that the world says is FUN. They will want to go after things that God says to DO.

READ: Isaiah 47:8-9
        1 Timothy 5:5-6

QUESTIONS

Does the scripture in Isaiah sound like God wants us to be given to the seeking of pleasures? (No, God did not like this.)
How is a widow that is a widow indeed act? (She trusts in God and continues in supplications and prayers night and day.)
What is the opposite in 1 Timothy? (The opposite is one who lives in pleasure.)
What does the Word say this woman is? (It says that she is dead while she lives.)
Is she dead as in dead in herself, alive in Christ? (No!)
How is she dead? (Spiritually.)

THE NARROW WAY: Building Character Through Family Biblical Study

READ: Luke 8:14

QUESTIONS

Where did the seed fall in this scripture? (It fell among thorns.)
Did these people hear? (Yes.)
But what happens to them? (They are choked with cares, riches and PLEASURES of this life.)
Are they fruitful? (They bring NO fruit to perfection.)
Are we to be choked with the PLEASURES of this life? (No.)

READ: 2 Timothy 3:1-5

QUESTIONS

What will happen in the last days? (Perilous times will come.)
What does vs. 4 say people will love more than God? (It says men will be lovers of PLEASURES more than lovers of God!)
Will they look like Godly people? (Vs. 5 says that these will have a FORM of GODLINESS.)
Are we to be with such people? (No.)
Are we to BE such people? (NO!)

DICTIONARY: Pleasures

(1. Amusement, diversion, or worldly enjoyment. 2. Sensual gratification or indulgence. 3. A source of enjoyment, gratification, or delight.)

READ: Hebrews 11:24-27

QUESTIONS

What did Moses choose? (Vs. 25, he chose to suffer affliction with the people of God.)
What was his other choice? (Vs. 25, to enjoy the PLEASURES of sin for a season.)
How did he do this? (Because of what he believed, or FAITH!!!)
What came with his choice? (Vs. 26, Reproach.)
How did he look upon this reproach? (He esteemed the reproach of Christ greater than the treasures of Egypt.)
What did he forsake? (Egypt. The world of his day.)
What are we to forsake? (The world.)
What are we to do? (Endure ANYTHING for Christ's sake.)

PARENT: Are we to take PLEASURE in the things the world takes pleasure in? ... We are to not walk according to the pleasures of the world, but according to the PLEASURE of our Father, which is to do His WILL!

Lesson Six
TEMPERANCE
Covetousness

PARENT: The Lord wants us to turn aside from the world and its ways. We learned in the last lesson that we are not to SATURATE ourselves in the pleasures of the world. Today we are going to learn about covetousness. This is another area of the flesh that we need to put to DEATH! Do you know which of the Ten Commandments deals with this issue? ... The Commandment "Thou Shalt Not Covet!" We are not to covet what other people have. We are not to LUST for material objects! Let's read some of the scriptures that talk about COVETOUSNESS.

READ: Luke 12:13-21

QUESTIONS

In vs. 15, what did Jesus warn people to beware of? (Take HEED, and beware of COVETOUSNESS.)

What did Jesus say about this? (For a man's life consists not in the abundance of the things which he possesses.)
What does the world think is very important? (Money!)
Why? (Because it buys THINGS that the world has to offer.)
Are we to be wrapped up in buying THINGS? (No. We are to only have what we NEED, not what we WANT.)
What did the man in the parable do? (Vs. 21, he laid up treasure for himself.)
Was he rich towards God? (No!)
What did he spend his whole life doing? (Getting material THINGS!)

READ: Romans 1:28-32

QUESTIONS

What are the people filled with in this Scripture? (Vs.29-31.)
Do they like to do these things? (Vs. 32 says that they have PLEASURE in doing them!)
Is COVETOUSNESS one of the things they do?
What is covetousness? (It is storing up for yourself material goods and THINGS of this world as in Luke 12.)

READ: Ephesians 5:1-7

QUESTIONS

Are BELIEVERS supposed to be COVETOUS? (No!)
Is it to be named among us ONCE? (No!)
What does vs. 5 say about covetous people? (It says a covetous man has no inheritance in the kingdom of Christ and of God.)
What will happen to the children of disobedience? (Because of these things (covetousness, vs. 6) comes the wrath of God.)
What are we to do? (Not be partakers with them.)
How do we avoid COVETOUSNESS? ...

READ: Colossians 3:5-8

QUESTIONS

In vs. 5, what does the Bible say covetousness is? (It says it is idolatry.)

READ: Revelation 21:8

QUESTIONS

In this scripture what happens to idolaters? (They shall have their part in the lake which burns with fire and brimstone; which is the second death.)
How do we not DO these things? (With TEMPERANCE, the controlling of our earthly flesh!)
Are we righteous because we DO these things? (No, we are RIGHTEOUS because of what we BELIEVE.)

READ: Hebrews 13:5

QUESTIONS

How is our conversation to be? (Without COVETOUSNESS.)
What are we to be? (We are to be CONTENT with the things we have.)
Does Jesus know when we need things? (Yes.)
How does He know? (Because He is with us ALL the time, and He sees what we need and sees the things we do.)
What scripture tells us this? (Vs.5, "For He has said, I will never leave you nor forsake you!!!!")

PARENT: We need to be TEMPERATE and control our fleshly bodies. Today we learned about COVETING or WANTING things that are not necessary in our lives. The Bible says that this is a form of idolatry. God will give us everything that we need and Jesus is with us ALWAYS and knows these things. We need to learn to be content with what we have and not strive for anything more than that, but be THANKFUL for what we have.

Lesson Seven
TEMPERANCE
Saying "No"

PARENT: The Bible teaches us to NOT follow along with what the world is doing.
We are learning what temperance means which is to control the lusts of our flesh! We can do this with our LOVE of the Lord and with the help of the Holy Spirit teaching us to RENEW our minds. With the Holy Spirit's help, we won't WANT to do the things of the world anymore, but will WANT to do the things GOD would have us to do!!!
We are going to learn today what the Bible tells us to ABSTAIN from which means to say "NO" to. Let's read the definition of ABSTAIN...

DICTIONARY: Abstain

(1. To refrain from something by one's own choice!)

DICTIONARY: Refrain

(1. To hold one's self back; to curb.)

READ: 1 Thessalonians 4:1-4
             1 Thessalonians 5:22

QUESTIONS

In the first Scripture, what are we to abstain from? (From fornication, which is to lust after a harlot or any other type of IDOLATRY.)
How are we to possess our vessels, or our bodies? (In sanctification and honour.)
What are we to abstain from in the second Scripture? (We are to abstain from ALL appearance of evil!)
What does it mean to abstain from the APPEARANCE of evil? (Even if you are not sinning, but you look like you are, you should not do it. For example, if you go into a bar, and are not participating in the lasciviousness going on inside, but just went in to rest your feet, it would LOOK like you were going to that bar! It would APPEAR as if you were just there taking in the world's evil entertainment!)
What are some other examples of appearing to be evil, even though they might seem to be harmless?

READ: 1 Peter 2:11-12

QUESTIONS

What are we to say "NO" to in this Scripture? (Say "NO" to ALL fleshly lusts!)
What are we to do? (The non-BELIEVERS are to see our GOOD works.)
Are we SAVED by our GOOD WORKS? (No! By what we BELIEVE!)

READ: 1 Peter 3:10-11

QUESTIONS

What are we to refrain from? (Refrain our tongues from evil.)
What are we to eschew? (We are to eschew evil!)
What does ESCHEW mean? (It means to SHUN and to AVOID.)
What are we to DO? (We are to DO good.)
How are we to do these things? (Through our KNOWLEDGE of the Word of God.)

How do we know what is GOOD? (Through READING what is good in the Bible!)
What is a MATURE Christian? (One who through practice has discerned what is good from what is evil and does what is GOOD! Hebrews 5:14)

READ: James 3:1-13

QUESTIONS

What is the TONGUE likened to in vs. 6? (The tongue is a fire, a world of iniquity.)
What does the tongue defile? (The whole body.)
Can the tongue be tamed like animals? (It says in vs. 8, "But the tongue can no man tame.")
What is the tongue? (Vs. 8 says it is unruly evil, fully of deadly poison.)
What do we do with our tongues? (We bless God and we curse men.)
What comes out of our mouths? (Both blessings and curses.)
Is this good? (Vs. 10 says this OUGHT NOT to be.)
What are we to show out of our mouths? (Good conversation.)
How are we to speak? (With meekness of wisdom.)

PARENT: One of the most important things we need to have TEMPERANCE in is in speaking! We need to learn to control our tongue. We argue and fight with our tongue and say things that BELIEVERS shouldn't say. According to Scripture, this is something that we need to bring under the cross of Jesus. We need to put EVIL conversation from us!

ACTIVITIES

Talk with the children about controlling the TONGUE.

Lesson Eight
TEMPERANCE
Dying to Ourselves

PARENT: The Bible teaches us many things about no longer LIVING to sin but being DEAD to it. This is a form of TEMPERANCE, which is bringing our bodies under control of the Holy Spirit. It is to allow CHRIST to live in us! This means that we love God more than we love anything else on earth! If we can't give up something it is because we REALLY must like it. If this is something of the world, we REALLY must like doing this thing that the world offers. But God will help us to LOVE Him more than anything else. He will help us to not LIKE that thing anymore if we ask Him to help us and repent and turn from that sin. We are to DIE to the cares of this world. Remember the parable of the seed sown among thorns? It was the CARES of this world and the PLEASURES of it that choked the seed, and it never was fruitful.

READ: Romans 6:1-10

QUESTIONS

What does baptism show? (Vs. 4, We are buried with Jesus by baptism into death, and when we are raised up we should walk in the NEWNESS of life.)
What happens to the OLD MAN, which means the person that lives according to the lust of the flesh? (He is CRUCIFIED with Jesus that his body of sin might be destroyed that henceforth we should not serve sin.)
What does vs. 8 say we should be? (Dead with Christ.)
Why? (So we will LIVE with Him.)
What did Jesus die to in vs. 10? (He died unto sin once.)
How does He LIVE? (He lives unto GOD!)

READ: Romans 6:11-15

QUESTIONS

What are we to do in vs. 11? (We are to reckon ourselves to be DEAD indeed unto sin.)
What are we to be alive to? (We are to be alive to GOD through Jesus Christ our Lord.)
How are we to view SIN? (It is not to REIGN in our mortal bodies.)
What does reign mean? (To rule! To govern or to have CONTROL!)
Are we to obey our MORTAL BODIES? (Vs. 12 says that we should NOT obey it in the lusts thereof.)
Will we sin? (1 Jn says yes, but we have an advocate, Jesus Christ, the RIGHTEOUS.)
Do we WANT to sin? (No! We will have no pleasure in it and will hate EVIL. This is the FEAR of the Lord!)
What are our bodies to be? (Vs. 13, Instruments of righteousness unto God.)
Will a BELIEVER have Jesus reign over them or sin? (Vs. 14 says sin shall not have dominion over you, for you are not under the law, but under grace.)
Do we go ahead and follow the LUSTS of our bodies because we are under GRACE? (Vs. 15 says GOD FORBID!!!)

READ: Romans 8:1-8

QUESTIONS

In Vs. 1, who is no longer under condemnation? (Those who walk NOT after the flesh.)
What do these people walk after? (The Spirit.)
What are we free from through Jesus? (We are free from the law of SIN and DEATH.)
In vs. 4, what is fulfilled in those who do NOT walk after the flesh? (The RIGHTEOUSNESS of the law is fulfilled in them.)
What do those that are of the flesh think of? (They that are after the flesh do MIND the things of the flesh.)
What do those that are after the Spirit MIND? (They mind the things of the Spirit.)
What is it to be carnally or fleshly minded? (Death!)
What is it to be spiritually minded? (Life and peace.)
What is the carnal mind towards God? (It is ENMITY against God.)
Can they that are in the flesh please God? (No.)
Are we to be after the things of the flesh? (No!)
How are WE to walk? (After the ways of God, not letting our fleshly bodies control us.)

PARENT: We are to bring our fleshly bodies under control of the Spirit of God. It is to even bring our BODIES under OBEDIENCE to the Word of God. For example, if the Word of God tells us not to be a glutton or a winebibber, we need to not allow our bodies to be such things! It is LOVING the ways of God more than LOVING the ways of the flesh. It is in WHOM you serve. Either you will serve the world and your FLESH, or you will serve God... But you can't do both!

Lesson Nine
TEMPERANCE
Review

What is temperance? (Temperance is being temperate; having moderation or self-restraint. It is controlling our fleshly body.)
What did Paul talk to Felix about? (Righteousness, temperance and the judgment to come.)
Should we be speaking about these things? If we are talking about these things had we better be living them? (Yes.)
What are we to master? (We are to master our bodies.)
Who are they to be under subjection to? (They are to be under Jesus!)
Is temperance a fruit of the spirit? (Yes.)
What are Christ's people to do with their bodies? (They are to crucify the flesh with the affections and lusts.)

What is lust? (It is extreme, excessive or unrestrained cravings.)
What are some lusts of the flesh? (Overeating, drunkenness, smoking and other things, i.e. drugs...)
What happened to the seeds that were sown among thorns? (They were choked.)
What choked them? (The cares of this world, riches, and the LUSTS of other things.)
How were the children of Israel idolaters? (In 1 Cor. 10:1-7 it said that the people sat down to eat and drink, and rose up to play, and so they were called idolaters.)
How are we to live? (We are to deny ungodliness and worldly lusts.)
Who are we to live for? (Once we choose to follow Jesus, we are to now LIVE for Him, and please our King!)

What is lasciviousness? (It is basically having VICES.)
What are some VICES? (Smoking, overeating, overworking, or any bad habit that has control over us and causes us to be a SLAVE to it.)

Where is lasciviousness? It is in people's hearts.
What does it do to them? (It defiles them.)
What is constantly working against the Spirit? (Our flesh.)
What does the flesh want to do? (Live after its own lusts.)
What do we need to do with our flesh? (Bring it under control of the Holy Spirit.)
How do we do this? (By CHOOSING to follow the Spirit and DENY ourselves.)
What other bad characteristic goes along with lasciviousness? (Greed.)
What do ungodly men do? (They turn the grace of God into lasciviousness.)
How do they do this? (They say you that through grace you can sin!)
What is this doctrine? (It is false and deceptive. It is a doctrine of the flesh.)

What is a glutton? (A glutton is a person who cannot control his appetite.)
What is a winebibber? (A person who gets drunk with wine.)
If we are given to appetite, what should we do? (Bring it under control of the Holy Spirit.
Is this pretty serious? (Yes, because it is a form of idolatry.)
How do we control these things? (By putting off the old man and putting on the NEW.)
How is this new man renewed? (By the knowledge of God)
How are we to possess our bodies? (In sanctification and honour.)

What happened to the seed that fell among thorns? (It was choked by the cares and riches and PLEASURES of this life.)
Do we need to be careful with this? (Yes, especially in our society.)
What does God warn us to watch for in the last days. (It says that men will be lovers of PLEASURES more than lovers of God.)
What did Moses choose to do? (He CHOSE to suffer affliction with the people of God rather than to enjoy the PLEASURES of sin for a season.)

Is sin pleasurable? (Yes, it is.)
Should we be deceived by it? (We need to be careful that we are not.)
What did Moses also forsake? (He forsook Egypt, the world of his day.)
What are we to forsake? (The world of our day.)

What is COVETOUSNESS? (It is coveting or lusting after THINGS.)
What did Jesus say about covetousness? (Take heed and BEWARE of covetousness.)
Do you remember the parable Jesus told us about laying up treasure for yourself...? What did the rich man spend his whole life doing? (Getting material things as his security.)
What did God have to say about this? (That it was wrong, for he worried more about his physical life, than his own soul.)
Are we as believers to be covetous? (No!)
What does the Bible say covetousness is? (It says it is idolatry.)
Are we to make it a HABIT of being idolaters? (No! We are to keep ourselves from idols. We need to control our flesh!)
How are we to live our lives? (We are to be content with the things we have, not always on the lookout for more THINGS.)
Does God know what we NEED?
Is there a difference between a want and a need? (Yes.)
What is the difference?
How are we to live this?

What does it mean to abstain? (It means to choose not to do something.)
What does refrain mean? (It means the same thing, you choose to NOT do something.)
What are we to abstain from? (We are to abstain from the lusts of the flesh.)
What does James tell us to control? (Our tongues.)
Why is this? (It is very hard to control our tongues, and if we can do this we can tame our whole bodies.)
What do we do with our tongues? (We bless and we curse.)

Which should we try to always do? (Bless. We are to BLESS those who persecute us. Even our enemies do we bless.)
How are we to speak? (With meekness of wisdom.)

Why did Jesus wish us to be baptized? (To show the death of the old man and being risen to a NEW man that has put to death the lusts of his flesh.)
How are we supposed to be living? (Scripture tells us we are to live as one dead with Christ to the world, but alive in Him.)
How are we to view sin? (We are not to let it reign in our mortal bodies.)
What does REIGN mean? (It means to rule.)
Are we to obey our mortal bodies? (No, we are to bring them under the control of our Lord Jesus.)
If you are of the flesh, what do you think about? (You think of things of the flesh.)
What do people who are after the Spirit think of? (They think of things of the Spirit.)
What is the carnal mind towards God? (It is enmity against God.)
What helps us to put to death the carnal mind? (The renewing of our minds through God's Word.)

TEMPERANCE

There was once a boy who was a loyal subject of the King of All. This boy served His King in every way he could because he Loved His King and wanted to please him. The boy received great pleasure in obeying and walking his life in the commands of the King. One day the King told the boy to go out into the land and spread the news of His Kingdom. He was to proclaim the news that all you had to do was believe in the King, and then when the time was right, all who believed would be able to enter into the most wonderful Kingdom that had ever been or ever would be.

The boy went all throughout many villages and towns and told whoever would listen about the King. In one particular village he decided to spend more time, for the people there received the news with joy and wanted to know more about the King and His Kingdom. They believed in the King and asked the boy to tell them what the King required of His subjects.

The boy answered, "All the King requires of you is that you love him more than anything else…Be ready at all times for the King to come back and collect you into his Kingdom!"

The boy then gave the people in the land each a copy of the King's Book of Wisdom and told them that this would guide them in all they needed to know about the King. He then left them and told them that he would be back to visit them again, but to be very careful that they loved the King more than any other thing.

For a time, the people didn't do anything but read the King's Book of Wisdom and fellowship in the love of the King.

Then, some of women saw that a man had come into town selling beautiful items for their homes. He had pictures of how homes should look and had many ideas of patterns for decorating and many objects to make them exactly pleasing to the eye. At first, they just looked in longing at the shop, but then went in to buy just a few things, then more things, then more things to decorate their houses with and spent less and less time in the reading of the King's Book and fellowshipping with the other people who loved the King. They still believed in the King... "We just feel that it is more important to be making our houses into homes," they stated when questioned about what they were doing.

Another group of men believed in the King with great exceeding Joy and in the beginning spent much time in His Book and with the other believers, but soon realized that they needed to be getting back to work. They saw the people who did not believe in getting the best positions and promotions, and thought that a King's Subject should have the best positions and not be outdone by a non-believer, so they put all their effort into becoming the best at their jobs. They soon spent less and less time reading the King's Book, and spent more and more time in reading things that pertained to their jobs.

Soon, every bit of spare time was spent in just resting and seeing their family and they had no time for getting together with other believers. They still believed, but things had to be put into perspective, they said, and a job was the most important thing for the family to survive!

Another group of believers had spent much time in the King's Book of Wisdom, but they saw many things in the land that looked like so much fun! They saw many viewing boxes, where one could sit for hours and just live in another world that was so much more fun than the world they did exist in. They saw plays and entertainment that the non-believers saw and they looked like so much fun also!

There was no way that just a little bit of non-believing entertainment could hurt them, right? So they started enjoying a little bit of non-believer entertainment, which lead into a little bit of less enjoyment of the King's Word... Then a little bit more entertainment, ... and a little bit more, until they anxiously awaited the newest play, the newest show, that tickled their minds and made life SO much better! Why, life wasn't meant to be dull was it? they reasoned. In the back of their minds they knew they should spend more time in the King's Word, but, they would, after the next show!!!

Some other believers loved the King and spent much time in fellowship. But they soon began to center all the fellowships around food. In the beginning it was just for the nourishment of the believers, but soon it turned into baking luscious foods that had no nourishment for the body but were created for the taste! These people started getting their pleasure, not from the fellowship of believers, but from the newest recipes that tantalized and fed their flesh, not their Spirits! This pleasure moved into all aspects of their lives where their thoughts were constantly on what would be the next thing they put into their mouth. But, they reasoned, the King had made food, so they were to enjoy it, right? And enjoy it they did!

After the boy had left, there were a small group of believers that had forsaken every other thing that the world had to offer them. They grew into the King's Book of Wisdom and received their pleasure from just reading His Words and waiting until the King would proclaim that it was time for them to come to His Kingdom. Their thoughts were not on the things of the world they lived in then, but in the world that was coming! They lived simply, looking after one another's needs, not wants, and were content with whatever situation they were in. They were ready and waiting for the King and His Kingdom for they loved their King above any other thing!

One day, the boy came back to the village with wonderful news ...

"The King has declared it is time to go to His Kingdom. It is all prepared!!! It is now time to leave!"

He went to the doors of the women that had gone off to take care of their homes. He eagerly told them the news that the King had beckoned for them to come! Each of the women told the boy, "I have just finished redecorating my house, and right now am waiting for a new item to be delivered. I'll come just as soon as it get's here." The boy only shook his head in sadness and went on.

He went to each of the men that worked so hard at their jobs, but the men each said, "I'm up for the big promotion, at last! Please tell the King that I will come just as soon as I get that raise!" And the boy sadly shook his head and went on.

He went to the next group of people who were just getting ready to leave to go to the newest play in town. The boy told them that the King was waiting for them but they replied, "We've been waiting for these tickets to this opening for ages. Tell the King we'll come just as soon as this show is over!!!"

The boy shook his head with sorrow and went on.

He went to the people that received their pleasure from eating and earnestly told them that it was time to go! They looked at him and mumbled through a mouth filled with food, "Great! Just give me an hour until this cake I'm baking is through. We can bring it to the King!" The boy shook his head and wearily walked on.

He came at last, to a small group of people who were earnestly studying and talking about the King. They looked up in surprise when they saw him and warmly greeted him with hugs. "The King has proclaimed that it is now time to go Him!" the boy proclaimed.

The people gave a great shout of JOY and hugged one another in excitement. "Now? Do we get to go now?" they eagerly questioned.

The boy nodded his head and asked cautiously, "Are you ready?"

The people responded, "We have been waiting for a long time now. We are ready!!"

The boy beamed with a smile of happiness and said, "You have loved your King above any other thing. Let's go, now! His Majesty is waiting!!!"

And all who were ready went and lived with the King, and were happy in His Kingdom forever after!!!

Patience

Lesson One
PATIENCE

PARENT: Today we are going to be learning the next characteristic. It is PATIENCE. Do you remember ALL the ones that we have been learning so far? We have learned about FAITH, KNOWLEDGE, TEMPERANCE and now we are going to add PATIENCE. Do you know what patience is? ... Let's read the Strong's definition of the word PATIENCE in the context of 2 Peter.

STRONG'S: Patience

(Greek # 5281 & # 5278; means cheerful endurance; constancy; enduring, patience, patient continuance (waiting); and to undergo, bear trials, have fortitude, persevere; abide, endure, take patiently, suffer, tarry behind.)

DICTIONARY: Patience

(1. The capacity of calm endurance.)

DICTIONARY: Patient

(1. Capable of bearing affliction with calmness. 2. Persevering; constant. 3. Understanding. 4. Forbearance.)

PARENT: We need to learn PATIENCE. When you say the word patience, most people think of just WAITING, that it means to wait. We will read some scriptures where it does mean this, but it ALSO means to calmly bear affliction. When we are HATED by the world we bear this with patience. Let's take a look at what the Bible has to say about patience...

READ: Luke 8:10-15
             Luke 21:16-19

QUESTIONS

According to Luke 8:15, how do those seeds which bear fruit bring forth fruit? (It says with PATIENCE.)
What type of hearts do these people have? (Honest and good.)
After they hear the Word of God, what do they do with it? (They keep the Word!)
In Luke 21:19, how will these believers possess their souls? (In their PATIENCE.)
Do you know what this patience means? (Enduring affliction calmly.)
In this scripture are they being afflicted?

READ: Romans 5:1-4
             Romans 15:4,5

QUESTIONS

What does this scripture say tribulations (afflictions to believers) do in us? (They WORK PATIENCE!)
What does patience work in us? (Experience, this means in the Greek #1382 means being TRIED and proved TRUSTABLE.)
In Romans 15, why were the scriptures written? (Vs. 4, says for our learning.)
What do they do? (They give us hope through patience and comfort of God's Holy word.)
What does vs. 5 call God? (The God of PATIENCE and consolation.)

READ: 2 Corinthians 6:4-5
             James 1:2-5

QUESTIONS

According to this scripture, how are we to be as ministers of God? (We are to have MUCH patience, it says.)
How are we to endure afflictions? (With MUCH patience?)
How are we to endure distresses, being whipped, being in prison and other things for the Word of God's sake? (We are to endure it all with CALM.)
In James, when we fall into different temptations what are we to do? (Count it all joy!)
What does the TRYING or being TRIED in

our faith do? (It works PATIENCE!)
What is patience going to do in us? (It will make us PERFECT (means complete), entire, and not wanting for anything.)

PARENT: We have been reading some scriptures about PATIENCE. It says that patience comes through TRIALS and AFFLICTION and that this is a GOOD thing.
Trials and afflictions do not sound as if they are going to be anything fun to go through, but God says to ADD patience. If we must add PATIENCE, then the only way to obtain it is through these. But if God is the one that is in control of our lives, and He is, we need to never fear or doubt HIM! He will take care of us and raise us up as His children just as you will someday train your own children!

❀❀❀❀❀

Lesson Two
PATIENCE
Being Patient

PARENT: In the last lesson we learned the definition of PATIENCE. Do you remember what it was? Patience is the ability to endure affliction with calmness. It also means to persevere and to forbear. We will learn about perseverance and forbearance later. Today we are going to read more Scriptures on PATIENCE.

READ: Ecclesiastes 7:8
               Romans 2:7

QUESTIONS

What is it better to have, a patient or proud spirit? (The Word says PATIENT!)
In Romans, what are we to be doing with patient continuance? (Well doing, vs. 7 says, for by well doing we seek for glory and honour and immortality, and eternal life!)
How do we continue in this? (With patience.)

READ: 1 Thessalonians 5:14-15

QUESTIONS

How are we to be toward all men? (Patient!)
When someone does evil to us, are we to turn around and do evil to them? (No, we are to do good to them. We are called to bless those who persecute us.)
How can we do this? (Through patience with all men.)
What is patience? (Calmly enduring afflictions.)
When someone does evil to us, what are we to do? (Be patient! Do good to ALL men.)

READ: James 5:1-10

QUESTIONS

In vs. 7, what are the believers commanded to be? (PATIENT.)
How long are they to be patient? (Until the coming of the Lord.)
What does the Word compare this patience to? (A husbandman, or farmer, who waits for the precious fruit of the earth, and has LONG patience for it until he receives the early and latter rain.)
How long does a farmer wait? (Many months.)
What does he do as he waits, just sit and wait? (No, he cultivates his fruit with mulch, he waters his fruit, and he weeds around it.)
Is he happy to see his fruit bloom? (Yes!)
What happens when he sees blooms on his plants? (He knows his fruit will soon be coming.)
Are we to be looking for Jesus' return in the same way? (Yes, with PATIENCE.)
What does patience mean in this scripture? (Waiting and watching. Patience does not mean to be LAZY as we wait.)

READ: Mark 13:28-37

QUESTIONS

What does the Lord liken the time of His return to? (To the ripening of a fig tree.)
In vs. 33, what are we commanded to do? (WATCH! and pray.)
What are we to be careful of? (That He does not come suddenly and find us sleeping.)
Are we to be working for Him until He comes? (Vs. 34 says yes!)
What are some ways we can do this? ...
How are we to watch and wait for the Lord? (James 5 says PATIENTLY!)
So, in what are we to be patient? (In our waiting for the Lord to return.)

READ: Hebrews 12:1-3

QUESTIONS

What race are we to run? (The race of being a believer in our Lord Jesus Christ.)
How are we to run this race? (With patience.)
If we are tempted to be weary and faint in our minds, what are we to think of? (Of Jesus and what HE endured for us! We have not yet ENDURED to blood.)

PARENT: Patience means to calmly endure afflictions, but it also means to WAIT. We are to PATIENTLY and faithfully look towards the return of Jesus. He is coming soon!

ACTIVITIES

Take paper cups and plant vegetables seeds with the children tending them until they produce fruit.

Lesson Three
PATIENCE
Forbearance

PARENT: One of the definitions of PATIENCE was FORBEARANCE. Have you any idea of what this means? We are going to find out, because this is something we are going to need to have! Let's look up in the dictionary Forbearance and Forbear.

DICTIONARY: Forbearance

(1. The act of refraining from something. 2. Tolerance and restraint in the face of provocation. 3. Patience.)

DICTIONARY: Forbear

(1. To ENDURE. 2. To hold yourself back. 3. To be patient.)

PARENT: According to the definition of FORBEARANCE, it also is another term for PATIENCE! Let's read in the Word of God all the scriptures that talk about forbearance.

READ: Romans 2:4
Romans 3:25-26

QUESTIONS

According to Romans 2, who has forbearance in this verse? (God!)
Who does God show forbearance to? (Us!)
In Romans 3, how did God show His forbearance towards us? (By sending Jesus for the remission of sins.)

PARENT: God has forbearance towards us! He is PATIENT to us in all our sin. He sent His own Son to die for us for the remission of that sin. We are also to have forbearance.

READ: Proverbs 24:11-12
Proverbs 25:15

QUESTIONS

How is FORBEAR used in Proverbs 24? (It means to delay or to hold back.)
What are they FORBEARING to do? (To deliver them that are drawn unto death...)
In Proverbs 25, what does it mean by long FORBEARING? (It means endurance and PATIENCE.)
According to this Proverb, are we to FORBEAR? (Yes, for by this you can persuade princes!)
What should we want to persuade people to? (To the knowledge of Jesus Christ, our Savior.)

READ: Ezekiel 2:5-7

QUESTIONS

In Ezekiel, was this a good FORBEAR? (NO!)
How was it not good? (They FORBEAR AGAINST the Lord!)
What does forbear mean here? (That they held back from Him and didn't HEAR Him.)
Should WE ever FORBEAR against Him in this manner? (Never!)
What manner of forbearance should we cultivate? (The type of forbearance that endures and is patient. We need to HOLD BACK from SIN!)

PARENT: We have found that the Word of God talks about two types of forbearing. The first is forbearance in the way of patience and endurance. God is everlastingly patient with us. He endured seeing His only Son die on a cross because He loved us and wanted us free from the law of sin and death. He is patient with us in all our imperfection and by His Holy Spirit will grow us into the knowledge of Him. So, our God has forbearance, patience and endurance towards us. The next meaning that we learned was to HOLD oneself back; to restrain ourselves. We read in the book of Ezekiel that the children of Israel held back from the knowledge and obedience of God. We are NEVER to do this.

We are to restrain ourselves from evil. In the chapters on TEMPERANCE we also learned that we are to restrain or control our flesh and its lusts. The next thing we are going to learn is FORBEARANCE towards our brothers and sisters in the Lord Jesus Christ. We are to FORBEAR one towards another...

❦❦❦❦❦

Lesson Four
PATIENCE
Forbearing

PARENT: There are many scriptures that talk about having patience and forbearance among the believers. We are commanded to love one another and forbearance is a part of this love.

READ: Ephesians 4:1-6

QUESTIONS

How are we to walk? (Vs. 1 says we are to walk worthy of the vocation wherewith we are called.)
What is our VOCATION? (Our vocation is the walk of a BELIEVER in Jesus Christ. This is our life.)
How are we to walk worthy? (With all lowliness and meekness, with longsuffering, FORBEARING one another in love.)
How are we to forbear one another in love? (With all patience. This is the meaning of FORBEAR here.)
Why are we to FORBEAR one another? (We are to endeavor to keep the unity of the Spirit in the bond of peace.)

READ: Colossians 3:12-12

QUESTIONS

What are the ELECT of God to put on? (Bowels of mercies, kindness, humbleness of mind, meekness, longsuffering.)

How are we to treat our brothers and sisters in the Lord? (Vs. 13 says that we are to FORBEAR one another.)

What goes along with forbearing one another in this scripture? (Forgiving one another.)

Who forgave us? (Christ.)

If He can forgive us, should we forgive others? (Yes! The Word of God says so.)

If we have a complaint or quarrel with a brother, what are we to do? (We are to forbear and forgive.)

Are we to forbear even when people treat us wrongly? (Yes.)

READ: Luke 6:28

QUESTIONS

How are we to be towards those that curse us? (We are to bless them.)

How are we to be towards those who despitefully use us? (We are to pray for them.)

Does it say NOT to be despitefully used? (No. It says they despitefully USE us, meaning we are USED! We do not hold back from being despitefully used.)

Is this a type of FORBEARANCE? (Yes!)

READ: 2 Timothy 2:23-26

QUESTIONS

How is a servant of the Lord to be? (Vs. 23 says he is to be gentle unto all men, apt to teach, PATIENT or the definition of patient here is FORBEARING.)

How are we to instruct those that oppose themselves? (Vs. 25, says in MEEKNESS.)

READ: Revelation 1:9

QUESTIONS

What does John say he is IN? (He is a companion in tribulation, and IN the Kingdom and PATIENCE of Jesus Christ.)

Why was he exiled to the isle of Patmos? (Vs. 9 says for the Word of God and for the testimony of Jesus Christ.)

How will the world regard the Word of God and the testimony of Jesus Christ? (The world will hate us as it also hated Jesus)

How are we to act when it hates us? (With forbearance and patience.)

PARENT: It is very important that we learn to have patience and forbearance. We are to be patient and kind towards one another, forbearing and forgiving. If the Bible says that we will have to forgive one another, do you think there was a reason for it saying this? We will probably offend one another and we will not all be at the same belief at the same time in our growth. This is why we need to be patient with one another and forbear and forgive. This should be in our hearts. Remember the Words we studied about LIVING the Word of God by being DOERS? We need to DO patience! Our Lord Jesus Christ will enable us to cultivate patience. He wouldn't tell us in His Word to ADD it if it wasn't possible!!!!

Lesson Five
PATIENCE
Endurance

PARENT: The Bible tells us that we are to add to our Temperance - Patience. We have learned two types of patience so far. First, there is a type of patience that calmly endures affliction. The second was forbearing one another. Do you remember what FORBEARANCE is? Forbearance means to endure, to restrain oneself, and to be patient towards others. For example, if someone is doing something DIFFERENT from the way you would do it, but the way they do it isn't WRONG, just different, you must quietly endure the way they do it. This is patience. God is patient with us and so we should be patient with fellow BELIEVERS.

Today we are going to study scriptures on ENDURANCE. We read that FORBEARANCE means to endure. Do you know what ENDURE means?

DICTIONARY: Endure

(1. To carry on through, despite hardships; undergo. 2. To bear with tolerance; put up with. 3. To suffer patiently without yielding. 4. Persevere.)

DICTIONARY: Endurance

(1. The act, quality, or power of withstanding hardship or stress. 2. The state or fact of persevering.)

PARENT: In the world that we live in today, it is very rare to find anything that teaches us to endure hardships for the sake of TRUTH. The world believes that you do what FEELS good. But the Bible tells us that being a Christian all the time might not feel so good to our flesh. Through temperance we are to temper or bring our flesh into submission to Jesus. This will not FEEL good. The next step is that we need to learn that in the days to come, when the world we live in gives us trouble for the Word's sake, we must ENDURE whatever it throws our way, but NEVER leave our love and our stand for TRUTH, which is the Word of God. Like John, in the Book of Revelation, we might be exiled to an island like Patmos. Will we give up our BELIEF in order to live a better life in our flesh? No! This is what it means to ENDURE. John endured. Paul endured. Stephen endured. JESUS endured! And WE must endure!

READ: Mark 4:16-17

QUESTIONS

Where do these seeds land? (On stony ground.)
Do they receive the Word? (With gladness!)
Do they have a root? (No, they have no root in themselves.)
What happens? (They only ENDURE for a time.)
What happens to them that causes them to be offended? (When affliction or persecution arises for the Word's sake.)
How long did they ENDURE? (Only a while.)

READ: 2 Timothy 2:1-10

QUESTIONS

In Vs. 3, what are we to endure? (We are to endure hardness.)
How are we to endure hardness? (As a good soldier of Jesus Christ.)
In vs. 10, what did Paul ENDURE? (He endured ALL things for the elect's sake.)
Why? (So they may also obtain the salvation which is in Christ Jesus with eternal glory.)

READ: James 1:12-16

QUESTIONS

In this scripture, who is blessed? (Vs. 12 says blessed is the man that ENDURETH temptation.)
What happens during this time of enduring temptation? (He is tried.)
What tempts a man, God? (No, a man's own lust.)
What does the Bible say we are to do to the lusts of the flesh? (Put them away with the old man.)
If a man ENDURES temptation, does this mean he gives in to it? (No. It means he stands firm and does not give in to it.)
What does ENDURE mean? (Endure means to suffer patiently without yielding!)
Can you think of things that we ENDURE through temptation?
In order to ENDURE, what keeps us standing firm? (Our LOVE of Jesus.)

✿✿✿✿✿

Lesson Six
PATIENCE
Enduring Afflictions

PARENT: Do you remember the first definition of PATIENCE? It was being capable of bearing affliction with calmness. Today we are going to read in the Word what the Bible says about afflictions. There are many Christians today who are facing terrible afflictions and persecutions. In America, we do not have it very severe yet. Did you know in Israel, if you are a BELIEVING Jew, and the government finds out, you are terribly persecuted, just as Jesus and the disciples were? Did you know that many of the religious Jews still believe in taking out these BELIEVERS and stoning them to death? This is still going on, almost 2000 years after our Messiah. According to the Word of God, affliction comes with being a BELIEVER. But, we are to learn PATIENCE through these troubles.

READ: 2 Corinthians 4:8-18

QUESTIONS

When these believers are troubled on every side are they distressed? (No! vs.8)
When they are perplexed do they despair? (No!)
When they are persecuted, are they forsaken by God? (No!)
When they are cast down, are they destroyed? (No!)
Should we ever fear death? (Never!)
Why? (Because God has CONQUERED death through Jesus Christ our Lord.)
What will God do to our body whether it is alive or dead? (He will raise us up by Jesus, vs. 14.)
In vs. 16, it says "but though our outward man perishes" ... what happens to our inward man? (He is renewed day by day.)
What does vs. 17 say affliction is? (It is light and is just for a moment!)
Through affliction, what are we to look at? (We are to look at things that are ETERNAL!)

READ: 2 Corinthians 8:1-4

QUESTIONS

What was the grace that God bestowed on the churches of Macedonia? (Vs. 2, that in a great trial of affliction the abundance of their joy and their deep poverty abounded unto the riches of their liberality, or simplicity!)
What did these believers have in their affliction? (Abundant JOY!)
What did their deep poverty abound unto? (It allowed them liberality or simplicity!)
Are afflictions and poverty regarded as BAD in the Word of God? (No!)
How does the world regard it? (They DESPISE the afflicted and the poor.)

READ: 1 Thessalonians 1:6

QUESTIONS

How did the believers in this scripture receive the Word of God? (In much AFFLICTION.) How did they receive the Word in this affliction? (With JOY of the Holy Ghost.)

READ: Hebrews 11:25-27

QUESTIONS

What did Moses choose to do? (He CHOSE to suffer AFFLICTION with the people of God.)
What did he CHOOSE not to do? (He chose NOT to enjoy the pleasures of sin for a season.)
Why did Moses endure? (Vs. 27 says He endured, as seeing HIM who is invisible!)
How shall we endure affliction? (As seeing HIM who is invisible, our eyes always fixed on GOD!)

READ: James 5:10-11

QUESTIONS

Who are we to look at for our examples in this scripture? (The prophets.)
What are they an example of? (An example of suffering affliction, and of patience.)
In vs. 11, what does it say about those which ENDURE? (It says we count them HAPPY which endure.)
What happened to Job in the end? (He was restored with MORE than he ever had before, after he was tried.)
Was Job patient? (Yes! The Word says Job calmly endured afflictions.)
Should we be like Job? (Yes!)

❀❀❀❀❀

Lesson Seven
PATIENCE
Being Afflicted

PARENT: The Word of God is very clear about the life of a believer. If we are BELIEVERS, it will not matter what anyone does or says to us because we KNOW the Truth. We will stand firm and calmly endure anything it offers us, never repaying evil for evil. This is PATIENCE!

READ: Acts 20:22-27

QUESTIONS

When Paul went to Jerusalem, what did he say waits for him, or abides with him in every city? (Bonds and affliction.)
Did this stop him from preaching the gospel? Who told him this would happen in every city? (Vs. 23, says that the Holy Ghost witnesses in every city saying that bonds and afflictions wait for him.)
What is Paul's attitude towards this? (Vs. 24, these things do not MOVE him.)
How does he regard his fleshly life? (He didn't count his life dear.)
What did this regard towards his life do? (It says that this way, he could finish his course and his ministry with JOY.)
What was the most important thing to Paul? (That he declared to every man the counsel of God.)
What is the most important thing in your lives?

READ: 2 Corinthians 6:1-10

QUESTIONS

How are we to walk in vs. 3? (We are not to give offense in any thing.)
Why? (So that the ministry, or Jesus' name is not blamed.)
What are we to do in all things? (We are to

approve ourselves as the ministers of God.)
How do we approve ourselves? (Vs. 4 says in much patience.)
How does vs. 6 say we can endure these things? (Through pureness, by knowledge, by longsuffering, by kindness, by the Holy Ghost, by love unfeigned, by the Word of Truth, by the power of God, by the armour of righteousness...)
In God's eyes do we have honour? (Yes.)
Do we in the world's eyes? (No, they think us fools.)
In God's eyes are we of good report? (Yes.)
What does the world think of us? (Evil.)
What does the world think of it when a person is won to Christ? (They think we are deceived!)
When we never seek to BE someone and want to live quiet, humble lives, does God know us? (Yes.)
Is this the world's way? (No, a person of the world seeks recognition and fame. They seek to have THEIR names known.)
Many believers have died for their faith, did they really die? (No, they LIVE!)
In this world we will have persecution and suffering. What does the Bible say to do in persecution for the Word's sake? (To rejoice!)
Can the world understand this? (No.)
How does the world view it? (They look on it and see suffering, believers look at persecution and rejoice!)
When we do not strive after being rich and having worldly things, what does the world regard us as? (Poor.)
Where are our treasures? (In heaven.)
Are we RICH? (Yes!)
Telling others about the Word of God and our testimony of Jesus makes us ... ? (Rich!)
Are the ways of the world opposite to the ways of the Lord? (Yes. 100%.)

READ: Hebrews 10:32-39

QUESTIONS

In vs. 32, what did the believers endure? (A great FIGHT of afflictions.)
How were they reproached? (Vs. 33, they were made a gazing stock by reproaches and afflictions.)
In vs. 34 how did they take these things? (Joyfully!)
How did they have this in them to take it joyfully? (Because they were looking towards heaven and knew the things to come are MUCH better than the things which are here.)
What does vs. 36 say they need? (They have need of patience.)
For what? (For when Jesus would come.)

PARENT: We are to endure afflictions knowing that at the end of the road is our Lord and Savior! We are to bear these afflictions with JOY, knowing that we are not of this earth, but of another KINGDOM. We are simply aliens here waiting for our true home!

❁❁❁❁❁

Lesson Eight
PATIENCE
Enduring Tribulations

PARENT: According to the Word of God, we are to endure anything thrown our way with calm assurance in Jesus! Do you remember what Romans 5:3 says? It says "But we glory in tribulations also; knowing that tribulation worketh patience!" If this is true, and it is, then we should welcome tribulation! Today we are going to study out the scriptures which talk about tribulations. Do you know what tribulation is? ...

DICTIONARY: Tribulation

(1. Great affliction, trial, or distress; suffering.)

STRONG'S: Tribulation

(Greek #2346 & #2347; Pressure, affliction; anguish; burdened; persecution; tribulation; trouble; to crowd; afflict; narrow; throng; suffer tribulation; trouble.)

PARENT: The Word tribulation has, for hundreds of years, meant persecution against believers. Let's read the scriptures which tell us more about tribulation.

READ: Matthew 13:21

QUESTIONS

This scripture should be very familiar to you by now. Why is this person offended? (Because of tribulation or persecution that comes from standing for the Word of God.)
How long does he endure? (It says he only endureth for a while.)
Is he faithful? (No.)
How are we to be when we go through tribulation because of the Word's sake?

READ: John 16:33

QUESTIONS

In the scripture in John 16, What will we have in the world? (In the world you shall have tribulation.)
What does Jesus tell us to be in this? (He says to be of GOOD CHEER.)
Why? (For Jesus has overcome the world!)
When tribulation arises because of the Word's sake, how are we to be then? (Of good cheer.)
Will this be hard? (No, we can do all things through Christ who strengthens us.)

READ: Acts 14:21-22

QUESTIONS

What did the apostles in this scripture exhort the believers in? (They exhorted them to continue in the faith.)
What else? (That we must through much tribulation enter into the kingdom of God!)
Do you think this will be a very popular verse with most people?
What will tribulation do in us? (Remember Romans 5:3 which says we GLORY in tribulations also knowing that tribulation worketh patience!)
When we GLORY in tribulation, what will we be perceived as? (That we are crazy...?)

READ: Romans 12:12-21

QUESTIONS

What are we to rejoice in? (Hope.)
What are we to be in tribulation? (PATIENT!)
What are we to do through our tribulation? (Always be talking to the Lord, continuously.)
Are we to pay people back with evil when they do evil to us? (No.)
Are we to avenge ourselves? (No.)
Who does vengeance belong to? (The Lord.)
Will God repay? (It says in vs. 19 that He will.)
How do we treat our enemies that afflict us? (We feed them if they are hungry.)
How do we overcome evil? (With good.)
What is the definition of tribulation? (Great affliction, trial or distress, suffering.)
Did Jesus have tribulation? (Yes! They hung Him on a cross.)
Should we perceive it as STRANGE that we go through tribulation? (No, it should be NORMAL. It should be strange if we do not. Remember the scripture in John 16:33 that says in the world you WILL have tribulation.)
What should our attitude be when it arises? (We should be of good cheer.)

Lesson Nine
PATIENCE
Through Tribulations

PARENT: Do you remember why we are studying the scriptures on tribulations? It is because of the scripture in Romans 5:3 which says, "But we glory in tribulations also; knowing that tribulation worketh patience!" We need to be finding out what the Word of God has to say about tribulation because this is one way PATIENCE comes. Without this knowledge we will be unfruitful and not be unable to add the rest of the characteristics that we need. Let's read some more about tribulations.

READ: 2 Corinthians 1:1-4

QUESTIONS

In vs. 3, what do they call God? (The God of all comfort.)
What does he comfort us in? (In all our tribulation.)
After we are comforted by God, what are we to do? (We are then to comfort others which are in any trouble.)
How? (By the comfort wherewith we ourselves are comforted by God.)
In tribulation, will we need comfort? (Yes.)
What is the definition of tribulation? (Great affliction, trial or distress, suffering.)

READ: 2 Corinthians 7:1-4

QUESTIONS

What are we to cleanse ourselves from? (From all filthiness of the flesh and spirit.)
In vs. 4, what was Paul filled with? (Comfort.)
How did he handle tribulations? (He was exceedingly JOYFUL in all their tribulations.)
What happened to them in Macedonia? (Their flesh had no rest, and they were troubled on every side.)
In vs. 6, who does God comfort? (God comforteth those that are cast down.)
How did God comfort them? (He comforted them by the coming of Titus.)
In our tribulations, what will God do? (He will comfort us so we can bear them.)
Will Jesus ever leave us? (No, He will never leave us nor forsake us.)
What will we learn through our tribulations? (PATIENCE.)

READ: Ephesians 3:13-21

QUESTIONS

What does Paul say his tribulations are? (The believer's GLORY.)
What does Romans 5:3 say about this? (But we GLORY in tribulations also.)
How do we GLORY in tribulations? (Knowing that tribulation worketh PATIENCE. It is good for us.)
In vs. 16, how are we to be strengthened? (By God's Spirit.)
Where are we strengthened? (In our inner man.)
In vs. 21, where is God's glory? (In the church.)
Is this a building? (No, it is in the people that BELIEVE in Jesus Christ throughout ALL ages or time.)

READ: 2 Thessalonians 1:2-10

QUESTIONS

In vs. 4, what did they GLORY in? (In the churches or the people that BELIEVED, for their patience and faith in all their persecutions and TRIBULATIONS that they endured.)
What is a manifest token of righteous judgment of God, in vs. 5? (Their persecutions and tribulations.)
Why? (That they may be counted worthy of the kingdom of God, for which they also

suffer.)
Will God recompense tribulation to those that trouble believers? (It says in vs. 6 yes.)
Should we wish evil on those who do evil to us? (No. We are to do them GOOD.)
Who will Jesus take vengeance on? (Vs. 8, 1. Them that know not God; and 2. Them that obey not the gospel of our Lord Jesus Christ.)
When tribulations happen to us, how long are we to endure? (Until they are over.)
How do we endure? (With joy and good cheer.)
How can we do this? (Through God who will comfort us.)
Will God comfort us during our tribulations? (Yes. He is the God of comfort!)

❀❀❀❀❀

Lesson Ten
PATIENCE
God is Longsuffering

PARENT: Another attribute of PATIENCE is LONGSUFFERING. Have you ever heard of this word before? It is mentioned many times in the Bible. We need to learn to be longsuffering. It was very important to learn the character traits in 2 Peter in exactly the order that they were given. If we hadn't learned about TEMPERANCE first, longsuffering would be very difficult to obtain. Let's read the definition of LONGSUFFERING.

DICTIONARY: Longsuffering

(1. Patiently enduring wrongs or difficulties. 2. Patient endurance.)

READ: Exodus 34:4-7

QUESTIONS

Who did the Lord stand with? (Moses.)
Do you remember what Moses endured? (He chose to endure hardship with the people of God rather than the pleasures of sin for a short while.)
What did the Lord proclaim? (In vs. 6 He proclaimed that the Lord God is merciful, gracious, LONGSUFFERING, and abundant in goodness and truth.)
Can you think HOW God is longsuffering? (He patiently endures all our wrongs with the hopes that men will turn towards His SON for salvation... He is not willing that any man should perish.)

READ: Numbers 14:18-21

QUESTIONS

In vs. 18, what is the Lord? (The Lord is LONGSUFFERING, and of great mercy.)
How is He LONGSUFFERING and of great mercy? (Forgiving iniquity and transgression.)
How do we make God suffer? (By doing evil against the Lord.)
Will He forgive us? (Yes.)
How? (Through Jesus Christ our Lord!)
When we sin, why does this make God suffer? (Because He is sinless and He hates what is evil.)
What is the FEAR of the LORD? (To hate what is evil.)

READ: Psalms 86:15-17

QUESTIONS

In vs. 15, what is God? (He is full of compassion, and gracious, LONGSUFFERING and plenteous in mercy and truth.)
In vs. 17, what did God do for him? (He helped him and comforted him.)
Who comforts us in our tribulation? (God.)

READ: Romans 9:18-24

QUESTIONS

Should we question God for the way He chooses to do things? (No, vs. 20 says who are YOU that repliest against God. Shall the thing formed say to Him that formed it, Why hast thou made me thus?)
What does God endure? (Vs. 22, He endured with much LONGSUFFERING the vessels of wrath fitted to destruction.)
How does He endure them? (With LONGSUFFERING.)

READ: 1 Peter 3:20
        2 Peter 3:9-15

QUESTIONS

In 1 Peter, during what time did God wait in LONGSUFFERING? (During the time of Noah.)
What were the people like then? (They were very ungodly and did much evil.)
What does the Bible say the world will be like when Jesus returns? (He says, "As it was in the days of Noah, so shall it be also in the days of the son of man", Luke 17:26.)
Is God enduring LONGSUFFERING now? ...
In 2 Peter, how is God towards us? (Vs. 9 says that God is longsuffering to usward.)
What does He will all men to do? (That they should come to repentance.)
What is the LONGSUFFERING of our Lord? (Vs. 15 says it is SALVATION.)
In what way will the day of the Lord come? (As a thief in the night.)
What are we to look for? (For new heavens and a new earth, wherein dwelleth righteousness, vs. 13.)

Lesson Eleven
PATIENCE
Longsuffering

PARENT: In Lesson Ten we learned that God is LONGSUFFERING. Do you remember the definition for longsuffering? LONGSUFFERING is patiently enduring wrongs or difficulties. Today we are going to read the scriptures that tell us to be longsuffering.

READ: Romans 2:4-5

QUESTIONS

What does the goodness of God lead people to? (It leads to repentance.)
Are we to despise the riches of God's goodness and forbearance and LONG-SUFFERING? (No!)

READ: 2 Corinthians 6:6
        Galations 5:22-26

QUESTIONS

How are we to approve ourselves in 2 Corinthians? (By pureness, by knowledge and by LONGSUFFERING ...)
In Galations, is LONGSUFFERING a fruit of the Spirit? (Yes.)
What have those that are Christ's done? (Vs. 24 says they have crucified the flesh with the affections and lusts.)
Which characteristic is this under? (Temperance.)
So, in order to be fruitful and not barren, do we need to learn LONGSUFFERING? (Yes.)

READ: Ephesians 4:1-3

QUESTIONS

How are we to walk? (Worthy of the calling.)
What are we to be? (Lowly, meek, LONGSUFFERING, forbearing one another in love.)

Why are we to do this? (To keep the unity of the Spirit.)
What bond do BELIEVERS have? (Vs. 3 says the BOND of peace.)

READ: Colossians 1:10-12
        Colossians 3:12

QUESTIONS

In most of these scriptures that mention longsuffering, what does it mention before it? (In most of the scriptures it talks about how we are to walk.)
What does it mean WALK? (It means how you live your life. A "WALK" is how we walk out our lives.)
How are we to live our lives? (Colossians 1:10 says we are to live our lives worthy of the Lord unto all pleasing, being fruitful in every good work, and increasing in the knowledge of God.)
How are we to be patient and longsuffering? (With joyfulness.)

READ: 1 Timothy 1:15-17
        2 Timothy 3:10

QUESTIONS

Why did Jesus come into the world? (To save sinners.)
How did Jesus show forth all longsuffering? (Paul or Saul persecuted His church. Paul was the one who stood by and watched as Stephen was stoned. And yet, Paul repented and was forgiven.)
How was this a pattern to them which should hereafter believe? (It showed the depth of Jesus' mercy and longsuffering!)
Who is talking in this scripture? (Paul)
What did he say he was like? (That he had FAITH, LONGSUFFERING, CHARITY and PATIENCE.)
Are we to learn from him? (Yes! He was made an apostle by Jesus.)
If Paul was longsuffering and patient and he was just a man, do you think we can be to? (Yes!)
Who helped him to be this way? (Jesus.)
Will Jesus help us?

READ: 2 Timothy 4:1-5

QUESTIONS

What are we to do? (Preach the Word, be instant in season, out of season; reprove, rebuke, exhort.)
How do we exhort? (With all longsuffering and doctrine.)
What is NOT sound doctrine? (Anything that does not line up with God's Word.)
What if something is 99% right with God's Word? (The 1% error makes it NOT sound.)

✿✿✿✿✿

Lesson Twelve
PATIENCE
Suffering Long

PARENT: We are learning about LONGSUFFERING. Now we are going to see what the Bible has to say about "suffer". Do you know what it means to SUFFER? It sounds like such an awful word, but the definition isn't really that much different from tribulation, affliction or longsuffering. Do you want to suffer? It sure doesn't sound like anything we WANT to happen to us. But, the disciples of our Lord had a much different way of looking at it. They REJOICED when they suffered for Jesus' sake. They had TRUE faith in KNOWING Jesus and His coming Kingdom. We need to read what the Word of God will tell us to encourage us in this.
Let's look up SUFFER in the dictionary...

DICTIONARY: Suffer

(1. To feel pain or distress. 2. To tolerate or endure evil, injury, pain, or death.)

READ: Romans 8:16-18

QUESTIONS

If we suffer with Jesus, what else will we do? (We may be also glorified together.)
How can we suffer WITH Jesus? (Remember Him telling us that He is WITH us always?)
When we suffer is He suffering? (Yes.)

READ: Acts 9:1-5
QUESTIONS

What did Saul want to do? (He wanted to bring BOUND anyone who believed in Jesus as the Messiah to Jerusalem for punishment.)
Was Jesus risen at this time? (Yes.)
What did He say to Saul? (Vs. 4,5)
Was he persecuting Jesus when he was persecuting the believers? (Yes.)
So in Romans 8:16-18, are we persecuted WITH Jesus when we are suffering? (Yes.)
Isn't this comforting? (Yes! We are never suffering or enduring things alone.)

READ: 1 Corinthians 4:11-13

QUESTIONS

Were the disciples given glory and honour on earth? (No.)
What were their lifestyles? (Vs. 11, they were hungry, thirsty, were naked, were buffeted, and had no certain dwelling place. They worked with their own hands.)
How did people treat them? (They were reviled and persecuted and defamed.)
How did the world consider them? (They were made as the filth of the world and are the off scouring or GARBAGE of all things unto this day.)
How did they handle persecution? (It says they SUFFERED it.)

READ: 1 Corinthians 6:6-11

QUESTIONS

What is the trouble in this scripture? (The believers were going to sue one another in courts of law.)
What does Paul say to do? (He says to SUFFER yourselves to be defrauded, vs. 7)
What does this mean? (It means rather than go against a brother GIVE them what they want and SUFFER being taken in your material goods.)
Does the world teach this? (No, they say that would be FOOLISH.)

PARENT: When we suffer troubles in this world because of the Word of God, are we going to be alone? The Bible tells us that Jesus will always be with us. If we REALLY know this, should we ever be afraid of anything anyone will do to us? .... Jesus says when evildoers persecute us they are persecuting Him. And if we partake of His persecutions the Word promises that we shall also be glorified with Him. What better hope to ENDURE anything than to have the knowledge that we are not of this world but of another, that is going to be so much better than anything here. Jesus, Himself, will be with us through ALL things. We need to always remember this. When we are suffering, He is there suffering with us! This is TRUE! Even though we do not see Him with our earthly eyes, He is right HERE! At all times! He promises to NEVER leave us or forsake us. Don't ever forget this!

❀❀❀❀❀

Lesson Thirteen
PATIENCE
Sufferings for Righteousness

PARENT: It is very important to remember Romans 5:3. Do you remember the scripture? It says that tribulations work PATIENCE. Do you remember what tribulations are? Strong's said that it was to SUFFER tribulation. Do you know WHY the believers have always suffered tribulations and persecutions? There are scriptures that tell us one reason is to TRY us, and to PURIFY us, and to make us WHITE. In the Book of Daniel it states that this is why persecution is allowed. We need to know that whatever happens to us here on earth that it is always for GOOD! When parents discipline and chastise their children, it is not pleasant, but afterwards it yields good fruit. We need to TRUST God that He is our Father and will take care of us even MORE than our earthly fathers. And Jesus will always be with us, enduring the same afflictions as we do!

READ: Philippians 1:27-30

QUESTIONS

Are we to be terrified by our adversaries? (No! vs. 27.)
What is it when we are not? (An evident token of perdition.)
What is it to US when we are not terrified of our adversaries? (Evidence of salvation and that of God.)
What is given to us? (Vs. 29 says it is given in the behalf of Christ, not only to believe on Him, but also to SUFFER for HIS sake.)
Did Paul go through this too? (Yes.)
Did all the rest of the disciples? (Yes.)

READ: Philippians 3:9-10

QUESTIONS

Do we have our OWN righteousness? (No, only that which is BY faith!)
What does the scripture say they wanted? (That I may KNOW Him; and know the power of His resurrection; AND the FELLOWSHIP of His SUFFERINGS!)
Did Paul WANT the fellowship of His sufferings? (Yes!!!!!)
How could Paul feel this way? (He was madly in love with Jesus and couldn't wait to be with Him in His resurrection of the dead! He truly believed in Jesus and His coming Kingdom and wanted it to COME!)
Should we feel this way? (Yes.)

READ: Philippians 4:11-13

QUESTIONS

Is this a very important scripture? (YES!)
How are we to live our lives? (CONTENT in whatever situation we find ourselves.)
Even in sufferings? (Yes!)

READ: Colossians 1:23-24
         2 Thessalonians 1:5

QUESTIONS

In Colossians, did Paul WEEP in his sufferings? (No. He REJOICED.)
Why did he suffer? (The religious people considered Paul a heretic and stoned him, put him in jail and basically wanted to kill him for what he had to SAY! They wanted to SHUT him up.)
Could they? (No. He continued to speak the TRUTH for those who would believe regardless of the danger.)
Why do believers suffer? (They suffer FOR the Kingdom of God.)
Willingly? (Yes. All they would have to do to stop suffering is quit speaking truth and there would be no reason to make these people suffer.)

READ: 1 Timothy 4:10
2 Timothy 1:11-14

Why do we both labour and suffer reproach? (Because we TRUST in the living God! 1 Tim.)
In 2 Tim. why did Paul suffer? (Because of what he BELIEVED.)
Will God keep us? (Yes.)
How often is God with us? (ALL the time.)

PARENT: The only reason we could suffer for something is because we BELIEVE in it. This is the same thing that we learned with VALOR. The only reason we are brave is because of what we BELIEVE. If you BELIEVE something you can endure ANYTHING!

Lesson Fourteen
PATIENCE
Suffering With Patience

PARENT: We have been reading the scriptures on the BELIEVER'S attitudes towards suffering. Do you think that teachings on suffering are very popular? They probably are not very popular because this is not something most people want to hear. Do YOU want to suffer? But, according to the Word of God, they took their afflictions JOYFULLY. Somehow, when we are suffering for righteousness sake, it will be a JOYFUL thing. It is because of their STRONG belief! They BELIEVED and would not back down because of fear. This is what we need to learn. This is patience!

READ: 2 Timothy 2:8-13

QUESTIONS

Are we to suffer for doing evil? (No!)
But will the world look upon our beliefs as GOOD? (No!)
How was Paul suffering as an evil doer? (They punished him for doing righteousness as if he was doing evil!)
In vs. 12, how will we reign with Him? (It says if we suffer, we shall also reign with Him.)
What will happen if we deny Him? (He will deny us.)
Should we ever deny Him? (NEVER!)

READ: 2 Timothy 3:12-14

QUESTIONS

Who will suffer persecution? (All that will live Godly in Christ Jesus.)
Does this just mean the believers during Jesus' day? (No, it says ALL that will live Godly in Christ Jesus.)
Are we trying to live Godly in Christ Jesus? (Yes.)

Then will we suffer persecution? (Yes.)
How will we suffer it? (Joyfully.)

READ: Hebrews 2:9-16

QUESTIONS

Who is our King? (God, Jesus.)
Did our King suffer? (Yes.)
How? (He died on a cross and suffered death.)
Why did He do this? (Because He loved us.)
How can we ever endure suffering? (Because of our LOVE for HIM!)
What will all tribulations work in us? (Patience.)
So, are they good or bad? (They are good, and we are to GLORY in our tribulations.)

READ: Hebrews 11:25-50

QUESTIONS

This scripture should be very familiar to you by now. HOW did Moses choose to suffer affliction with the people of God? (By FAITH! By what he BELIEVED!)
In vs. 35, why did some believers choose torture? (They did not accept deliverance because they wanted to obtain a better resurrection.)
What does it say about these people who wandered about in sheepskins and goatskins, being destitute, afflicted, tormented? (It says in vs. 38 that the WORLD was not WORTHY of them.)
Is this how the world views the destitute? (No, they DESPISE these types of people.)
Should we despise them? (No! We might be called to be ONE of them.)
How did they live like this? (Through FAITH, through what they BELIEVED which was in Jesus Christ!)

READ: James 5:10
1 Peter 4:12-19

QUESTIONS

What are we to do when we have sufferings? (1 Pe. 4:13 says to REJOICE!)
How will we be when we see His glory? (We will be glad also with exceeding joy!)
If we are reproached for the name of Christ, what are we? (Vs. 14 says HAPPY are ye.)
What does it say is on us? (THE SPIRIT OF GLORY AND OF GOD RESTETH UPON YOU!!!!!!!!!!!!!!!!!)
Isn't this wonderful? Could you handle suffering now? (God's Spirit of glory rests upon us!)
What are we forbidden to suffer as? (As an evildoer.)

❀❀❀❀❀

Lesson Fifteen
PATIENCE
Persecutions

PARENT: As we have been reading many of these scriptures under PATIENCE, we have been seeing the word "persecution". Do you know what persecution is? What ideas do you have that it is? ...

STRONG'S: Persecute

(Greek #1377; To pursue; to persecute; ensue; follow, suffer persecution.)

DICTIONARY: Persecute

(1. To oppress or harass with ill-treatment. 2. To annoy persistently.)

READ: Matthew 5:10-16
        Matthew 5:44

QUESTIONS

What does it say we are when we are persecuted for righteousness' sake? (It says we are BLESSED!)
What is theirs, in vs. 10? (Their's is the Kingdom of Heaven!)
If this is true, and it is, then is it GOOD to be persecuted? (Yes, we will have the Kingdom of Heaven and be blessed!)
How else are we blessed? (We are blessed when men shall revile us, and persecute us, and say all manner of evil FALSELY, for Jesus' sake.)
What does it say to do when this happens? (REJOICE! and be exceeding glad.)
Why? (Because GREAT is our reward in heaven.)
What are we? (We are salt. We give flavour to the earth.)
How do we give flavour? (By speaking the Truth which is the Word of God.)
Because of FEAR of persecution, should we NOT speak the Word of God? (No!)
How are we to treat those who persecute us? (We are to love them and pray for them.)

READ   Matthew 10:22-28

QUESTIONS

Will the world love us? (No, vs. 22 says we will be hated of ALL men for Jesus' name sake.)
When we are persecuted in a city, what are we to do? (We are to flee to the next city.)
Are we to FEAR those who persecute us? (No, read vs. 28.)
How long are we to endure persecution? (Until the end.)
What will happen to those that endure till the end? (Vs. 22 says he that endureth to the end shall be saved.)
What did the world call Jesus? (Beelzebub or devil.)
What does Jesus warn us? (That if they felt that way about HIM how much more would they feel about us?)
What will persecutions and tribulations work in us? (Patience.)
Is this supposed to be a NORMAL thing for BELIEVERS? (Yes. It says we are blessed when it happens.)

READ: Matthew 13:20-21
        Mark 4:16-17

QUESTIONS

How long did these people endure? (Just for a while.)
What caused them to fall away? (Persecution or tribulation that came because of the Word.)
Are we to be like this? (No, we are to stand firm when persecution comes.)

READ: John 15:18-27

QUESTIONS

Who did the world hate before it hated us?

(Jesus.)
How do you know you are not of the world? (Vs. 19, it says the world would love you, and if it hates you, you are not of the world.)
Does Jesus say we will be persecuted? (Vs. 20 says if they have persecuted me, they WILL also persecute you.)
Do the people that persecute you know God? (No!)
If a person hates Jesus, who do they also hate? (God, the Father.)
Did they have a reason to hate Jesus? (It says they hated Him without a cause.)
What did Jesus send us? (He sent the Comforter or the Holy Spirit!)
Why is He called the Comforter? (Because He comforts the believers.)

✿✿✿✿✿✿

Lesson Sixteen
PATIENCE
Enduring Persecutions

PARENT: We learned in the last lesson that persecution is a normal thing for believers. Many people do not want to ever suffer persecution so they compromise the Word of God. They would rather save their flesh and not have trouble so they never speak the Truth of the Word of God. We need to learn that we must STAND for truth no matter what comes our way because of it. This is an aspect of VALOR and PATIENCE!

READ: Romans 8:35-39

QUESTIONS

Are we separated from Jesus' love during perils and tribulations? (Never. He is there suffering with us.)
Are we conquerors or losers during these things? (We are more than conquerors through Jesus!)
When these things happen to us, will God help us through them? (Yes. It is our LOVE for Him that helps us to endure! He will never leave us nor forsake us.)

READ: Romans 12:14-21

QUESTIONS

How are we to treat those who want to hurt us? (We are to bless them.)
Will this be easy? (It will depend on how you look at persecution.)
We are to treat our enemies with what? (Love.)

READ: 1 Corinthians 4:10-14

QUESTIONS

How will this knowledge be perceived by the world? (It will be foolishness.)

What will they call us? (Fools.)
When we are reviled, what do we do, revile them back? (No, we bless!)
When we are persecuted do we fight back? (No, we suffer it.)
When we are defamed, do we tell THEM what THEY are? (No, we entreat.)
What is this called? (It is "turning the other cheek", as Jesus told us to do.)

READ: 2 Corinthians 12:9-10

QUESTIONS

What did Paul say he took pleasure in? (I take pleasure in infirmities, in reproaches, in necessities, in persecution, in distresses for Christ's sake.)
When we are weak, what are we? (We are strong.)
Who can use us when we are weak? (Jesus can.)
How? (In vs. 9 it says that I will gladly glory in my infirmities, that the power of Christ may rest upon me. It is JESUS who will do every-
thing when we are weak!)

READ: 2 Thessalonians 1:3-12

QUESTIONS

What is to be growing exceedingly? (Vs. 3, says our FAITH!)
How did the believers handle their persecutions and tribulations? (They endured them with patience and faith.)
How should we live our lives? (So that the name of our Lord Jesus Christ may be glorified in us. We are AMBASSADORS for Christ!)

READ: 2 Timothy 3:10-17

QUESTIONS

Does God deliver us out of persecutions? (Yes, vs. 11.)
Are we to endure them? (Yes.)
Who will be persecuted? (ALL who will live godly in Christ Jesus shall suffer persecution.)
What will get worse and worse as time goes on? (Evil men and seducers.)
What are seducers? (According to the Greek, it is one who entices people away from sound doctrine. They seduce away from the TRUTH with religious, false doctrines that tickle ears.)
How are we to live? (We are to LIVE the Word of God, continuing in it and growing in it.)
What will this do? (It will increase our KNOWLEDGE of Truth!)

🌀🌀🌀🌀🌀

Lesson Seventeen
PATIENCE
Bearing Trials

PARENT: *In God's Word, we are taught to bear different trials. Have you ever thought that you might be going through a trial when persecution or tribulation happens? Let's read in the Word of God what it has to say about going through TRIALS.*

DICTIONARY: Trial

(1. The act or process of testing, trying, or putting to the proof by actual or simulated use and experience. 2. A single complete instance of such testing. 3. A state of pain or anguish caused by a difficult situation or condition. 4. A test of patience or endurance.)

READ: 2 Corinthians 8:1-5

QUESTIONS

What does the scriptures say their afflictions were? (It says in vs. 2, "A great TRIAL of affliction". They were trials.)
What happened in their trial? (They abounded in the abundance of their joy!)
How did the believers come through this trial? (They first gave their own selves to the Lord, vs. 5.)

READ: Hebrews 11:36

QUESTIONS

What trials did these believers endure? (They had trials of cruel mockings and scourgings, yea, moreover of bonds and imprisonment...)
What is a trial? (It is a process of testing, or trying.)
Is a trial a bad thing? (No, the world and its people would look upon it as a bad thing, but we are to glory in these things.)
What does a trial do to a believer? (A trial builds our faith and we get stronger through our weakness. It teaches us to depend on the Lord.)

READ: 1 Peter 1:3-9

QUESTIONS

Where is our inheritance? (Vs. 3, says that our inheritance is reserved in heaven.)
Does this mean God has it for us now? (Yes!)
How are we kept? (By the power of God through FAITH.)
How are we to be even in the heaviness of our temptations? (We are to GREATLY rejoice.)
What does it say the trial of our faith is? (It is much more precious than gold.)
Do you TRY gold? (Yes. It is refined again and again by heating it in very hot fire. The impurities then come to the surface and you skim them off. This is purifying gold.)
What is being compared to this gold being tried in fire? (Our faith.)
Will God purify us? (Yes, for our faith is more precious than gold and He is faithful to perfect or purify us.)
When we go through trials, what do we need to remember? (That we are being purified, just like gold.)
Even though we do not see Him, who do we love? (Jesus!)
What is the END of our faith? (It is the salvation of our souls!)

READ: 1 Peter 4:12-19

QUESTIONS

Is it NORMAL that we have trials? (Yes, vs. 12 says think it not STRANGE!)
What will trials do for us? (They will TRY us.)
What are we to do when trials come? (We are to REJOICE!)
So are trials good for us? (Yes. And they are normal to every BELIEVER. It is not normal

to not have them according to the Word of God.)

DICTIONARY: Try

(1. To test in order to determine strength, effect, or worth. 2. To put on trial. 3. To melt to separate out impurities!)

PARENT: Trials are to TRY us. They refine us and purify us. Trials build our FAITH and we need to regard trials as something GOOD, not bad.

❀❀❀❀❀

Lesson Eighteen
PATIENCE
Being Tried

PARENT: In Lesson Seventeen we learned that trials are to TRY us. Do you remember the definition of being TRIED? It means to test to determine strength, or to melt to separate impurities. Did you know that God TRIES His people? He purifies us!

READ: Jeremiah 11:20
              Jeremiah 20:12

QUESTIONS

What does God do? (It says that He triest the reins and the hearts.)
What are the reins, do you remember? (Hebrews #3629 says the reins is the mind, as in the interior self... who you are INSIDE.)
What does God do when He TRIEST the reins and hearts? (He tests and purifies.)
In Jeremiah 20, WHO does God try? (He tries the RIGHTEOUS.)
Why does God TRY us? (Because He loves us and wants us refined.)

READ: Psalms 7:9
              Psalms 11:5

QUESTIONS

In these two scriptures, what does it say God does? (He tries the righteous and their hearts and reins.)

READ: Daniel 11:33-35
              Daniel 12:10

QUESTIONS

According to our Unit on KNOWLEDGE, who are those that have understanding? (Those that know the Word of God.)
In Daniel, what shall the people that have understanding do? (Vs. 33 says they shall

instruct many.)
What will happen to these of understanding? (They shall fall by the sword, and by flame, by captivity, and by spoil, many days.)
Does this sound like tribulations to you? (Yes. Afflictions, persecutions, etc.)
Why does God allow this? (Vs. 35 has the answer. To TRY them, and to PURGE, and to make them white.)
Will God TRY us? (It says so in the Word.)

READ: 1 Thessalonians 2:4

QUESTIONS

Who does it say God tries? (It say OUR hearts, which would mean BELIEVERS, since it is a BELIEVER writing this.)
Who does God want our hearts to be loyal to? (To Him!)
Are we to fear men and be men pleasers? (No!)

READ: Hebrews 11:17-19

QUESTIONS

Was Abraham tried? (Yes.)
Do you know HOW he was tried? (God wanted to see how much Abraham trusted Him and almost had him offer up Isaac, Abraham knowing God would raise Isaac from the dead.)
Did Abraham pass the test? (YES!)

READ: James 1:12

QUESTIONS

In this scripture, how are we tried? (By temptations.)
Does God tempt us? (No! We are tempted by our own lusts.)
What do believers that are tried in this scripture receive? (They receive a crown of life.)
Who gets this crown of life? (It says those who love Him get it.)

READ: 1 Peter 1:7

QUESTIONS

Do you remember this scripture?
What is tried? (Our faith.)
What does this do for us? (It refines us and make us pure.)
Do we need to be tried? (Yes, it purifies us, purges us, and makes us white.)

ACTIVITIES

Have the children draw what they think the crown of life looks like!

✿✿✿✿✿

Lesson Nineteen
PATIENCE
Review

PARENT: We have learned that patience is being able to calmly bear afflictions. It is also patiently continuing and waiting with hope. We have been reading many scriptures that are helping us to understand PATIENCE. Our tribulations, afflictions, persecutions and sufferings help to work PATIENCE in us. The Word of God says that these things are good and we are to REJOICE when they happen. Right now, our flesh may not think so highly of it, but the more we grow OUT of this world, and INTO God's Kingdom, we will be renewed in our minds. God wants us to add PATIENCE and we must do this, but it is the Lord who allows trials for us to be tried. We cannot go out and chase these afflictions to get patience. They will come soon enough as we are being SALT to the earth! One of the definitions in the Strong's of PATIENCE was perseverance. This means to continue on in the faith even when times get rough. There are many scriptures that talk about the believers continuing in the FAITH. We need to encourage one another daily in walking out the Word of God, and helping one another through our trials and tribulations!

What are some definitions of PATIENCE? (Patience is to endure afflictions with calmness. It also means to faithfully wait.)
What works patience is us? (Tribulations.)
What does patience work? (Experience or being TRIED.)
Is God patient? (Yes.)
How is God patient? (He is longsuffering with us, and is patient and kind in all our sin, through Jesus Christ.)
How are we to endure afflictions? (With much patience.)

How are we to be towards all men? (Patient.)
When someone does evil to us, are we to pay them back with evil? (No, we are to do good to those who are evil to us.)
How can we do this? (Through PATIENCE.)
How are we to be like husbandmen or farmers? (We are to be patient as we wait for the coming of the Lord.)
Are we to wait for Jesus to come with laziness? (No, we are to be waiting and watching!)
What are we to be careful of regarding His coming? (That He does not come suddenly and find us sleeping.)

What is FORBEARANCE? (It is endurance in the face of being provoked. It is another form of patience.)
Does God have forbearance? (Yes.)
How are we to treat one another? (With forbearance.)
What does the scripture tell us also to do to one another? (We are to forbear and to forgive one another.)
How are we to be towards those that spitefully use us? (We are to forbear.)

What does it mean to endure? (Endure means to carry on through hardships. It means to suffer patiently without yielding.)
What causes some people to stop enduring? (In the parable of the seeds, those who have no root only endure until persecution or affliction arises because of the Word's sake.)
How are we to handle temptation? (We are to ENDURE it.)
What does this mean? (This means we are to stand firm and not yield to the temptation.)
What allows us to endure? (Our belief and our love of God.)

What are afflictions? (Afflictions are things that happen to us because of the Word of God that are to make us stronger in God.)
How are we to regard afflictions? (We are to look at them as just being temporary, while our hope is in things that are ETERNAL.)
How did the believers of the Word receive affliction? (With great joy.)
Are afflictions and poverty something we

should despise as believers? (No!)
How does the world regard afflictions and poverty? (They despise them.)

What does TRIBULATION mean? (Tribulation means great affliction, persecution, trials or suffering.)
What does tribulation do for us? (It works patience in us.)
Is it STRANGE that we go through tribulation? (No, this is a normal part of the life of a BELIEVER.)
What did Jesus tell us we would have regarding tribulation? (He said, in the world you will have tribulation.)
Are we to avenge ourselves when the world afflicts us? (No, we are to bless those who persecuted us.)
Who will avenge us? (It says that God will avenge us. God will repay, the Word says.)
What was Paul's GLORY? (His tribulations.)
What are we to do in tribulations? (We are to glory in our tribulations.)

How are we to endure earthly sufferings? (With patience.)
Does God suffer long? (Yes, He is full of long suffering.)
Are we to be living our lives with the concerns of this world? (No, we are to be concentrating on heavenly things, those which are of the Spirit, not of the natural.)

Are we to suffer for wrong doing? (Never.)
What are we to rejoice in? (When we are persecuted for righteousness sake.)
Who will suffer persecution? (All who desire to live Godly in Christ Jesus.)
Are we to fear this persecution? (No! This is a normal thing for believers to endure.)
Why will the world hate us? (Because it hated Jesus before it hated us. If they hated our Master, how much MORE will they hate us.)
How are we to regard these who hate us? (We are to love our enemies. We are to bless those who persecute us.)

When we are persecuted, who is persecuted with us? (Jesus.)
How do we know this? (The Word of God tells us this.)
What are we to do in afflictions? (Rejoice! For great is our reward! Ours is the Kingdom of Heaven!!!!!)
What will afflictions and tribulations work in us? (PATIENCE!!!!!)

PATIENCE

There was once a King who loved righteousness and goodness. He proclaimed that the law of the land would be that the people should do righteousness and goodness and those that did not follow the law, would be brought to trial.

The King looked down upon the people in the land and saw that in the beginning, they sincerely were trying to do good, but over a period of time, they simply loved the pleasures of evil, more than they loved doing what was right.

Now the King loved His people and wanted more than anything, that they should have hearts that loved righteousness and goodness. He was filled with sorrow that they would be brought to trial and He would have to execute judgment towards them in the form of banishment. The King was not willing that even one of His people should be banished forever, away from Him, and so sought a way to change their hearts to prevent this.

He pondered and came up with a thought, "I know! I will send them messengers that I hand pick myself, to tell them to turn back to their King and serve Me with obedience. My messengers will tell them the danger of their folly. Maybe they have forgotten that they will be judged and that those who practice evil will be banished."

So, the King went and chose His messengers to tell the people to turn from their evil ways and obey the laws of the King.

The messengers went into all the land and proclaimed the news. There were a few people who listened to the messengers and turned their hearts from evil, but the majority of the people continued on in wickedness. When the messengers continued to try to persuade them into obeying the King they became angry and wanted to silence the messengers. They spit on them, and beat, and killed them and then continued on in their pleasures.

The King watched in grief as the people continued to love evil more than righteousness. He knew they had no idea of the extent with which He must judge them. But, He had given His Word that He would execute sound judgment on law breakers and no matter how much he loved His people, He would have to judge them according to their deeds. Those who were found innocent would be able to live in the land in peace. Those who were found guilty would be banished forever.

But the King loved His people so much... There must be a way to save them from their evil deeds.

So the King thought and thought, and came up with an idea that surely would work! "I will send them my Son! Surely the people will listen to Him! When they see My Son, it will be as if they were seeing Me, and maybe He will turn their hearts to do good."

So the King told His Son to prepare Himself for He would have to go into the world and proclaim His Kingdom. The Son, loved the people as much as His Father, and willingly sought a way to find a way to stop His people from facing banishment.

After a long discussion between Father and Son, they came up with a solution to save their people. Knowing what must be done, the Son left the Castle and went out alone, filled with the love of His Father.

The Son traveled all throughout the land and told them that His Father had sent Him and that they needed to turn back to obeying the laws of the land or they would soon face banishment.

A few souls believed the Son, and followed and listened to Him talk about His Father, the King and ways to please the King, but they still couldn't seem to stop themselves from doing evil here and there. It seemed to be inborn in them. They told the Son that they didn't wish to do this evil, but it just warred with their wanting to do what was good. The Son told them that He was aware of their problem and had a solution for it. But, they would have to wait a while for the answer.

Most of the people in the land didn't believe the Son when He said that He was the Son of the King. They laughed and ridiculed, and made great fun of Him.

But, this didn't stop the Son from speaking, and soon more and more of the people in the land were listening to Him. Many of the leaders of the villages became angry when the people started listening more to Him than to them, and decided to put an end to this troublemaker now and forever!

They plotted and plotted and finally came up with a solution... They would put Him to death! They had their evil deed all planned out and when the time was right, took the Son into custody and prepared to kill Him!

The King received news of what was happening to his Son. He became very sorrowful at the hardness of the people's hearts. The King realized that He could save His Son by sending His army to rescue Him. But, in His love for His people, He considered their problem of their bondage to doing evil. The King and His Son had planned beforehand that no rescue would be possible.

"The people must be punished," he thought to Himself. "Anyone who breaks the laws of the land needs to face a trial and must be banished. But there are people who are warring against doing evil, and when they do it, they are not willing to do it and are sorry. There is only one way to save them..."

The King sat for a long time with a very sad, solemn look on His face. "This is a very difficult decision, but it must be done," he said to himself. "If I allow my Son to die for the evil that the people do, they no longer will face banishment. His punishment will be good enough for whatever evil they commit. The only thing the people must do is to love and believe in My Son. They must believe that He is my Son and that His punishment is payment for their evil doing."

So, resolved, and because of His patience and love of His people, the King allowed His Son to be put to death...

And to this day, anyone who believes in the King's Son, does not face banishment for the evil that he has committed, but can live in the land of the King and His Son forever!

Godliness

Lesson One
GODLINESS

PARENT: Today we are going to start a new Unit on GODLINESS. Can you tell me what the characteristics we have studied are? ... In order? We have learned about FAITH, VIRTUE, KNOWLEDGE, TEMPERANCE, PATIENCE, and now we are going to study GODLINESS. The Bible tells us that we are to add GODLINESS. Before we can do this we have to know what Godliness means. Do you have any idea of what Godliness is? ...

DICTIONARY: Godliness or Godly

(1. Having great reverence for God. 2. Pious.)

STRONG'S: Godliness

(Greek #2150 in 2 Peter; From #2152; piety; spec. the gospel scheme; godliness; holiness.) (Greek #2152; Well-reverent; Pious; Devout; godly.)

PARENT: According to the definition of Godliness, we are to be well-reverent, pious, devout, godly, and holy. We are going to study what God's Word says about being these things.

READ: 1 Timothy 2:1-15

QUESTIONS

Who are we to be praying for, according to this scripture? (Vs. 1 says we are to pray for all men; and for kings, and for ALL that are in authority.)
What are we to pray for? (Vs. 2 says to pray that we may lead a quiet and peaceable life in all godliness and honesty.)
How are we to live our lives? (Quietly and peaceably.)
In WHAT do we live our lives? (It says in all godliness and honesty.)
What is godliness? (Having great reverence or fear of God and living your lives in this.)
Why are we to live like this? (Vs. 3 says for this is good and acceptable in the sight of God our Saviour.)
What do women PROFESS in vs. 10? (It says women professing godliness.)
How is a godly woman to adorn herself? (Vs. 9 and 10.)
Are women that profess godliness different than women that are non-believers?
How are they different?

READ: 1 Timothy 3:16

QUESTIONS

What is a great mystery? (Vs. 16, the mystery of godlinesss.)
What is the mystery of godliness? (The mystery is that God was manifest in the flesh, justified in the Spirit, seen of angels, preached unto the Gentiles, believed on in the world, and received up into glory.)
Who can understand this mystery? (Those that BELIEVE.)
How do we start adding GODLINESS, according to 2 Peter? (We start it with believing the mystery of Godliness. We start adding Godliness when we receive and believe these Truths.)

READ: 1 Timothy 4:6-10

QUESTIONS

How are we to be nourished, by food? (Vs. 6, by the words of faith and of good doctrine.)
What are we to refuse? (We are to refuse profane and old wives' fables.)
Can you think of some things that would be considered old wives' fables? ...
Is anything not TRUE considered a FABLE? (Yes, for a fable is a story that is not true.)
What does it mean to REFUSE something that is profane or a fable? (To refuse something would be to not even entertain talking

about it. To refuse means to not discuss.)
What do we exercise ourselves in? (Vs. 7 GODLINESS!)
What does it mean to exercise ourselves in GODLINESS? (It means to live according to God and His Word. It would mean to turn aside from anything that is contrary to Him or the Bible.)
How do we be GODLY? (We live according to God and His standards rather than the world and its standards.)
How much do we profit from bodily exercise? (Vs. 8 says LITTLE!)
What is profitable for ALL things? (GODLINESS.)
If we live Godly, what will happen? (Vs. 10 says we both labour and suffer reproach because we trust in the living God.)
Is this a good thing? (Yes! For this is what happens to those who are not of this world but of heaven! It is a great thing to rejoice in!)

Lesson Two
GODLINESS
Following Godliness

PARENT: Do you remember what Godliness is? So far, the definition has been that it is living a life that is lined up with the Word of God in the fear of the Lord. Do you remember what it means to have the fear of the Lord? ... We studied what the word FEAR meant, and it meant to REVERENCE God. Fear means to REVERENCE Him. We are to live our lives in REVERENCE to God. We are to line our lives up and LIVE out the Word of God. Do you remember what the fear of the Lord is? It is to HATE what is evil. We will not DO evil. Part of GODLINESS is to BE a doer of the Word. It is doing what the Bible tells us to do.

READ: 1 Timothy 6:3-11

QUESTIONS

If a person is teaching that it is ok to have sin in your life, is this a teaching of godliness? (No.)
If a person simply OMITS, or never speaks, about obeying the Word of God and not doing evil, does this person teach things according to godliness?
What does vs. 4 have to say about people which do not teach things according to GODLINESS? (It says he is proud, knowing nothing, but doting about questions and strifes of words, whereof cometh envy, strife, railings, evil surmisings (concepts of men, not concepts of God), perverse disputings of men of corrupt minds, and destitute of the truth...)
What are WE, as BELIEVERS in Jesus to follow after? (Vs. 11, we are to follow after righteousness, GODLINESS, faith, love, patience, meekness.)
Does this sound as if we are to live according to the way the world lives? (No, we will not live anything like the world lives. We learned in Temperance that we are to put to death the lust of the flesh, and this is what the world lives their lives in.)
Can you give some ideas of what a person that lives GODLY, lives like? ...

READ: 2 Timothy 3:1-5

QUESTIONS

What will happen in the last days? (Vs. 1, perilous times will come.)
What will men be like? (Vs. 2-4)
What will they have a form of? (It says in vs. 5 that they will have a form of GODLINESS.)
Even though they may have a form of godliness, in vs. 2-4, are they living as doers of the Word? (No.)
Have they died to the lusts of their flesh? ...
What do they love more than God? (Pleasures.)
Are we to have this type of godliness? (No! The Bible teaches just the opposite.)

When you see this type of godliness, what are you to do? (From such turn away.)

READ: Titus 1:1

QUESTIONS

What type of TRUTH are we to follow? (The Truth which is after godliness.)
Is godliness part of faith? (It says here that it is what we are to acknowledge, or KNOW of.)

READ: 2 Peter 3:10-13

QUESTIONS

In this scripture, what will happen to this world? (It will pass away with a great noise and melt with heat.)
Knowing this, what type of persons are we to be? (It says in vs. 11, we are to be in ALL holy conversation and godliness!)
What do you think it means to have holy conversation?
Is making jokes at another person's expense holy conversation?
Is fighting with your brothers and sisters holy conversation?
Is speaking about God and His Word, holy conversation?
How are we to be godly? (By doing that which is PLEASING to God.)
Are we to take PLEASURE in the things of this world? (No, for this is a world ran by sin.)
What are we to look for? (This day of God, when this earth is going to be dissolved!)
What will happen when this world and heavens are dissolved? (God will have a NEW heaven and a NEW earth.)
What will be so different about this new heaven and new earth? (RIGHTEOUSNESS, not sin, will DWELL there!)
How should we live our lives until this new earth and heaven come? (In GODLINESS!)

Lesson Three
GODLINESS
Being Godly

PARENT: Many believers today think that we are living in the last days. We read in one of our scriptures that perilous times will come, for men will be living abominable lives in God's eyes, but still claiming a form of godliness. We need to learn to have the REAL form of godliness that lines up with the Word of God. Our standing for the Word of God, which is GODLINESS, will cause many to feel uncomfortable. When a person is standing for TRUTH and living a godly life, it will cause others who are not yet doing this know that they need to line their lives up with the Word of God. They will either become convicted and line their lives up with God's Word or they will become angry and hate you, and then comes persecution, because they still wish to have a form of godliness but do not want to give up the world.

READ: 2 Timothy 3:10-12
          2 Peter 2:9

QUESTIONS

What does the scripture say will happen to those that will live godly? (They will suffer persecution.)
Did God deliver Paul in his persecutions? (Yes, vs. 11 says God delivered him out of them.)
In 2 Peter 2:9, what will God deliver us from? (He knows how to deliver the godly out of temptations.)
Who does He deliver out of temptations? (The Godly!)
So even if we are going to have temptations and persecutions, will God deliver us? (Yes.)
Who suffers with us through these things because we are trying to live godly? (The Word of God says Jesus suffers with us and is with us always! He never leaves us.)
Who is our deliverer? (God!)

Because the Bible says that we are going to suffer persecutions if we live godly, should we NOT want to live godly? (NO!)
If we do want to be persecuted, should we live ungodly lives? (No, we must realize that this is a part of the Christian walk.)
How are we to live? (We are to live godly lives.)
Are we to fear men persecuting us? (No, do not fear men who can do things to your flesh, but fear God, who can do things to your SOUL!)

PARENT: It is very important to know in the age we live in that we WILL be persecuted for trying to live godly. It is also important to learn that this is normal! It is scriptural! We all need to be careful that we do not love our FLESH above loving Jesus. If we love Him we can endure anything. He is our deliverer and our Saviour! The most important thing in our heart should be living Godly lives regardless of what ever happens to us. Pleasing God should be NUMBER ONE!!!!

READ: Psalms 4:3-4

QUESTIONS

What has God done toward those that are godly? (He has set them apart.)
Who has He set them apart for? (For himself!!!)
Isn't this a wonderful REWARD!!!???
Who will the Lord hear when we call to Him? (The godly!)
When we are ever in trouble, who should we call out to? (God!)
Will He hear us? (Yes!!!)
Should we ever fear? (No, for the Lord is with us and hears us.)
Should we be talking to Him? (Yes, we have been set aside for the Lord. He takes pleasure in the godly! We are His!)
What is it called when we talk to God? (Prayer.)

STRONG'S: Prayer

(Hebrews 8605; intercession; supplication)
(Greek #1162; petition; prayer; request; supplication.)

DICTIONARY: Pray
(To address a deity or other object of worship.)

DICTIONARY: Address
(1. To speak to.)

PARENT: God has set aside for Himself those who are godly. He wants us to talk to Him and whenever we are in trouble it should be to HIM we call out to! He will hear us and deliver us!

Lesson Four

GODLINESS
God Has Set Us Apart

PARENT: The Lord has clearly told us throughout His Word that He would have us be Godly. Can you tell me what this means? It means that you are living to PLEASE God in accordance to His Word. We learned that God sets apart those that are godly for Himself! This is a wonderful thing to know. We are set apart!

STRONG'S: Apart

(Hebrew #6395; means to distinguish, put a difference, show marvellous, separate, set apart, sever, make wonderfully.)

PARENT: God has set apart the godly for Himself. We are going to look in the Word of God and find the scriptures that give more information on this. Did you know that we are not to be of this world. Did you know that the word CHURCH, means Ecclesia, or THOSE WHO ARE CALLED OUT. Even the very word Church, means people that are separated from the world... called OUT of the world.

READ: Ezra 10:10-11

QUESTIONS

Did you know that God wanted the children of Israel to separate from the people of the land and to separate from the wives that did not serve the one true God. Why do you think this was? (Because they caused God's people to turn away from God and be enticed to serve idols and other gods.)
What does vs. 10 say it did? (It increased the trespass of Israel.)
What is a trespass? (A trespass is an offense, a sin, being guilty, a fault.)
Do you think that we can learn from this scripture also?
In what way?

READ: 2 Corinthians 6:14-18

QUESTIONS

Who are we not to be unequally yoked with? (With unbelievers.)
What does it mean to be yoked? (Yoked in the Strong's #2086 means to ASSOCIATE discordantly. It means that we are not to associate with people that are unbelievers.)
Why are we not to? (Vs. 14 says we do not have any fellowship, for what fellowship can righteousness have with unrighteousness.)
Do you think a non-believer would have fun sitting around talking about Jesus? (No.)
If you associate with people like this, will you have to compromise and talk about things of the world? (Yes.)
Would they want you to start doing worldly things with them in pursuit of worldly pleasures?
Do you think this would be pleasing to God?
If a person doesn't mind talking about the Word of God and you can talk about the Bible and Truth, is this different than associating with them? (Yes. This is called spreading the Gospel!)
What communion can light have with darkness? (None.)
Do you remember what it means to have light? (It means those that have ENLIGHTENMENT or knowledge of God's Word.)
Can those of Christ have fellowship with those of the devil? (It says no.)
Who is the temple of the living God? (We are.)
Who dwells in us and walks in us? (God! We are His temple.)
What are we to do in vs. 17? (We are to come out from among them and be separate.)
What does it mean to be separate? (It means that we do not be yoked together with those that are not His, lest we learn their ways like the children of Israel.)
When we are separate, what does it say God will be to us and we to Him? (Vs. 18 says

God will receive us and will be a Father unto us and we shall be His sons and daughters, SAITH THE LORD ALMIGHTY.)

Does being separate mean we do not tell people about the Gospel? (No! It just means that you do not associate or be yoked together with those that are not believers. If a person will listen to the Word of God, we are to speak Truth! We are to be fishers of men, and we throw out bait to see if their hearts love God and would like to hear Truth!)

What happens if they do NOT want to hear it? (They will not want to talk about God or His Son or His Word.)

Lesson Five
GODLINESS
Guarding Our Hearts

PARENT: *We have been learning about what God has done with those that are godly. Do you remember? God has set apart for Himself those that are godly. The Bible also told us to come out from among the world and be separate. We are not to be unequally ASSOCIATED or yoked, with unbelievers. This does not mean that we do not witness to the lost, but it means that we do not have close associations with those who refuse the Gospel of Jesus Christ. What could we ever have in common with those who hate our Lord? We are going to study in the Word about companionship. How far are we to take this separation that God tells us to take from the world and its people?*

READ: Exodus 23:2
        Exodus 23:32-33

QUESTIONS

When multitudes of people do evil, what are we to do? (We are not to go the way of the masses, but to go the NARROW way of the Word of God.)

Do you remember how narrow the narrow way is? (The Greek word was as NARROW as a NEEDLE.)

In the world we live today, how do the multitudes train their children? (In the public school system, which does not educate their children in the Word of God, but in the wisdom of the world.)

What is the wisdom of the world in the eyes of God? (It is foolishness.)

When you grow up, how are you going to educate your children? (In the WORD OF GOD!!!)

What did God tell His children not to do in vs. 32-33? (It says He said to make no covenant with the world of their day.)

Why did God tell them not to? (Lest they make you sin against God, and serve their gods, and be a snare to you.)

Do we need to guard our hearts today from this same thing? (Yes! The Bible teaches us to be separate in the New Testament. We do not want to be a part of the world nor love the things of the world.)

Does the world teach us to be set apart? (No, today everyone is teaching that love is just getting along, and we are to accept everything, even sin.)

What did we learn through TEMPERANCE in regards to our flesh? (That we are to put to death the lusts of our flesh, and living according to the lusts of this world.)

Does godliness and separation go hand in hand? (The scriptures teach that we are to deny the ways of the world.)

READ: Psalms 1:1

QUESTIONS

What type of counsel are we to walk in? (GODLY, not ungodly!)

What is counsel? (It means advice.)

Should we listen to advice from people who do not believe or live God's Word? (This scripture says no.)

What type of advice do we listen to?

(Godly!)

READ: Psalms 101:3-4
       Psalms 101:7
       Psalms 141:4

QUESTIONS

What are we not to set before our eyes? (Anything wicked.)
How do you think television and movies line up with this scripture? (It says, "I will set no wicked thing before my eyes", are the things we watch godly?)
Are we to make friends with the wicked? (It says in this scripture that we are not to KNOW a wicked person.)
How are we to regard wickedness? (We are not to be associated with it!)
What do we need guard? (Our hearts and not incline them to ANY evil thing.)
Does it sound as if we are to be careful? (Yes!)

ACTIVITIES

Talk with the children about things that we need to guard our hearts in in regards to things in their own lives.

Lesson Six
GODLINESS
Company We Keep

PARENT: The opposite of godliness is worldiness or wickedness. We are not to be partakers of anything that is wicked in the eyes of the Lord. We are going to read today what the Word of God has to say about the company we keep. The Bible is very clear when it tells us to be careful of those we spend our time with. The reason WHY we are to be careful is that our very own hearts are treacherous and we need to guard them! The Bible states very clearly that a GOOD person will never make a wicked person good, but rather a wicked person will make a GOOD person WICKED! This belief is found in both the New and Old Testaments. Again, we are to witness to the world as the disciples and Jesus did, but then Jesus always withdrew, and so did the disciples, after they were finished telling them TRUTH!

READ: Proverbs 4:14-15

QUESTIONS

Does vs. 14 sound as if we are to spend much time in companionship with evil men? (No. It says not to enter their path, as in partaking in their evil.)
Are we to be careful of their deeds? (Yes!)
What are the FOUR warnings of going in the way of evil people? (1. Avoid it! 2. Pass not by it! 3. Turn from it! 4. Pass away!)
Should we listen to these warnings? (Yes!)

READ: Proverbs 13:20

QUESTIONS

If we have friends that are wise, what does the Bible say we will be? (We will be wise!)
What type of wisdom are our friends to have? (The Wisdom of God!)
What type of wisdom are our friends NOT to

have? (The wisdom of the world!)
What type of friends are we NOT to have? (We are not to be a companion to fools.)
Why? (Because then we will be destroyed.)
What is a fool? (A fool is someone that does not know God, nor what is Holy.)

READ: Proverbs 14:7
        Proverbs 20:19

QUESTIONS

What are we to do when we are around a fool? (It says that we are to leave. We are to not keep company with him.)
Why is this? (Because a companion of fools will be destroyed.)
When do you leave? (After you find out that he is a fool.)
How do you know a person is a fool? (When they do not love God, nor want to obey His Word.)
Who are we not to meddle with? (One who flatters with his lips.)
What is flattery? (According to the dictionary, flatter is to compliment excessively and often insincerely, especially in order to win the favor of; to court; blandish.)
Why do you think we are NOT to meddle with a flatterer?

READ: Proverbs 22:24-25

QUESTIONS

In this scripture, who are we to NOT make friends with? (We are not to make friends with an angry man.)
What does James say about being angry? (We are to be SLOW to anger, SLOW to speak, and quick to hear.)
Will an angry man follow these three things? (No.)
Why does this scripture say not to befriend a person that is quick to anger? (Because you will learn his ways and get a snare to thy soul.)
Is it a dangerous thing to be a friend of an angry man? (Yes, to our very SOULS!)

READ: Proverbs 24:1
        Ecclesiastes 9:18

QUESTIONS

When we see wicked people that have lots of material things, should we be envious of them? (No! We are not to want the things of the world. We are to set our sight on things above!)
Should we desire to be with evil people? (No!)
What is an evil person? (Anyone who rejects the Truth of Christ! ...)

Lesson Seven
GODLINESS
Who We Associate With

PARENT: *We are going to read some more scriptures that deal with who BELIEVERS should be around. Again, it is very important to know that we are to witness and spread the Gospel of Jesus Christ to every person we can, but like Jesus and His disciples, we are to withdraw ourselves after witnessing. We do not "hang", as the term goes, with those that do not love the Lord.*

READ: 1 Corinthians 5:6-13

QUESTIONS

In this scripture, who are we not to keep company with? (It says with fornicators.)
What else? (With covetous, or idolaters or a railer, or a drunkard, or an extortioner.)
What is very important here? (He is talking about people who claim to be BELIEVERS that are practicing these things.)

Are you to eat dinner with "Christians" that are doing these things? (The Bible says to not keep company with them or even to eat with them.)
What is the danger of being with people that call themselves Christians but still walk according to the things above? (One very important thing is that we are to abstain from even the APPEARANCE of evil, and we would then be condoning wickedness. You are known by the company you keep.)

READ: 1 Corinthians 15:33

QUESTIONS

What are we not to be deceived in? (Thinking that it is okay to have steady companionship with evil doers.)
What will happen to a person that continuously has evil communications or associations? (The Bible says that evil communications corrupt good manners.)
Can we trust ourselves? (No, we are to put our trust in God. We also need to be careful of whom we yoke ourselves together with.)

READ: Ephesians 5:1-11

QUESTIONS

Who are we not to be partakers with? (People that walk not in love, but in fornication, uncleanness, covetousness, filthiness, foolish talking, jesting... etc.)
What are we to walk as? (Vs. 8, we are to walk as children of light! Those who have understanding of the knowledge of God.)
What are we not to have fellowship with? (The unfruitful works of darkness.)
What are we to do? (Vs. 11 says we are to reprove them!)

READ: 1 Timothy 5:22

QUESTIONS

How does this scripture tell us to keep ourselves? (It says to keep ourselves PURE.)
What does this mean? (It means to keep us pure from the world and its evils.)
How do we do this? (Through the renewing of our minds through the Word of God.)

READ: 2 John 9-11

QUESTIONS

Does a person that does not stay in the TEACHINGS or doctrines of Jesus have God? (No.)
What happens to this person? (Vs. 9 says WHOSOEVER TRANSGRESSETH, and abideth not in the doctrine of Christ has not God.)
Who has both the Father and the Son? (Those who abide in the teachings of Jesus.)
What does it mean to abide in the teachings of Jesus? (It means to stay and be faithful to them; to do Jesus' commandments.)
Is this godliness? (Yes, to abide in the teachings of Jesus.)
What does it mean to be godly? (It means to follow after and do what God would have us do and have attributes of our King.)

PARENT: *God wants us to be godly, or to do things that HE would have us do. When you add "LY" to a word it is the form of the root word. For example, to do something "wickedly" would be to be wicked. To do something "Kindly" would be to be KIND. To do something "harshly" would be to be HARSH. To do something "GODLY" would be to do it as GOD would. We are to live our lives to please GOD. This is godliness.*

Lesson Eight
GODLINESS
Living for God

PARENT: The opposite of being godly is to be wicked. We are learning that the godly, those who God has set apart for Himself, are to be a separate people and are not to follow after the ways of the world. Part of godliness is a separation from the world!

READ: Titus 2:11-15

QUESTIONS

What has the grace of God taught us? (To deny ungodliness and worldly lusts.)
How are we to live? (We are to live soberly, righteously, and GODLY!!!! in this present world.)
What are we looking for? (The appearing of Jesus.)
What does He want to purify unto Himself? (A peculiar people, zealous of good works.)
Are we to teach these things? (Yes, vs. 15 says these things speak! and exhort! and rebuke! with all authority.)
Should believers despise this teaching? (It says let no man despise thee.)

READ: James 4:7-8

QUESTIONS

Who are we to SUBMIT ourselves to? (It says to God.)
Is this godliness? (Yes!)
Who are we to resist? (The devil.)
Does the devil want us to live godly? (No. He wants us to do wickedly.)
What will happen when we resist him? (The devil will flee from us.)
Who are we to draw near to? (God.)
What will happen when we do this? (God will draw near to us.)
What are we to do? (Vs. 8 says to cleanse our hands and purify our hearts.)
Is this a part of godliness? (Yes, it is telling us to put away wickedness and live godly.)

STRONG'S: Godly

(Greek #2316; a deity; the Supreme Divinity; Godly, ward)

PARENT: Part of godliness is that we are looking Godward ... or towards our God. It means that we are allowing Him to be the ruler of our lives. To live godly would be to live for GOD! Godliness is to live for God, not for the world. It means to be sold out for Him and to be dead to ourselves. We are to no longer live according to the world.

READ: 1 John 2:15-17

QUESTIONS

What are we not to love? (We are to NOT love the world.)
What else are we NOT to love? (The things of the world.)
What does it say about people that love the world? (Vs. 15 says if any man love the world, the love of the Father is not in him.)
Are the things of this world of our Father, God? (Vs. 16 says all that is in the world is not of the Father, but is of the world.)
What are the three things that make up the world? (1. The lust of the flesh. 2. The lust of the eyes. 3. The pride of life.)
What is going to pass away? (This world will pass away.)
What is going to happen to this world? (It is going to burn up. We are to look for this to happen because then the new heaven and new earth will come and there will dwell righteousness.)
What are some things that are the lust of the flesh? (The Bible says drunkenness, gluttony...)
What are some of the lusts of the eyes? (Wanting, not needing. Covetousness, which is idolatry...)

What does God think of pride? (Pride is an abomination to Him.)
Who will abide forever? (Vs. 17 says that He that doeth the will of God abideth forever.)

PARENT: We are to live our lives being NOT of this world. Do you know what an alien is? The world says it is someone from another planet or country. We are citizens of heaven, not citizens of earth. We are not to set our hearts on things on earth, but we are to look forward to the coming of our King. God is our King and we are to be godly, by doing things that are of HIS Kingdom to please HIM. When we do not love the ways or things of this world, we are living godly. We need to do the will of our Father!! Won't it be wonderful to abide with Him forever?!

Lesson Nine
GODLINESS
Training Children To be Godly

PARENT: We are reading in God's Word that God wants us set apart for Him. He does not wish us to live as the world does, but according to the Word of God. This is going to be a very NARROW walk, as the Bible tells us it is. When you grow up it is very important that you also raise your children to be Godly. Do you remember why God chose Abraham and His seed to be His chosen people?

READ: Genesis 18:16-19

QUESTIONS

What would Abraham become? (Vs. 18, says Abraham shall surely become a great and mighty nation, and all the nations of the earth shall be blessed by him.)
How were all the nations blessed by Abraham? (Jesus was a seed of Abraham, and by Jesus, all the earth is blessed! Jesus was a descendant of Abraham. Jesus was a Jew.)
What did God know about Abraham? (That he would command his children and his household after him, and they SHALL KEEP THE WAY OF THE LORD, to do justice and judgment! Vs. 18.)
What was very important to God? (That Abraham trained his children and his household after HIM and His ways!)
Are we to do this today? (Yes!)

READ: Malachi 2:14-15

QUESTIONS

What does God seek? (God seeks a GODLY SEED.)
What is seed? (It is children.)
Why does God make husband and wife ONE? (It says because He seeks a godly seed!)

READ: 2 John 1-6

QUESTIONS

Who does John write this letter to? (The elect lady AND HER CHILDREN.)
In vs. 4, what did John rejoice in? (That he found her children walking in TRUTH!)
Were her children GODLY SEED? (Yes! They were walking in TRUTH!)
What is love? (Vs. 6, that we walk after Jesus commandments.)
What are we to train children up in? (The commandments of God's Word!)
How important is it that children are trained up to be godly? (Very important! YOU, dear children, are the next generation of believers! If parents allow compromise with the world, THEIR children will allow DOUBLE the compromise, because not only will they have the compromise they were trained up with, but THEY will compromise with the world ALSO!)

READ: Ecclesiastes 12:1

QUESTIONS

When are we to remember our Creator, God? (In the days of our YOUTH!)
When are we to start learning about God? (From the time we are weaned from our mothers.)
When we are trained in the knowledge of God, what are we being trained to BE? (Godly!)

PARENT: The reason why God chose Abraham was because he would train his children up in the knowledge of Him. It is very important that you learn that the only important thing is THE KNOWLEDGE OF GOD. You must have it instilled in YOU, as children, to train YOUR children in the knowledge of God. God seeks a godly seed. He wants children that are living according to HIS ways, not the ways of the world. We need to learn to be like the elect lady in 2 John, who was known for her training of her children. Her children were godly seeds, being full of the KNOWLEDGE of the TRUTH. Jesus is the way, the TRUTH and the LIFE. There is nothing more important on the face of the earth than to be GODLY, which is living a life pleasing to our GOD!

Lesson Ten
GODLINESS
Instructing Children to Godliness

PARENT: We are going to read scriptures today on what God says about what YOU, as children, are to be trained in. You are to be trained in godliness! This is very important to know, so that you can train YOUR children up to be godly ALSO!

READ: Deuteronomy 6:6-9

QUESTIONS

HOW are you to teach God's ways to YOUR children? (DILIGENTLY.)
What does this mean? (Diligently means with attentive care and heedfulness. To be consistent!)
Are you to be slothful in this? (No!)

READ: Deuteronomy 11:16-21

QUESTIONS

What were the people to HEED? (That their hearts not be deceived.)
What were they not to turn aside to? (To serve other gods, and worship THEM!)

What would happen if they did this? (God's wrath would be kindled against them, and he would shut up the heaven so there would be no rain and that they would perish.)

Who were they to teach the Word of the Lord to? (It says in vs. 19, to teach them to their children.)

How often were they to teach their children the ways of the Lord, or godliness? (All day long, vs. 19.)

Does this sound as if it were just a few minutes each day?

How was this going to TRAIN their children? (The children were to be with the parents ALL day long, watching the parents as THEY walked the ways of the Lord, instilling in them habits of the ways of the Lord, and explaining what the Lord wanted them to do!)

Does the world train their children? (No, they send their children to have someone else train them in knowledge that is VOID of God.)

Should you train your children up in this way? (No! For the wisdom of the world is foolishness to God.)

What is the wisdom of God to the world? (Foolishness to the world.)

READ: Deuteronomy 31:12-13

QUESTIONS

Who were gathered together all at one time? (Men, women, children and thy stranger.)

Why were they to be gathered? (To listen and learn the ways of God.)

Why were the children supposed to be there? (To HEAR and learn to fear the Lord your God.)

What is the Fear of the Lord? (Scripture says it is to HATE what is evil.)

How do we know what is evil? (We read the Word of God and it will tell us. Evil is to do things that God does NOT want us to do.)

Why is it important to teach the children at the same time the adults are learning about God? (Because the children are the next generation of GROWN UPS!)

What will the children then learn to do? (The children will then learn to teach THEIR children the fear of the Lord.)

READ: Psalms 34:9-11

QUESTIONS

What are the children to hearken, or listen, to? (They are to listen to the Psalmist.)

What will this Psalm teach them about? (The fear of the Lord.)

Why is it so important that children learn the fear of the Lord? (Because this is wisdom! A child has to have the fear of the Lord in order to walk in wisdom.)

What is the fear of the Lord? (To hate what is evil.)

How young are we to learn the fear of the Lord? (The Bible says from the time one is weaned from his mother.)

FACT

According to the Colorado Springs Gazette, the worldwide average age that a child is weaned, is 4 years old! America is the only nation to have an average age of weaning at 6 months!

PARENT: According to the Word of God, it is very important that YOU as children learn to train YOUR children up in the Ways of God, and not in the ways of the world. You will be the next generation of BELIEVERS!

Lesson Eleven
GODLINESS
Teaching Our Children to Train Their Children!

PARENT: We are learning in these lessons on Godliness that it will be up to YOU to train the next generation of BELIEVERS! We have read some of the scriptures that tell us that the parents and children are to be learning the word together and that you are to be learning the ways of the Lord all day long, gleaning from the lifestyles of your parents! God desires a godly seed, or godly children, and the only way you can be godly is to learn the ways of the Lord. Then we can follow Him and do what HE would have us do and this is godliness! Then you are to pass it on to YOUR children!

READ: Psalms 78:1-8

QUESTIONS

Will people that know God understand parables? (Yes. Jesus said many times, "He who has an ear let him HEAR!" And he who had an ear to know TRUTH, understood.)
Are we to just learn great truths of the Word and not share them with our children? (No! Vs. 4 says we will not HIDE them from our children.)
What are we to tell the next generation? (We are to show to the generation to come the praises of the Lord, and His strength, and His wonderful works that He has done.)
Who are we to think of, when we instill God's word in our children? (Their children! Vs. 6)

READ: Proverbs 22:6

QUESTIONS

What does it mean to train a child? (It means what the other scripture in Deut. 11:16-21 said, that they are to train them ALL DAY LONG!)
Will he depart from it? (No!)

READ: Isaiah 28:9-10

QUESTIONS

Who will God teach knowledge? (Those that are weaned.)
Will we learn the Word of God all in one day? (No, the Bible says precept upon precept, line upon line.)
How are we to learn? (A little at a time.)
Is a 4 year old too young to teach the Word of God! (No! As soon as a child is weaned, he is to be trained in the knowledge of God!)

READ: Joel 1:1-3

QUESTIONS

When Joel received the Word from the Lord, who did he say to tell it to? (To the children.)
Who were their children to tell it to? (To there children.)
When you learn new things about God, and you have children, who are you going to be excited to go tell? (YOUR children!)

(Dear Parent, please note in the rest of the chapter of Joel, that his WORD from the Lord was a very hard one. We should never be afraid to tell our children TRUTH regardless of how hard the truth is. Joel commanded this to be taught to the children and we should tell our children both the HARD and the easy to handle TRUTHS of the Word.)

PARENT: Godliness starts at a very young age. When you are trained up in the Word of God from tiny children, it will become a HABIT, to do that which is of the Word. This is why God said to TRAIN your children and when they grow up they will not depart from God's Word. Do not be deceived in thinking that training is simply by saying scriptures and then not LIVING the Word. Many people say that they have trained their children because they send them to Sunday School once a week. Then they are greatly grieved when their children do not have hearts to follow God when they are older. Training involves much time and contact with your children. It means you spend most of the day training them up in the Bible!

ACTIVITIES

Discuss with the children the importance of WHAT they should be training their children. It is important that THEY learn what and how to be training the next generation. This is a very important job that we as parents must learn to do, as many parents of our generation were not taught HOW to train their children in a manner pleasing to God.

Lesson Twelve
GODLINESS
Piety

PARENT: God wants us to live with attributes of Himself. He wants us to live our lives to be pleasing to Him! This is Godliness. GODLINESS is what we are to add to PATIENCE. Part of the definition of GODLINESS was piety. Do you know what PIETY means?

DICTIONARY: Piety

(1. Devotion and reverence to God. 2. Being devoted.)

PARENT: Being PIOUS means to be devoted and to reverence God. We are going to read in God's Word all the scriptures that talk about being devoted or pious.

READ: 1 Timothy 5:4

QUESTIONS

This is the only scripture that uses the word piety. Who is to learn piety? (A widow's children or nephews are to show piety by taking care of the widow when her husband is gone.)
What does piety mean here? (The Greek #2151 says to be pious; towards God to worship, or towards parents to respect (support); show piety, worship.)
Are there scriptures that tell us to show piety towards our parents? (Yes, honor thy father and thy mother.)
Is this being godly? (The Bible tells us to honor our parents, so when we are obeying this we are doing what God wants us to do, so YES, we are being godly.)
Is this a part of godliness? (Yes, any obedience to the scriptures is godliness, for we are then doing what GOD wants us to do!)

READ: Psalms 119:38

QUESTIONS

What is the Psalmist praying here? (That God will establish His Word in Him.)
What is this servant devoted to? (The fear of the Lord.)
What is the fear of the Lord? (To hate what is evil.)
What should we be devoted to? (The fear of the Lord.)

PARENT: Do you remember the definition of PIETY? It meant to be devoted and to REVERENCE God. Let's read the following scriptures on what the Bible says about reverencing God.

READ: Matthew 21:33-40
        Mark 12:1-12
        Luke 20:9-18

QUESTIONS

In this parable, did the religious Jews REVERENCE God's Son? (No.)
What did they do to Him? (They killed Him.)
Are we to reverence God's Son? (Yes.)
How do we do this? (By listening to His Words and obeying them.)

READ: Hebrews 12:9
        Hebrews 12:28-29

QUESTIONS

Are we to give reverence to our earthly fathers? (The Bible says yes.)
How much MORE are we to give Father God reverence?
What does being reverent also means in verse 9? (That we are in SUBJECTION to the Father of spirits.)
How are we to serve God? (Vs. 28, acceptably with reverence and godly fear.)
Does this go along with Psalms 119:38 where it says that we are to be DEVOTED to the fear of the Lord?

What does vs. 29 say that our God is? (It says that our God is a consuming fire.)
How are we able to serve God? (Vs. 29 says, "Let us have GRACE whereby we may serve God ...")
What does grace enable us to do? (It enables us to serve God!)

PARENT: The Lord wants us to serve Him with reverence and godly fear. Through GRACE we can serve God acceptably with reverence and godly fear. This is very important to know. Many people believe that grace is given to us so that we do not have to obey God. This is very wrong. Grace is given to us so that we can obey God and serve Him. This is Godliness ...

Lesson Thirteen
GODLINESS
Being Devoted to God

PARENT: We learned that PIETY means to be devoted. We are to be DEVOTED to God. This means that we no longer live our lives for ourselves, but we live according to the Word of God, for God's good pleasure! To be devoted to God means He is NUMBER ONE in our lives. God is our God, and we will have no other gods but HIM!

DICTIONARY: Devoted

(1. To give or apply (one's time, attention, or self) entirely to a particular activity, pursuit,

cause, or person. 2. To set apart by or as if by a vow or solemn act; dedicate; consecrate.)

DICTIONARY: Devout

(1. Deeply religious; pious. 2. Displaying reverence or piety. 3. Sincere, earnest, devoted.)

READ: Luke 2:25-35

QUESTIONS

What was Simeon like? (Vs. 25 says he was just and devout.)
What was he devoted to? (It says he was waiting for the consolation of Israel and that the Holy Ghost was upon him.)
What did God show him? (That he would not see death, before he had seen the Lord's Messiah.)
Did he see Jesus? (Yes!)
Are we to be devoted to God? (Yes!)
What should our hearts be devoted to? (Serving God in all reverence and godly fear.)

READ: Acts 2:5, 41

QUESTIONS

What were dwelling at Jerusalem? (Devout men.)
What were they devoted to? (Serving God.)
Where were they from? (Every nation under heaven.)
In vs. 41, how many of these devout men soul's were added to being a believer? (3,000.)
Why did they receive the truth about Jesus? (Because they were devoted to learning about God and knew this to be truth.)

READ: Acts 10:1-8

QUESTIONS

What was Cornelius like? (Vs. 2 says he was a DEVOUT man, and one that feared God with all his house, which gave much alms to the people and prayed to God always.)
What nation was Cornelius from? (Vs. 1 says he was an Italian.)
Was he a Gentile? (Yes.)
Which God was he serving? (The Greek word for God hear is #2317 devoutness; piety; GODLINESS. He served the One True God and yet he was a Gentile Italian!)
Who else feared God? (All of his house.)
In Vs. 7, who else was devout to God? (One of his soldiers.)
When a person is devout, does this show towards other people? (Yes, because it is how you live your lives unto the most Holy God in ALL that you do.)
Did Cornelius' devoutness effect others? (Yes. All his household feared the lord, his servants, and even some of his soldiers!)
When we are DEVOTED to God, will we be effective for God? (Yes! Because our one true purpose in life is to serve our KING!)

READ: Acts 22:11-16

QUESTIONS

What was Ananias? (Vs. 12 says he was a devout man according to the law.)
What did God tell Ananias to do? (To go and pray for Saul to receive his sight.)
Did he receive it? (Yes.)
Are we to be devout? (Yes.)

PARENT: God wants us to be DEVOTED solely to Him. He wants us to be a people SET APART for Himself. When you are devoted to God, you have made a decision to be HIS and to serve Him, not just part of the time, but ALL of the time! It's very important to remember that CHURCH is not a place you go ONCE a week, but is a lifestyle all day long!

❀❀❀❀❀

Lesson Fourteen
GODLINESS
Holiness

PARENT: If you look at the definition of GODLINESS and PIETY, you will find that one word used to describe it was HOLINESS or HOLY. What do you think of when you think of something being HOLY? ... God is very Holy. If you read the story of Moses, you will find that when he came to Mt. Sinai and saw the burning bush, God told Moses to take off his shoes, for he was standing on HOLY ground. The presence of God is Holy. God Himself is Holy. But did you know that WE are called to be HOLY also? Today we are going to find out more about HOLINESS, which is an essential part of GODLINESS.

STRONG'S: Holy (Old and New Testament)

(Hebrew #6944; Kodesh; means a sacred place or thing; sanctity; consecrated; dedicated; hallowed; holiness; holy; saint; sanctuary. The roots of this word used in the Old Testament all have this meaning also.)

(Greek #40; Hagios; sacred; pure, blameless or religious; consecrated; most holy; saint.)

(Greek #3741; right; holy, mercy, shalt be.)

PARENT: This is a very interesting thing to study. Did you notice that in both of the first definitions that SAINT is used to define HOLY? Do you know what a SAINT is? A SAINT is a person who is RIGHTEOUS, or one who BELIEVES! We are called SAINTS! Let's read the scriptures that call us Saints...

STRONG'S: Saints

(Hebrew #6918; Sacred; God; an angel; a saint; a sanctuary; holy one; saint.)

(Greek #40; Sacred; pure, blameless; consecrated; most holy one or thing; saint.)

PARENT: This is a very interesting thing! Did you know that the word for HOLY in the Greek and the word for SAINT, are the VERY SAME WORD?!! A saint is a person who has dedicated themselves to God. A saint is one who is a BELIEVER! A saint or a believer is HOLY!

READ: Psalms 31:23
        Psalms 34:9

QUESTIONS

In the first scripture, what are God's saints to do? (They are to love the Lord!)
In Psalms 34:9, what are God's saints to do? (They are to fear the Lord.)
What does it say about those who fear God? (There is no WANT.)
What does this mean? (That God takes care of them.)

READ: Psalms 97:10
        Psalms 116:15

QUESTIONS

What are the people that love the Lord supposed to do in Psalms 97? (We are to hate evil.)
What are some things that God does for His saints?
What is our death to God? (Psalms 116 says that our deaths are precious in the sight of the Lord.)

READ: Ephesians 2:19
        Colossians 1:12
        Philemon 5-7
        Jude 3

QUESTIONS

When we become BELIEVERS, or when we BELIEVE, what are we? (Eph. says that we are fellowcitizens with the saints, and are of

the household of God.)
What are we partakers of in Colossians? (We are partakers of the inheritance of the saints in light.)
What do we inherit? (We are now citizens of the Kingdom of God.)
Are we saints? (Yes. When we believe!)
What does Paul call the believers in Philemon? (He calls them saints.)
Are they Holy? (Yes, they are Holy and Righteous.)
What makes a righteous person righteous? (Their belief!)
What will a person DO after they believe? (They will DO the Word of God.)

🌹🌹🌹🌹🌹

Lesson Fifteen
GODLINESS
Being Holy

PARENT: *We learned yesterday that the same word is used in the Greek for the words HOLY and SAINT. We are SAINTS! We are also HOLY! When we receive Jesus as our Way to God, we are no longer considered evil as Jesus cleanses us from ALL unrighteousness. We also are to be Holy in the way that we are to do things that are pleasing to God. Let's look in the dictionary and find what HOLY means.*

DICTIONARY: Holy

(1. Belonging to, derived from, or associated with a divine power; sacred. 2. LIVING according to a religious or spiritual belief. 3. Specified or set apart for a religious purpose.)

READ: Psalms 22:3
        Psalms 33:21
        Psalms 71:22

QUESTIONS

Who is Holy in Psalms 22? (The one who inhabits the praises of Israel.)
Who is this? (It is God.)
Should we PRAISE God? (Yes!)
What does "praise" mean? (In the Hebrew here it means Laudation. Hymn. Praise. The dictionary says LAUD means to give or express DEVOTION to; glorify; praise.)
What is God's name? (Holy.)
Who in Psalms 33 do we trust in? (In God's Holy name.)

READ: Psalms 99:3-9

QUESTIONS

What is God's name? (It is a great and terrible name.)
What is holy in this scripture? (His holy hill.)

Is God holy? (Yes!)

READ: Psalms 111:9

QUESTIONS

What has God sent to His people? (Redemption.)
What is redemption? (It means to be redeemed.)
In this scripture, what is God's name? (Holy and reverend is His name.)

READ: Psalms 145:21

QUESTIONS

Who is to bless God's holy name? (ALL flesh.)
How long are we to bless God's name? (For ever and ever.)

READ: Isaiah 1:4

QUESTIONS

Who did Israel provoke? (The Holy ONE of Israel.)
What is God called? (The holy ONE of Israel.)

READ: Isaiah 6:3

QUESTIONS

In this scripture, what is the Lord called three times? (Holy, holy, holy.)
What is full of God's glory? (The whole earth is full of His glory.)
What have we learned about God in these scriptures? (That God is Holy. He has a Holy Hill where we are to worship. God's name is Holy...)

READ: 1 Peter 1:13-16

QUESTIONS

Are we to fashion ourselves as before we BELIEVED in Jesus? (Vs. 14 says no.)
What are we called to be? (We are to be holy in all manner of conversation.)
What does vs. 16 say we are to be? (We are to be holy, for God is holy.)

STRONG'S: Conversation

(Greek #391; from 390 to busy oneself, i.e. remain, live, abide, behave, have conversation; behavior.)

PARENT: *We have learned that God is holy. Everything ABOUT Him is holy and WE are called to be holy also. The very word SAINT is the same as HOLY!*

🌹🌹🌹🌹🌹

Lesson Sixteen
GODLINESS
Being Holy as HE is Holy

PARENT: *In the last lesson we read scriptures that told us God is holy. We have also learned that the very word SAINT is the same as the word HOLY. 1 Peter told us to be holy in ALL our behavior, for we are to be holy as God is holy. We are learning that when we put to death the lusts of our flesh, we are living according to the Spirit of God. It is very easy when we decide to please God and not to please ourselves! But it is very difficult when we still want to please "self". Let's read scriptures on how we, as believers, are to live.*

READ: Romans 12:1-2

QUESTIONS

What does Paul beseech us to do? (That we present our bodies as a living sacrifice to God.)
In what manner? (Vs. 1 says HOLY, acceptable unto God.)
Should this be the normal behavior of a believer? (Vs. 1 says "which is your REASONABLE service".)
Are we to live according to the world? (Vs. 2 says "be not conformed to this world.")
How are we to be transformed? (By the renewing of our minds.)
Why are we to renew our minds? (To prove what is that good, and acceptable, and perfect, will of God.)
Why do we need to know the will of God? (To DO the will of our Father.)

READ: 1 Corinthians 3:16-17, 22

QUESTIONS

Where is the TEMPLE of God? (WE are the temple of God.)
How are we the temple? (The Spirit of God dwells within us.)
Is the temple of God holy? (Yes! It says it is in vs. 17.)
So WHO is holy? (We are! For we are the temple of God!)
Who do we belong to? (Vs. 22, we belong to Christ.)
And who does Christ belong to? (Christ is God's!)

READ: Ephesians 1:4

QUESTIONS

What does God want us to be? (We should be holy and without blame before Him in love.)
How can we do this? (Through LOVE!)
How does LOVE help us to do this? (If we love God more than any other thing, we will WANT to please Him, not because we are going to GET something from Him, and we know we are NOT saved by works but by BELIEF, ... but it is simply that we LOVE God and want to do His will.)

READ: Ephesians 2:19-22

QUESTIONS

Whose household do we belong to? (To God's.)
Are we a building? (Yes.)
What type of building? (A TEMPLE!)
What type of temple does it say we are in vs. 21? (A HOLY temple.)
What are we builded together for? (We are built together for a HABITATION of God through the Holy Spirit!)
Who lives in our building? (The Holy Spirit!)

READ: Colossians 1:21-23

QUESTIONS

How are we reconciled to God? (Through Jesus' death, vs. 22.)
What did His death do for us? (Vs. 22 says in the body of His flesh through death, to present us HOLY and unblameable and unreprovable in His sight.)
How? (All we have to do is confess our sins and Jesus is faithful to cleanse us from ALL unrighteousness when we believe in Him. 1 Jn.1:9.)

PARENT: The Word of God is clear that all we need to do is to BELIEVE in Jesus and then God looks at us THROUGH Him! He no longer sees our sins, but sees Jesus' blood that was shed for our wicked deeds! We are also to walk pleasing to God because we LOVE Him. This is how we are to be Holy... by doing what God would have us do in living our lives!

Lesson Seventeen
GODLINESS
We are Told to Walk Pleasing to God

PARENT: We are told in God's Word that we are to be a holy temple that belongs to Christ. Isn't this wonderful?! We belong to Jesus! We have been reading scriptures that tell us to be holy in all our behavior. Do you remember what it means to be holy? It means to be set apart for God in that we are living our lives NOT for ourselves any more, but we are now living for the will of God. Let's read more scriptures that talk about being holy.

READ: 1 Thessalonians 5:27
2 Timothy 1:9

QUESTIONS

In 1 Thessalonians, what do they call the brethren? (Holy brethren.)
What makes us holy? (What we believe.)
What will the actions be of someone who LOVES God? (Their actions will be according to the love of the Lord in doing what HE would want them to do.)
In 2 Timothy, are we saved according to our works? (No!)
Are we SAVED by doing things that are righteous, holy, or godly? (No! We only do things like this because we love the Lord.)
What type of calling are we called with? (A HOLY calling.)

READ: 1 Peter 2:1-9

QUESTIONS

What are we to lay aside? (We are to lay aside all malice, all guile, hypocrisies, envies, and all evil speakings.)
What are we to desire? (We are to desire the sincere milk of the Word that we may grow.)
What does vs. 9 say we are? (We are a chosen generation, a royal priesthood, an HOLY nation, peculiar people.)

STRONG'S: Peculiar

(Greek #4047; means acquisition; preservation; obtaining, peculiar, purchased, possession, saving.)

What should we show forth? (Vs. 9 says we are to show forth the praises of Him who has called us out of darkness into His marvelous light?)
Do you remember what this word "light" means? (It means to manifest or make known. It is understanding God's knowledge!)
What does "we are now a HOLY nation" mean? (We are now citizens of the Kingdom of heaven, regardless from where we are from. Now Gentiles and Jews can BOTH be part of the Kingdom of God, and God is preparing a place for us, a new heaven and a new earth for us to live where righteousness dwells!)

READ: 2 Peter 3:7-13

QUESTIONS

What is the heaven and earth now reserved for? (Vs. 7 says they are reserved unto fire against the day of judgment and perdition of ungodly men.)
What is the opposite of GODLY? (UNGODLY or wicked.)
What is this earth reserved for? (Vs. 7. the judgment and perdition of the UNGODLY.)
What will the next earth be for? (The dwelling of RIGHTEOUSNESS, or GODLINESS!)
How are we to be living our lives? (Vs. 11 says we are to be persons of HOLY conversation and godliness.)
What is "conversation"? (It means how we BEHAVE or live our lives.)
What are we to look forward to? (God's promise of new heavens and a new earth.)

READ: Revelation 22:11-14

Lesson Eighteen
GODLINESS
Being Blameless

QUESTIONS

What does it say about those that are holy? (He that is holy, let him be holy still.)
How fast is Jesus coming? (It says in this scripture that Jesus is coming QUICKLY!)
Will He reward us? (Yes.)
What does it say we will be awarded for? (It says, "My reward is with Me to give every man according as his work shall be.")
What does this word "work" mean? (Strong's #2041 says to work; toil; act; deed, doing, labour, work.)
Are we SAVED by our works? (No. We are only saved through BELIEVING in Jesus.)
What does this mean then? (That when we LOVE and BELIEVE in Jesus we will want to DO what is pleasing to the Father. We are not doing this for reward but because of our love.)

PARENT: The Lord wants us to walk Holy. Do you remember the definition of holy? It means to be living according to a religious or spiritual belief; or to be SET APART for a religious purpose. God has set aside those who are godly for himself. He has made us a PECULIAR people. According to all the scriptures we have read, the Lord wants us to be holy as He is holy. Today we are going to read what the Word of God has to say about being BLAMELESS. Do you know what this means?

DICTIONARY: Blameless

(1. Free from blame or guilt; innocent.)

READ: Luke 1:5-6

QUESTIONS

What was Zacharias? (He was a priest.)
Who was Elisabeth? (She was one of the daughters of Aaron.)
What were they before God? (They were righteous before God.)
How did they live their lives? (They walked in all the commandments and ordinances of the Lord BLAMELESS.)
Is what you DO going to save you? (No, but when you love God you will want to do things pleasing to Him.)
Does it seem as if Zacharias and Elisabeth loved God?

STRONG'S: Blameless

(Greek #273; irreproachable; blameless, faultless, unblameable.)

READ: 1 Corinthians 1:8

QUESTIONS

Look up BLAMELESS in this scripture in Strong's. What does it mean? (Greek #410; Unaccused; irreproachable; blameless.)

DICTIONARY: Irreproachable

(1. Beyond reproach.)

DICTIONARY: Reproach

(To do something which causes rebuke or blame.)

PARENT: There are two meanings for being blameless. We are now beyond blame and innocent because we believe in Jesus. God no longer sees all our wickedness when He looks upon us, but sees the blood of Jesus. We are now innocent because of our BELIEF in the Lord, and blameless because of Christ! The following scriptures talk about being BLAMELESS in how we behave ourselves. It is to abstain from the APPEARANCE of evil. It is to walk in accordance with God's ways so that we will never be accused of evil and then dirty Christ's name. It is not because we are rewarded for doing good, but again, because we LOVE God, that we walk in the ways of the Lord.

READ: Philippians 2:14-16

QUESTIONS

How are we to do all things? (Without murmurings and disputings.)
Why? (Vs. 15. That we may be BLAMELESS and harmless, the sons of God, without rebuke, in the midst of a crooked and perverse nation.)
What are we to be in this crooked and perverse nation? (We are to shine as LIGHTS in the world.)

READ: 1 Thessalonians 5:22-24

QUESTIONS

What does he pray to God for? (That our whole spirit, soul, and body be preserved BLAMELESS unto the coming of Jesus.) Who will do this? (Vs. 24 says Jesus will DO this!)

READ: 2 Peter 3:13-14

QUESTIONS

What are we to be diligent in here? (That we be found without spot and BLAMELESS.) What does blameless mean? (It means beyond reproach.)

❀❀❀❀❀❀

Lesson Nineteen
GODLINESS
True Religion

PARENT: We are learning that we are Godly, Holy, Blameless and Righteous, by what we BELIEVE. God then looks upon us through Jesus' blood, which makes us these things, for HE is Godly, Holy, Blameless and Righteous.. After we BELIEVE, we then want to do what is pleasing to our Father and then we DO the Word of God. We want to walk in a manner that is pleasing to the Father and NOT after the ways of the world. We are to then live according to the Scriptures and obey them because of our LOVE of God. We are going to read today what TRUE religion is.

READ: James 1:27

QUESTIONS

What is pure religion? (To visit the fatherless and widows in their affliction.)
What else is pure religion that is undefiled before God and the Father? (To keep oneself unspotted from the world.)

STRONG'S: Unspotted

(Greek #784, Unblemished; without spot, unspotted.)

QUESTIONS

How does this Scripture tie in with VIRTUE? (Part of virtue is to look unto the needs of others, Prov. 31.)
Does a virtuous woman look to the needs of the poor?
Do the righteous turn away from the poor or afflicted?
What does the Bible say about taking care of widows? (The believers were called upon to look after a widow indeed.)

READ: Ephesians 5:25-27

QUESTIONS

How much did Christ love the church? (He died and gave Himself for it.)
Why? (So that He would sanctify and cleanse it by the washing of water by the Word.)
How is the church to be? (Glorious.)
In what way? (Without spot or wrinkle or any such thing, but that it should be holy and without blemish.)
Who is the church? (The believers.)

READ: 1 Timothy 6:11-14

QUESTIONS

How are we to keep this commandment? (Vs. 14 says without spot, unrebukable (blameless) until the appearing of Jesus.)
What is this commandment? (Flee these things, and follow after righteousness, godliness, faith, love, patience, meekness.)
What does it mean to keep it without spot? (That means we will keep it purely, and DO this.)

READ: Hebrews 9:14

QUESTIONS

What are dead works? (It is thinking that you can BUY your way into heaven by doing good. Remember NO man is good; only God. We are to DO good only because we love God but are only SAVED by Faith!)
If we were saved by works, would Jesus have had to die? (No!)
What is Jesus? (He is our mediator!)

PARENT: *We are called to be a Holy people. We are to BELIEVE in God, which is what makes us righteous, then, after you BELIEVE, you simply want to do the will of the Father. We will want to live lives that are pleasing to God because of our belief. Godliness is living lives separated unto God for ONE reason ... to please Him, because of our LOVE of God! This is Godliness!*

ACTIVITIES

Talk to the children about how we are called to a life separate from the world. We should be instilling in them every day that we are not of the world but of the Kingdom of God. Ask them the differences of living a Godly life, compared to living a worldly life.

Lesson Twenty
GODLINESS
Review

What is GODLINESS? (It is living a life pleasing to God because we LOVE Him and are devoted to Him. It is also holiness, piety, being reverent...)

How are we to live our lives? (The scriptures say in all godliness and honesty.)

How do you start being godly? (By first BELIEVING in Jesus Christ.)

What are we to exercise ourselves in? (It says in godliness.)

What is profitable for all things? (Godliness.)

If we live godly in Christ Jesus, what will happen? (We will suffer persecution.)

Should we not want to live godly then? (No!)

What would this be? (Loving our lives more than loving God.)

When we are living godly lives, are we to live as the world lives? (No. We are not to live anything like the world.)

How can we live godly?

What does it mean to have a FORM of godliness? (It means they will have a form of godliness, but will be all the other things in 2 Timothy 3:1...)

When you have a form of godliness, have you denied the lusts of the flesh? (No, you are still living according to the flesh.)

When you see this type of godliness, what are you to do? (Turn away from it and not follow it.)

What will happen to this world that we live in now? (It will pass away with a great noise and melt with heat.)

Knowing this, how are we to live according to 2 Peter 3:10...? (We are to be in ALL holy conversation and godliness.)

What does it mean to be in ALL holy conversation? (It means our behavior.)

How are we to be godly then? (By doing things that are pleasing to the Father, NOT for salvation, but because we LOVE Him!)

What will happen after this earth is gone? (There will be NEW heavens and a new earth.)

What will dwell in this new earth? (Righteousness will dwell there.)

Do you want to be there? (YES!)

In Psalms 4:3-4, what has God done toward those that are godly? (He has set them apart.)

Who has He set them apart for? (Himself!)

Why has God done this? (Because He loves us.)

How much does God love us? (He loved us SO much, that He sent His ONLY Son to die on the cross for us. He also made it very easy to become children of the King in that ALL WE HAVE TO DO IS BELIEVE.)

Are we to live lives separate from unbelievers? (Yes, we are not called to be a part of the world.)

Does this mean that we do not spread the message of the Gospel? (No! We are simply not to yoke ourselves together with them. We are to tell all men about the news of the Gospel of Jesus!)

What are we called to be? (Fishers of men.)

When multitudes of people do evil, what are we to do? (We are not to go the way of the masses, but to go the NARROW way of the Word of God.)

How narrow is NARROW? (It is as narrow as a needle. This is pretty narrow.)

Does godliness and separation from the world go hand in hand? (We are to deny the ways of the world.)

What type of advice are we to walk in? (Godly.)

What type of advice should we not listen to? (Ungodly.)

What type of company are we to keep? (The Word of God tells us to be careful of the deeds of the wicked.)

Why? (Lest we learn their ways and become just like them.)

What is this called? (GUARDING OUR

HEARTS.)

What is the opposite of being godly? (Being ungodly or wicked.)
What has the grace of God taught us? (To deny ungodliness and worldly lusts.)
How are we to live in Titus 2:11-15? (We are to live soberly, righteously, and GODLY in this present world.)
What does Jesus want to purify unto Himself? (A peculiar people, zealous of good works.)
Are we to teach these things? (Yes.)
What does submitting have to do with godliness? (It means that we are submit to the ways of God because we LOVE Him. We want to PLEASE our Father.)

Godliness

There was once a girl who lived near the land of the One True King. The girl lived with her older brother near the edge of the border between the two lands.

The land that she lived in was full of wickedness and things that brought fear to her heart. It was a land that had no ruler whatsoever, and the people pursued anything that their hearts desired, disregarding if it hurt them or anyone else.

The girl would look with longing into the land of the King, and knowing she would never be allowed in, would turn wistfully back to her own little village.

One day, the girl was picking some flowers very near the edge of the border of the King's land. She suddenly heard a voice say kindly, "Hello."

There, standing by the edge of the border on the King's side was a little girl, who looked about her own age.

"Hello!" she said.

The two girls immediately started talking and soon they became fast friends. The girls sat down on the grass to talk some more and the girl from the land of NoRule pulled out a long tobacco stick so she could enjoy a smoke as they visited. She offered it to the other girl, but the girl quickly said, "Oh, no thank you. The King is not pleased when his subjects do things to their bodies that could hurt them. Because we love our king, we do not choose to partake of tobacco sticks."

The girl from NoRule had a puzzled look on her face, but put her tobacco sticks back in her satchel. Everyone in the land of NoRule smoked tobacco sticks. In fact, everyone in the land of NoRule did anything they wanted to, whether it hurt their bodies or not. They had always lived according to what was pleasure to themselves, not what gave someone else, like a King, pleasure!

The girls talked some more and then thought they had better be getting home, but promised to meet again at the same spot the following day.

The girl from NoRule went home to her miserable life with her brother. That night, as she lay awake in her bed, staring at the ceiling, she thought, "How I wish I could live in the land of the King. If only there was a way that I could live in the Kingdom..."

She sighed and soon fell asleep, dreaming of the land of the King and all the wonders therein.

The following day she eagerly went to meet her new friend. They sat on the grass and talked and after a while the girl from NoRule pulled out her wineskin to offer the girl some of her ale.

"Oh, No thank you! I couldn't possibly sit and drink ale with you as this would not be pleasing to my King. We are to love the King with all our hearts and souls and minds, and if I drink something that causes my mind not to think properly, how can I love Him as I should?! I want to please my King!"

The girl from NoRule wondered at how much this girl loved this King. This must be quite a love that could cause her to not smoke tobacco sticks, and not to drink ale!!! Curious, she asked the girl to tell her more about her King.

"He is a wonderful King, and he knows all His subjects personally. He loves us more than we love Him! ..." and the girl went on to tell her more of the wonderful King and His land.

The girls talked, but every so often the girl from NoRule would say words that the girl from the Kingdom would not like. After about the fifth time of saying something the girl asked, "What is the matter with these words I am saying?"

The girl from the Kingdom said, "You are taking the King's name in vain. This is my King, whom I love very much. Please do not use His name in a derogatory manner. Your words are dirty, also. I only want to speak things that are pleasing to the ears of the King. He hears everything we say and I want to do and say everything for His pleasure."

Again that evening, the girl lay awake wondering how she could be able to be in the land of the King. Finally she came up with an idea, maybe if she did all the things that the girl from the Kingdom did, she would be able to come into the land of the King.

The next day she purposed in her heart that she would not smoke tobacco sticks, nor drink ale for fun, nor say the King's name in a bad manner or speak any more filthy words.

That afternoon she rushed to meet her friend. She did not smoke, she did not say anything that was not nice, and she did not drink ale. To her shock, her friend didn't even seem to notice! But they still spent the day talking about the King and His land.

The girl decided to try even harder to do all the things that the girl of the Kingdom did. She wore her hair the same way, she made clothes that looked like the girls and copied her in every way imaginable. But the girl never even noticed!

After many afternoons, the girl was so frustrated that she finally asked the girl, "Don't you even notice that I am just like you now? Do you think I could possibly live in the land of the King now? I have given up my tobacco sticks, I dress just like you, I have long hair like you, I don't drink ale for fun, and I never say anything foul anymore! Can I please move into your Kingdom?"

The girl from the Kingdom looked at the girl in shock! Her mouth dropped open and she just stared at the girl for a moment in surprise.

Finally she spoke. "You mean you were doing all these things so that you could come into the land of the King?"

The girl from the land of NoRule nodded her head.

"Oh, don't you know that all you had to do was believe in the King? Anyone who believes in the King can come into His Kingdom. All He wants from His subjects is that they Love Him.

The only reason why I do anything is because of my Love for the King. When I first found out about the land of the King, all He wanted us to do was to make Him the King of our lives and to believe in Him. He simply let me in because I loved Him. When I first found out about the King I did many things that were not pleasing to Him. When I found out that He did not like what I was doing, I stopped only because I Loved Him, not because this is what would get me into His Kingdom. He wants us to have attributes that are pleasing to him because we are living to please Him because of LOVE. We don't do things for reward, but simply because it is our pleasure to please Him!"

The girl paused for a moment and smiled at the girl from the land of NoRule. "Do you love the King?"

The girl shyly smiled and nodded her head.

"Then come on!" And hand in hand, they both went running into the land of the Kingdom, to live in the love of their King forever after.

Brotherly Kindness

Lesson One
BROTHERLY KINDNESS

READ: 2 Peter 1:7

PARENT: *What are we to add to godliness? The scriptures tell us to add brotherly kindness. What do you think this means? ... It might mean to be kind to your brothers. We are going to find out what this means! Today we are first going to find if there are any more scriptures that tell us this same thing.*

READ: Romans 12:1-21

QUESTIONS

What is this whole chapter about? (It is how we are to behave ourselves.)
What word did we learn in the studies on GODLINESS that meant BEHAVIOR? (Conversation meant how we behave ourselves or live our lives.)
How are we to present our bodies? (Vs. 1 says to present them as a living sacrifice.)
Are we to be like the people of the world? (Vs. 2 says, "Be not conformed to this world.")
How are we to be towards one another? (Vs. 10 says to be kindly affectioned one to another with brotherly love; in honour preferring one another.)
Does this mean that we are to think of ourselves first? (No, it is to have other's interests at heart first.)
How are we to think of ourselves? (Vs. 3 says, "Every man that is among you, not to think of himself more highly than he ought to think; but to think soberly, according as God hath dealt to every man the measure of faith.")
What do you think we are to be towards one another? (Humble.)
Does every person that is a believer have something to offer other believers? (Yes. Vs. 4, says that as we have many members in one body, and all members have not the same office.)
What does OFFICE mean here? (It means function.)
What are the vs. 4-8 telling us? (That whatever you ARE, just function in it.)
Why is it telling us this? (So we love one another without dissimulation.)

STRONG'S: Dissimulation
(Greek #505; undissembled; sincere; without hypocrisy; unfeigned.)

DICTIONARY: Dissimulate
(1. To disguise one's intentions under a feigned appearance. 2. Hypocrisy.)

How are we to love one another? (Purely, and not pretending!)
Is each person valuable in their own way? (Yes.)
How are we to regard ALL believers? (We are to esteem each man higher than ourselves.)
Every person? (Yes.)
What is this called? (Humility.)
Does God like pride? (No, it is an abomination to Him.)
What are BELIEVERS together, likened to? (We are called a BODY.)

READ: 1 Thessalonians 4:6-9

QUESTIONS

Who does it say will teach us about loving one another? (Vs. 9 says, "For ye yourselves are taught of God to love one another.")
Should we defraud a brother? (No.)
What does defraud mean? (It means to take from or deprive of by fraud; it means to swindle.)
If you love your fellow believer, would you want to defraud them? (No!)

READ: Hebrews 13:1-3

QUESTIONS

What is to continue? (Brotherly love.)
If you love someone, will you be kind to them?
Why?
Who are we to entertain? (Strangers.)
Does this mean that we are to dance on tables and make sure they have a good time? (No! It means that we are to take care of their needs.)
Who might we be taking care of unawares? (Angels.)
Is this why we do this? (No, it is simply because we are concerned for others.)

ACTIVITIES

Talk with the children about how a physical body all functions together and draw a conclusion to how believers are a body.

Lesson Two
BROTHERLY KINDNESS
God, Our Father

PARENT: Yesterday we read some scriptures on Brotherly Kindness. Why are other believers called Brothers and Sisters? ... What does it mean to be a brother and a sister? It means that we have the same parent. We are brothers and sisters because of who our parents are. Did you know the reason why we call other believers brothers and sisters is because WE have the same parent. Who do you think this parent is? ... It is our Father, GOD!!!

READ: Matthew 7:7-12

QUESTIONS

To whom do we ask, seek, and knock? (To our Father, God.)
Will God give us evil gifts? (No! His will be even better for us than what our earthly Father would give.)
What scripture says God is our Father? (Vs. 11, says YOUR Father, and it is Jesus talking to believers.)
What is the "golden rule"? (It is vs. 12, therefore all things whatsoever ye would that men should do to you, do ye even so to them.)

READ: Matthew 12:46-50

QUESTIONS

Who is Jesus' family? (Vs. 50, "Whoever shall do the will of my Father which is in heaven, the same is my brother, and sister, and mother.")
Where do we find out what God's will is? (Through His Word.)
Do we want to be Jesus' brothers and sisters? (Yes!)
How are we His brothers and sisters? (By having the same Father!)

READ: Mark 11:25-26

QUESTIONS

What does this scripture say, that makes us a family? (It says in vs. 26, that YOUR FATHER, meaning we have the same Father if you are a believer.)
When we pray, what must we do first? (We must FORGIVE, if we have something against someone.)
Why do we have to forgive? (Because if we do not forgive, neither will your Father which is in heaven forgive your trespasses.)
Does this sound very serious? (Yes.)
If we love our brothers and sisters, will we WANT to forgive them? (Yes.)
What if we hold a grudge? (Then we are not humbling ourselves.)
How is this? (Because we are not remembering how many things that WE, ourselves,

have done wrong and then are forgiven!)
Is this a part of Brotherly Kindness? (Yes.)

READ: Luke 11:1-4

QUESTIONS

What did the disciples ask Jesus to teach them? (They asked Him to teach them how to pray.)
Who do we pray to? (To OUR FATHER.)
Does this mean that God is OUR father? (Yes!)

READ: Matthew 23:9

QUESTIONS

Who does this scripture say is our Father? (It says God is our Father.)
Where is He? (In heaven.)
Are we to call any man on earth Father? (No.)
Is it right to call a priest or minister "father"?
What does the word "father" mean in the Strong's? (It means PARENT or FATHER.)
Who is it better to have for our parent, a man or our God?

READ: John 8:39-47

QUESTIONS

According to this scripture, in vs. 42, how do you know God is your Father? (If you love Jesus!)
In vs. 47, how do we know we are God's? (It says if we hear God's words.)
Where are God's words? (In the Bible!)

ACTIVITIES

Read John 14:2-31 and discuss.

Lesson Three
BROTHERLY KINDNESS
The Family of God

PARENT: We learned in the last lesson that God is our Father. When the Bible is telling us to be kind to our Brothers, they are talking about other children of God! We are commanded to add brotherly kindness! Today we are going to read more scriptures that tell us about God as our Father, and the Family that we belong to now.

READ: 2 Corinthians 6:14-18

QUESTIONS

Who will be a Father to us? (Vs. 18 says that God will be a Father to us, and we shall be His sons and daughters says the Lord God Almighty.)
What does God want us to do? (Vs. 17, Wherefore come out from among them, and be ye separate, saith the Lord, and touch not the unclean thing; and I will receive you.)
What does God want us to come out from? (The world.)
Who is our brothers and sisters? (Anyone who comes out from among them, and is separate is who God will be a Father to.)
Is this what will SAVE us? (No, but when we read these scriptures, we will want to do what is pleasing to God.)
Will we be able to have fellowship with the world after we believe? (No, for we will not want to talk about what the world talks about or do what the world is doing.)
Who will we have fellowship with? (Our family.)
Who is our family? (Those who have God as their Father.)

READ: Galatians 4:1-7

QUESTIONS

How is an heir no different from a servant?

(Because he is under tutors and governors until the time appointed of the father.)
When we are children in the Lord, what are we in bondage to? (The elements, or things of this world.)
What does vs. 7 say we now are? (That we are no longer servants but SONS!)
And if we are sons, what are we? (It says heirs!)
What is an heir? (According to the dictionary an heir is one who receives or is expected to receive a heritage, or inheritance. Succession by right of BLOOD.)
What do we inherit? (The Kingdom of God.)
Who are we heirs through? (Vs. 7 says through Christ.)
So if those who believe are heirs and sons, what are we? (We are all brothers and sisters or a Family in God, our Father.)

READ: 1 Thessalonians 3:2-13

QUESTIONS

What is Timotheus called in vs. 2? (He is called our brother and minister of God.)
What is he also? (A fellowlabourer in the gospel of Christ.)
Are we all to be labourers in the gospel of Christ? (Yes!)
In Vs. 7, who are they writing to? (The brethren.)
Who are the brethren? (Those who have God as their Father.)
How does someone have God as their Father? (If they believe in Jesus, the Messiah.)
In vs. 9-10, how do they feel towards the brethren? (They give thanks to God for them; night and day they are praying exceedingly that they might see their faces. They are praying that they might perfect that which is lacking in their faith.)
How do we help one another? (We help others and they help us in areas where we lack faith!)

READ: 1 John 3:1-10

QUESTIONS

What are we now called? (The sons of God.)
Do we know what we shall be in the world to come? (No; but we shall know we shall be like Him.)
Shall we see God? (Yes, vs. 2 says we shall see Him as He is.)
Are we children? (Yes. vs. 7 says "Little children".)
How are God's children to behave themselves? (We are to love one another, vs. 10, and to live lives pleasing to God.)

Lesson Four
BROTHERLY KINDNESS
Who are Our Brothers?

PARENT: We are learning that those who believe in Jesus are now the children of God. There are more scriptures in which Jesus talks and tells us who His family is. Isn't this a wonderful thing to know that we are God's family? And when your earthly families all believe in Jesus, it is important to know that we will all live together forever in the New Heavens and New Earth that is coming with God our Father, and Jesus His Son! Even if our earthly, fleshly bodies die, we do not really die, but have simply gone ahead to be with the Lord. We will all be together again FOREVER, and will never be separated! We are families on earth, but also part of God's family that will live together FOREVER!

READ: Matthew 12:46-50
Matthew 25:31-40

QUESTIONS

Who does Jesus say is His mother and His

brethren? (Whosoever shall do the will of my Father which is in heaven.)
How does Jesus feel about His brethren? (He regards them as Himself.)
When we do things to the brethren, who have we done them to? (Jesus.)

READ: Hebrews 2:9-15

QUESTIONS

What did Jesus do for us? (Vs. 9, He tasted death for every man.)
How did Jesus bring us into His family? (It says in vs. 10-11, that He brought many sons unto glory to make the captain of their salvation perfect through sufferings. For both He that SANCTIFIETH and they who ARE sanctified ARE ALL OF ONE, for which cause He is not ashamed to call them BRETHREN!)
Who is Jesus' brethren? (Those who BELIEVE in Him.)
Who did God give us, as children, to? (It says in vs. 13, behold I and the children which God hath given me...We're given to JESUS!)
What did Jesus do for us? (He destroyed he who had the power of death, the devil.)
Are we in bondage to death now? (No!)
When we are of the family of God, will we live forever? (YES!)

READ: Acts 9:17
Acts 21:20

QUESTIONS

What did Ananias call Saul? (Brother.)
Why did he call him brother? (Because of what he believed.)
What did he believe? (That Jesus was God's Son.)
What did James and the elders call Paul? (Brother.)

READ: Romans 16:1-24

QUESTIONS

In vs. 1, who is Phebe? (She is our sister!)
In vs. 7, what does Paul call Andronicus and Junia? (He calls them his KINSMEN.)
What are KINSMEN? (The dictionary says KINSHIP means the state of being KIN or related by blood!)
Does it mean family? (Yes.)
By whose blood are we all related? (By Jesus'.)
Can you name all those who are our Kinsmen in chapter 16? (All the people listed!)
Why ARE they our kinsmen? (Because they still ARE. They are not dead! We will meet them and be with them with the Lord!)

PARENT: We know that we are all brothers and sisters in our Lord Jesus Christ. We are a family who will be together FOREVER, which is a long, long time! We will meet our brother Paul, who wrote much of the New Testament. We will meet Moses and Joseph, and ALL who believe in Jesus Christ that have lived down through the ages. It is a wonderful thing to know that Jesus has made a way for His family to be with Him forever! In this thought alone we should rejoice!!!

ACTIVITIES

Have the children talk about the fact that we are family, and brothers and sisters with all the believers of the Bible... !

Lesson Five
BROTHERLY KINDNESS
Considering Needs

PARENT: God has made a way, through His Son, Jesus Christ, for all who believe in Him to become a family. In your relationship with your own earthly family, if you saw your brother or sister in trouble, would you turn your head the other way, and ignore this fact? Of course not! How will you act towards other BELIEVERS who are also our family? If you see a brother or a sister in the Lord who are in need, will you turn your head the other way so that you do not have to get involved?

READ: Acts 2:41-47

QUESTIONS

How did the people who received the TRUTH continue? (They continued stedfastly in the apostle's doctrine and fellowship, and in breaking of bread, and in prayers.)
How did they treat their own belongings? (Vs. 44 says, "and all that believed were together, and HAD ALL THINGS IN COMMON.")
What does it mean to have all things in common? (Greek #2839 says common means shared by all.)
Did they regard what they owned as THEIRS? (No, they regarded their belongings as EVERYONE'S.)
What did they do with their possessions and goods? (They parted them, or shared them, with all men as every man had need.)
Should we have this attitude today, or was this only for then? ... (We should not have treasures stored up on earth, but treasures stored up in heaven.)

READ: Acts 4:31-37

QUESTIONS

When the multitude believed, were there divisions? (No, they were of one heart and of one soul, vs. 32.)
Did they say they OWNED anything, or that something was "theirs"? (Vs. 32 says neither said any of them that ought of the things which he possessed was his own.)
Did they share? (It says they had all things in common.)
Were there people among them who had need? (It says that neither was there any among them that lacked, vs. 34.)
What did they do if people lacked? (They sold lands or houses and brought the prices of the things that were sold and laid them down at the apostle's feet.)
What did the apostles do with the money? (Vs. 35 says, "And distribution was made unto every man according as he had need.")
Did they think it important to own these things? (No, they regarded their brother's needs as more important than owning a THING.)
How should we regard "things"? (As not important.)

READ: Ephesians 4:28

QUESTIONS

What is a person that was a thief, to do after they believe in Jesus? (He is to steal no more and to work.)
Why is he to work? (The Word says it is a good thing to work with your hands.)
Why is he to work, to get THINGS for himself? (No! It says so that he may HAVE to give to him that needeth!)
Are we to have attitudes of working to get belongings? (No.)
Why should we work? (To meet our family's needs and to GIVE to those who have need.)
Is this being kind to our brothers and sisters? (YES!)

READ: 1 John 3:16-18

QUESTIONS

What ought WE to do for our brethren? (Vs. 16 says we ought to lay down our lives for our brethren.)

Do we LOVE God if we do not willingly help a brother we see in need? (No.)

Does it say that we CAN help? (Yes, it says, "But WHO HATH this world's good, and seeth his brother have need, and shutteth up his bowels of compassion from him, how dwelleth the love of God in him".)

What is compassion? (Caring, affection, concern because of love.)

How are we to love? (Not in what we say, but in deed and in truth.)

Lesson Six
BROTHERLY KINDNESS
Preferring Others Above Ourselves

PARENT: We are learning that part of BROTHERLY KINDNESS is to consider others needs as much as we would our own. Can you think of something that you own, that is YOURS, that you like very much. Now, what would you do if you saw one of your sisters or brothers in NEED. Could you sell that item that you like so much? God wants us to care about others more than we care about earthly things. This is all part of BELIEVING. When we believe in God and His Kingdom, we are to be no longer concerned about earthly, carnal things. We are to consider the things of God's Kingdom rather than the world we live in now. Nothing that we have now will be able to go with us when we enter into God's Kingdom. The only "things" we can bring with us are people! For example, parents that are training their children up in the knowledge of the Lord are also making sure that their children will be going with them to live with the Lord! You can take your children with you into Heaven! But you cannot take "things"! We can also know that when we have brothers and sisters in the Lord, that THEY will be going with us also! What is it better to invest in, things that we CAN'T take with us, or things, meaning people, that we CAN? We had better have hearts that want to care for the people of God and consider their needs before the lusts of our flesh!

READ: Romans 12:10

STRONG'S: Kindly (In this scripture)

(Greek #5387; means cherishing one's kindred; fraternal towards fellow Christians.)

STRONG'S: Honour

(Greek # 5092; value; valuables; esteem of the highest degree.)

STRONG'S: Preferring

(Greek # 4285; means to lead the way for others; show deference; prefer.)

DICTIONARY: Prefer

(1. To give priority or preference to. 2. To value more highly.)

QUESTIONS

How are we to be towards our brethren? (Kindly affectioned.)

How are we to consider others? (We are to honour them.)

What does this mean? (It means we are to consider them more valuable than ourselves.)

What characteristic does this sound like? (Humility.)

How does God feel about Humility? (He wants all to be humble and to consider OTHERS before ourselves.)

What does it mean to prefer someone in honour? (It means that we hold someone in very high esteem and value them more than

ourself.)
Do we need to do this with EVERYONE? (Yes.)

READ: 1 Timothy 5:21

QUESTIONS

How are we to regard men? (As all being equal.)
Are we to be PARTIAL to any man? (No.)
What does it mean to be PARTIAL? (It means in the dictionary to favour one person or side over another. Having a particular liking for someone or something over others.)
Are we to hold some believers in esteem over others? (No. We are all a part of the body of Christ and the eye is just as important as the ear!)

READ: James 3:17

QUESTIONS

Does the wisdom that is from above show partiality? (No!)
Are we to consider ALL of the brethren's needs? (Yes. We cannot give to one without giving to another.)
Are we to show partiality in considering OURSELVES? (We are to consider all men above ourselves!)

ACTIVITIES

Talk with the children about how there is no partiality shown in a family relationship...

Lesson Seven
BROTHERLY KINDNESS
Submitting to One Another

PARENT: We have learned that we are to PREFER in honour other people before ourselves. Do you remember what it means to PREFER? It means to give priority or preference to someone else before you think of yourself. We read scriptures that told us that we are to prefer our brothers and sisters in the Lord. This is all a part of brotherly kindness. Today we are going to talk about submitting one to another. This would be a very easy thing to do if you are preferring others above yourself. We are also not to show partiality towards brothers or sisters but to love each one equally just as our parents love each of us equally. The same is with God!

READ: Acts 10:34

STRONG'S: Respecter

(Greek # 4381; means one exhibiting partiality.)

QUESTIONS

Are we to be partial towards people? (No!)
Is God partial to his children? (No, he loves us all the same.)

PARENT: Isn't this something, that God, our Father, loves us equally? Because God is perfect, He must love us PERFECTLY equally! What He does for one He will do for another?

QUESTIONS

Does God love us as much as He loved Moses?
Does God love us the same as He loved Abraham?

Does God love us the same as He loved David?
Does God love us as much as He loved Daniel?

READ:　　Ephesians 5:15-24

QUESTIONS

How are we as believers to walk? (Vs. 15 says we are to walk circumspectly, as wise.)
What is wisdom? (Vs. 17, Understanding what the will of the Lord is.)
How are we to speak to our brothers and sisters? (It says in vs. 19 that we are to speak to one another in psalms and hymns and spiritual songs, singing and making melody in your heart to the Lord.)
Who are we to submit ourselves to? (Vs. 21 says to submit ourselves one to another in the fear of the Lord.)
Who are wives to submit to? (To their husbands as if their husbands were Christ.)

STRONG'S: Submit

(Greek # 5293; means to obey or be subordinate; to submit self unto.)

READ:　　1 Peter 5:1-9

QUESTIONS

Are the elders to be "lords" over us, in the sense of a position? (No, vs. 3 says NEITHER as being lords over God's heritage, but being ensamples, or examples, to the flock.)
What are the younger people to do to the elders? (Submit themselves to them.)
Are we to be only subject to them? (No, we are all to subject ourselves one to another.)
What are we to be clothed with? (Vs. 5, we are to be clothed with humility.)
Why? (Vs. 5, for God resisteth the proud.)
What does He give to the humble? (He gives grace to the humble.)
How are the brethren to live their lives? (Casting all cares on God, being sober, being vigilant.)
Why? (Because our adversary the devil, as a roaring lion, walketh about, seeking whom he may devour.)
How are we to regard the devil? (It says, "...whom resist steadfast in the faith, knowing that the same afflictions are accomplished in your brethren that are in the world".)
So are all believers going through the same thing? (Yes, for God is not a respecter of persons, nor shows partiality to His children.)

Lesson Eight
BROTHERLY KINDNESS
Kindness

PARENT: We are commanded by God to be KIND to our brothers and sisters in the Lord. Did you know that God is KIND? Let's read all the scriptures that talk about God's Kindness...

READ: Nehemiah 9:13-17

QUESTIONS

Was God kind to the children of Israel? (Yes, vs. 17 says, "But thou art a God ready to pardon, gracious and merciful, slow to anger, and of great kindness, and forsookest them not.")
What were some of the things God did for them? (Many things, all throughout vs. 12-17.)
Was God rewarded for His kindness? (No, they refused to obey, and were not mindful of His wonders.)
Was God kind because He wanted a reward? (No, He was kind because He loved them.)

READ: Psalms 31:21-24

QUESTIONS

What type of kindness did the Lord show in this scripture? (His marvellous kindness.)
If we are of good courage, what will the Lord do to our hearts? (Vs. 24 says that He will strengthen our hearts.)
What does the Lord do to the faithful? (He preserves them.)
Is God being kind to us? (Yes.)
Why is God kind to us? (Because He loves us.)
When we love someone, what will we be? (Kind.)
How are we to treat our brothers and sisters in Christ? (Kindly.)

READ: Psalms 117:1-2

QUESTIONS

Is this a very long chapter? (No!)
Is it very important? (Yes!)
What type of kindness does God show in this scripture? (Merciful kindness.)
Is God "very" kind to us? (The Bible says His merciful kindness is GREAT toward us.)
What will endureth forever? (God's Truth!)
Who is the Way, the Truth and the Light? (Jesus!)

READ: Psalms 119:76-77

QUESTIONS

What type of kindness does God show in this verse? (Merciful.)
What will comfort us? (God's merciful kindness.)
How do we know this? (Vs. 76, says according to thy Word unto thy servant.)
What are God's tender mercies? (His kindness towards us.)

STRONG'S: Mercies
(Hebrew # 7356 compassion; as cherishing the baby in a mother's womb!)

What is God's kindness towards us like? (It is great and tender, and compassionate, which are all part of kindness.)

READ: Psalms 141:1-5

QUESTIONS

What is considered this man's kindness in this scripture? (If the righteous smite him.)
Why would he consider it a kindness? (Remember the scripture that says, "Rebuke a wise man and he will love you, Proverbs 9:8"?)
When the righteous reprove us, what is it likened to? (An excellent oil.)

When you care about a brother or a sister, and you see them in trouble or error, do you love them if you do not tell them? (No, true love is to love someone enough to show them error in loving kindness.)
Is this brotherly kindness? (Yes.)

PARENT: We are finding that God is Kind. According to the New Testament, God chastens us as children. God's kindness is very great and merciful towards us. We need to know that the God we serve is ever loving and ever kind. God's kindness is a PERFECT kindness. We need to learn to be kind towards our brothers. We are not to fight or strive with those we love. This is not preferring someone above ourselves. This is not to say that you do not tell someone if they are in error. This is kindness also!

Lesson Nine
BROTHERLY KINDNESS
God's Kindness

PARENT: Do you remember what we found out about God's kindness? ... God's kindness is very GREAT towards us. His kindness is also merciful and marvelous. Today we are going to read more scriptures which tell us about God's kindness. Everything we are to be, such as in the scriptures in 2 Peter, God is. God has all the attributes listed in 2 Peter! God is Kind, He is loving, He is temperate ... And He wishes us to to have these attributes also! We are to be kind to one another!

DICTIONARY: Kind

(1. Charitable; helpful; showing sympathy or understanding. 2. Forbearing; tolerant. 3. Courteous. 4. Generous. 5. Warmhearted, good, agreeable, hospitable, gentle.)

READ: Isaiah 54:5-8

QUESTIONS

How does God gather us? (Vs. 7, with great mercies will I gather thee.)
What type of kindness is mentioned here that God has for us? (Everlasting kindness.)
What does everlasting mean? (Neverending, infinite.)
How long will God's kindness last towards us? (Always!)
In God's everlasting kindness, what does He show towards us? (His mercy.)
So, does God's kindness and mercy go hand in hand? (Yes.)

READ: Joel 2:12-14

QUESTIONS

In verse 13, what is God? (God is gracious and merciful, slow to anger, and of great kindness, and repenteth him of the evil.)
Is God good? (YES!!!!)
Does God know who will return and repent to Him? (Yes, God knows all things!)

READ: Jonah 4:2

QUESTIONS

What did Jonah say about God's kindness? (That thou art a gracious God, and merciful, slow to anger, and of great kindness, and repentest thee of the evil.)
Who said this EXACT same thing before? (Isaiah!)
Did they know the same God? (Yes, they must have to say the EXACT same things about God!)

READ: Ephesians 2:4-9

QUESTIONS

What is God rich in? (Vs. 4 says that He is rich in mercy.)
How much does God love us? (Vs. 4 says, "For His great love wherewith He loved us!")
What is the greatest gift God gave us through His kindness? (The free GIFT of SALVATION!!!)
Is it by works that we are saved? (No, it is simply a gift, and all we have to do is to BELIEVE in Jesus Christ!)
What will God show us in the ages to come? (Vs. 7 says that in the ages to come He might shew the exceeding riches of His grace in His kindness toward us through Jesus Christ!)

READ: 2 Corinthians 6:1-10

QUESTIONS

In all things, what are we to do? (Vs. 4 says in all things approving ourselves as the ministers of God.)
In what way? (Vs. 7 says by pureness, by knowledge, by longsuffering, by KINDNESS...)
So are we to be kind? (Yes!)
What is this kindness? (It is a part of love!)
Why are we kind to our brethren? (Because we love them!)

READ: Proverbs 31:26

QUESTIONS

How does the virtuous woman speak? (She openeth her mouth with wisdom and in her tongue is the law of kindness.)
Can we be kind through what we say? (Yes.)
SHOULD we be kind through what we say? (YES!)

Lesson Ten
BROTHERLY KINDNESS
Being Gentle

PARENT: We are learning that God in His kindness, made a way for us to be with Him through His Son, Jesus Christ. Another aspect of kindness is gentleness. Did you know that God is gentle? God deals gently with us. Let's first look up the definition of GENTLE...

DICTIONARY: Gentle

(1. Considerate or kindly in disposition; amiable; patient. 2. Not harsh, severe, or violent; mild.)

READ: Isaiah 40:10-11

QUESTIONS

How will God feed His flock? (Like a shepherd.)
How shall He carry the lambs or babes? (In His arms.)
Where will He carry them? (In His bosom.)
How shall God lead those that are with young? (He shall GENTLY lead those that are with young!)

READ: 2 Samuel 22:32-36

QUESTIONS

What is God's shield? (He has given the shield of His SALVATION!)
What does God's gentleness do? (Vs. 36 says "Thy gentleness hath made me great.")

READ: Psalms 18:30-35

QUESTIONS

Is this the same scripture? (Yes!)
What does this GREAT mean? (The Hebrew word for GREAT is # 7235; it means to

increase.)
What would be the BEST thing to increase in? (The knowledge of the Word of God!)

READ: 2 Corinthians 10:1

QUESTIONS

What did Paul beseech the believers by? (By the meekness and gentleness of Christ.)
Is Jesus meek and gentle? (Yes!)
Is He also the Lion of Judah? (Yes!)
Is being meek and gentle a "sissy" thing to be? (NO!! It is the RIGHT way to be.)

READ: 1 Thessalonians 2:7-8

QUESTIONS

How were the disciples towards the brethren? (It says in vs. 7 that the disciples were GENTLE among you.)
How gentle were they? (They were as gentle as a nurse cherisheth her children.)

READ: 2 Timothy 2:24-26

QUESTIONS

What does the servant of the Lord do? (He is gentle unto all men, apt to teach, patient, in MEEKNESS instructing those that oppose themselves.)
What goes hand and hand with gentleness throughout the New Testament? (Meekness.)

READ: Titus 3:1-3

QUESTIONS

How are we to be towards all men? (We are to be gentle and SHOW meekness.)
So when we are gentle, what do we show? (Meekness!)

DICTIONARY: Meek

(1. Showing patience and humility; long-suffering.)

READ: Galations 5:22-23

QUESTIONS

What is the fruit of the spirit? (Love, joy, peace, longsuffering, gentleness, goodness, faith, joy, peace, longsuffering, goodness, faith, meekness, temperance.)
Are some of these part of the definition of meekness and kindness? (Yes!)

READ: James 3:17-18

Lesson Eleven
BROTHERLY KINDNESS
Being Hospitable

PARENT: We have learned that we are to be gentle and meek. These qualities are a part of being kind. Another way we are kind to our brothers and sisters is when we are hospitable to them. We have learned that the believers never considered anything that they owned as theirs. They considered everything as each other's and made sure that everyone had what they needed. How much more should WE be concerned about OUR family's needs, our HEAVENLY family's. God wants us to be kind, gentle and meek towards one another. He also wants us to show hospitality...

STRONG'S: Hospitality

(Greek # 5382 means to be fond of having guests.; hospitable.)

DICTIONARY: Hospitable

(1. Welcoming guests with warmth and generosity. 2. Well-disposed towards strangers. 3. Having an open and charitable mind; receptive.)

READ: Romans 12:13

QUESTIONS

How are we to take care of each other? (We are to distribute unto the needs of our brothers and sisters.)
What else are we to be? (Given to hospitality.)
Does this mean that we need to consider the needs of others before ours? (Yes.)
What if we are just too busy to have other people around? (This is not giving ourselves to hospitality.)
What if we do not have enough food to offer anyone? (Even if we do not have FOOD, which in America would be hard to understand, we can always offer someone a glass of water for refreshment.)

READ: 1 Timothy 3:1-5
        Titus 1:7-9

QUESTIONS

What is a bishop? (The Greek word # 1984 and #1980 means inspection; visitation; to inspect; to go see; relieve; look out, visit. A bishop was a person that visited the saints. According to the scriptures, the believers met in homes, Romans 16, and the bishop visited to see the needs of the saints.)
What must a Bishop be given to? (Hospitality.)
Does this go along with a person that visits and inspects the believers? (Yes, they must like being around other people!)
What would happen if they weren't hospitable? (They wouldn't make a very good bishop.)

READ: 1 Peter 4:9

QUESTIONS

How are we to be one to another? (Hospitable.)
Are we to do it grudgingly? (No!)
How are we to do it? (Kindly, meekly, and gently!)

PARENT: In the fast moving society that we live in, we barely have time for our families. It is often hard to find time to be hospitable to others unless we plan it out. But according to the Bible, the believers met daily. In our regimented lifestyles, it is hard to even imagine this, but we need to remember to be hospitable. We are commanded to be hospitable to others and to strangers. Many people, because of fear, make excuses to not invite strangers into their homes. We need to use wisdom from our precious Father, but we also need to remember that by entertaining strangers, some have entertained angels. I'd sure like to entertain an angel someday, wouldn't you? But keep in mind that whenever you are being hospitable to the least of those in the Kingdom of Heaven, you are also being hospitable to Jesus!!! Isn't that even better than entertaining an angel?!

Lesson Twelve
BROTHERLY KINDNESS
Being Gracious

PARENT: We read that God deals with us gently, kindly and meekly. Did you know that God is also gracious? According to the Word of God, WE are called to be gracious too! Let's look in the Strong's to find the meaning of gracious...

STRONG'S: Gracious

(Hebrews # 2587; gracious; from # 2603 means to favour, bestow; show favour, merciful, have pity upon.)

(Greek # 5485; graciousness, of manner or act; the divine influence upon the heart, and its reflection in the life; acceptable, benefit, favour, gift, gracious, joy liberality, pleasure, thanks-worthy.)

DICTIONARY: Gracious

(1. Characterized by kindness and warm courtesy. 2. Merciful; compassionate.)

PARENT: Let's read the scriptures that tell us about God's graciousness.

READ: 2 Kings 13:22-23

QUESTIONS

How was the Lord to Israel? (He was gracious to them.)
What did God show towards them? (He showed compassion.)
What else? (He had respect unto them and would not destroy them.)

READ: Psalms 86:15
        Psalms 103:8

QUESTIONS

What is God like? (He is a God full of compassion, and GRACIOUS, and longsuffering and plenteous in mercy and truth.)

READ: Psalms 111:2-4
        Psalms 116:5

QUESTIONS

What are the works of the Lord like? (His works are great!)
What else are they like in Ps. 111:3? (They are honourable and glorious.)
Why did God make His works? (Vs. 4, He hath made His wonderful works to be remembered.)
What is the Lord? (He is GRACIOUS and full of compassion.)

PARENT: We are to be gracious just as our heavenly Father is gracious. Let's read the following scriptures which talk about US being gracious...

READ: Proverbs 11:16

QUESTIONS

What does a gracious woman retain? (She retaineth honour.)
What does it mean to be GRACIOUS? (It means that we have characters that are kind and show warm courtesy. We are to be merciful and compassionate towards others, just as God is towards us.)
When we are gracious what does God say comes with this? (Honour.)

READ: Ecclesiastes 10:12

QUESTIONS

What are the words of a wise man like? (They are gracious.)
How does this mean a wise man speaks? (He

speaks graciously.)
Will a wise man speak kindly? (Yes.)
Will he speak courteously? (Yes.)
Will he speak with compassion? (Yes.)
Will he show mercy? (Yes.)

READ: Luke 4:22

QUESTIONS

What type of Words did Jesus speak? (Gracious words.)
So, can we be gracious by what we speak? (Yes. The three scriptures listed above are talking about how one speaks.)
So is being gracious a way one talks? (Yes. Also how one lives. It is an attitude.)

Lesson Thirteen
BROTHERLY KINDNESS
Forbearing

PARENT: We are already familiar with the characteristic of forbearing. Do you remember what forbearance is? It is an aspect of being patient. It is being tolerant with others and enduring wrongs. It is suffering things other people do to us unawares. This is why the Bible tells us not to be quickly offended. If we are not quickly offended we are tolerating others' mistakes. Remember the Bible scripture that tells us to treat people as we would like to be treated? We need to remember this. When we make mistakes we would like to be treated kindly. So would other people as they are growing in the Lord. We need to give others room to grow in Christ. Forbearance is also a part of Brotherly Kindness. It is being patient with one another. The Bible tells us there are mature Christians and Christians still on milk, which means they are babes. It is only right that the mature Christians be compassionate towards the babes!

God is forbearing towards us...

READ: Romans 2:4

QUESTIONS

Does God show us forbearance? (Yes, God is very forbearing towards us.)
In what way? (We continuously do things that are not pleasing to God, and instead of God wiping us off the face of the earth, He sees His Son's blood sacrificed for those sins. He is forbearing in that He even made a WAY for us to be forgiven.)
What goes along with forbearance? (Longsuffering.)
What does longsuffering mean? (It means to forbear LONG and patiently enduring wrongs or difficulties.)
Do we forbear when others do us wrong? (Yes.)
Is this a part of brotherly kindness? (Yes. We are not perfect and will sometimes offend others. We need to forgive others as they will forgive us.)

READ: Romans 3:23-26

QUESTIONS

What did God's forbearance do? (Through His forbearance He sent Jesus to make a way for our sins to be forgiven.)
What did God do when He sent Jesus? (He gave His ONLY begotten Son because He loved the world so much!)
Is this forbearance? (This is PERFECT forbearance. God loved us and He sent His only Son to die for us so that we would have a way to Him! He forgives us for all we do.)
How should we treat our brothers? (We should show the same type of forbearance

that loves our brothers so much that we forgive, always hoping that they will walk in the light of the Word!)

READ: Ephesians 4:1-6

QUESTIONS

How are we to walk? (We are to walk, or live our lives, worthy of the vocation wherewith we are called.)

How do we do this? (In all lowliness and meekness, with longsuffering, forbearing one another in love.)

When we are forbearing and longsuffering towards our fellow brethren, how is this showing brotherly kindness? (It is humbling ourselves in that we are knowing that they are being perfected in their weaknesses through Christ, just as WE are being perfected by Jesus. We must know that we are all in growing stages and must be patient with one another!)

PARENT: We have learned that we are now in a family! We are all brothers and sisters with those who love God, our Father! This family will never be separated, but will live with God throughout all eternity! We should treat our family with love and care, preferring others above ourselves. This is the summation of all the rest of this unit. When we prefer others above ourselves, we will be kind, gracious, hospitable, and gentle to all. God is all these things and He wants us to be kind to our brethren just as He is kind to us!

Lesson Fourteen
BROTHERLY KINDNESS
Review

How are we to behave ourselves towards others? (We are to show brotherly kindness.)
How are we to think of ourselves? (The Bible tells us not to think of ourselves higher than we ought.)
How are we to think? (Soberly.)
What are we to be in self-esteem? (Humble.)
What about the world's psychiatrists who say we need to have self-confidence? (That is not the wisdom of God. We are to consider all men before ourselves.)
What does God think of pride? (It is an abomination to Him.)
What does God call the believers? (He calls them the BODY of Christ.)
Who is the head of the Body? (Christ!)

What is the "golden rule"? (Therefore all things whatsoever ye would that men should do to you, do ye even so to them.)
Who is Jesus' family? (Whoever shall do the will of His Father, the same is His brother, and sister, and mother.)
How are we His brothers and sisters? (Because we have the same Father.)
When we pray to our Father, if we have something against someone what must we do? (We must forgive them.)
Why? (Because if we do not forgive others, neither will God forgive us, Mark 11:25-26.)
What is happening in our heart if we hold a grudge? (We are not humbling ourselves.)
Are we being KIND to our brothers then? (No.)

How do you know God is your Father? (If you love Jesus!)
How do we know we are God's? (If we hear His words, Jn. 8.)
What does our Father, God, want us to do, in regards to the world? (2 Cor. 6, says come out from among them, and be ye separate, saith the Lord, and touch not the unclean thing; and I will receive you.)
Is this separation from the world what saves us? (No! It is believing in Jesus that saves us! We simply want to obey because we LOVE Him.)

What is an heir? (An heir is one who receives or is expected to receive a heritage or inheritance. Succession by right of BLOOD.)
How are we heirs? (We are heirs and sons to God, our Father!)
Once we believe in Jesus are we God's children? (Yes.)
How does God want us to treat one another? (He commands us to LOVE one another!!!)

What did Jesus do for us so we could become part of His family? (He tasted death for every man.)
How? (He sanctifieth and they who are sanctified are all of one, for which cause He is not ashamed to call them brethren.)
Who is Jesus' brethren? (Those who believe in Him.)
What did Jesus do to death? (He destroyed the power of the devil over death!)
Do we die now? (No, those in God's family will never die!)

What is a kinsman? (A kinsman means the state of being Kin or related by blood!)
Is someone who is kin, family? (Yes!)
Are they related by blood? (Yes, Jesus' blood!)
Are WE related to the people in the Bible that believed in the Lord? (Yes. We belong to the family of God and they are our KIN!)
What about if they are dead? (They are still our kinsmen, and they are not dead. One who believes in Jesus does not die.)

How did the people who received the TRUTH continue in Acts 2? (They continued steadfastly in the apostle's doctrine and fellowship, and in breaking of bread, and in prayers.)
How did the believers regard their belongings? (They had all things in common.)

What did they do with their possessions? (They regarded their belongings as everyone's and they parted them, or shared them, with all men as every man had need.)
Is this an attitude of brotherly kindness? (Yes!)

What are we to do to every brother we meet? (We are to submit ourselves, one to another.)
What does this mean? (It means we are to consider them higher than we consider ourselves.)
Is this pleasing to God? (Yes.)
What does it mean to be "kind"? (It means we are to be charitable, helpful, showing sympathy or understanding, forbearing, tolerant, courteous, generous, warmhearted, good, agreeable, hospitable, and gentle!)

Brotherly Kindness

There was once in the land of the One True King, a village where many different types of people lived. In this village were people who loved to help others and were always making sure that everyone had enough food and clothing. Then, there were people who loved to go out and tell foreigners about the One True King, and try to win them into the Kingdom. There were also some people who loved to make peace when trouble arose, and their loving patience smoothed over many offenses. There were also some people who loved to go and encourage all the rest in their serving of the King.

Now, all the people in this village worked together very well, as they realized that each person had his own function that helped the others to function in what they were called to do!

One day, a man named Tom was sitting on his front porch, just thinking about how wonderful it was to be a "winner", as his function was fondly called. He loved to go into all the different lands and tell the foreigners about the One True King. It was His job to win them to the love of the king, where they could live fulfilling lives forever after!

He thought to himself, "Hmmmmm. There is nothing like being a winner. If only people knew how great it is to be winning people into the Kingdom! It is too bad that more people are not doing this. I think I'm going to go and talk to Sam about becoming a winner..."

And so off he went...

Now Sam was what the villagers lovingly called a caretaker, for it was his job to go throughout the village and find out if everyone's needs were met. If they weren't, he would make sure that they were given enough food and clothing or anything else that they were lacking in.

Sam was working out in his garden, as it was his great joy to grow plenty of food for whoever needed it. He saw Tom coming and happily went to greet him

The two men started talking and Tom finally brought up the subject that he came to talk about.

"Sam, I have just been sitting and thinking about how wonderful it is to be a winner. We go out into the unknown foreigner's lands and tell them about the King, and it is perhaps the most important thing that anyone can do. I was thinking, you should put aside this hobby of gardening for awhile and come on out and win foreigners!"

Sam scratched his head in thought, "Well, I know it is really important to be a winner! ... I guess it would be a great thing to do!... OK, ... I'm with you, Tom!"

And Sam dropped everything that he was doing and went with Tom, on his way to find foreigners for the Kingdom.

On their way through the village, Tom saw the peacemaker, Zeke, sitting in front of the village dry goods store. Zeke's function was to settle disputes when they arose, between the villagers. Zeke, Tom and Sam all greeted one another and Zeke asked them where they were off to.

"Oh, Zeke, it is such a wonderful thing to be winning foreigners into the Kingdom. There are so many unknown places to be reached, that it is very important that we get winners to as many foreigner places as possible, so that we can win them to the King!"

Zeke nodded his head in thought. "That sure is true! It is very important for these people to know about the King!"

"How about joining us?" urged Tom. "This is the most important function that anyone can do! We need as many men as possible!"

Zeke paused for a moment then said, "Sure! I'd be happy to go with you to tell the foreigners about the King! Let's go!" And Zeke dropped everything and went on with the winners.

On their way out of town, the tiny band met another man. It was Old Joe, the encourager. It was Old Joe's function to encourage all the people in the land of the King in what their functions were. He looked at the men and asked, "Where are you going?"

The men replied, "We have been firmly convinced that the most important thing that anyone can do is to tell all the foreigner's about the King. There are many unknown lands that need to know about the King! We are all on our way to tell foreigners about the Kingdom and win them to the King!"

Old Joe looked surprised, "Hmmmmmmm. Now that is a very important function! You are right! We should be telling the foreigners about the King! This sounds like a great idea! Can I join you?" And off they went.

As soon as they were gone, there was no one to go about and take care of the needs of the villagers. Soon there were some people who were lacking for their necessities. The people tried to help each other, but some received more food and didn't have enough clothing. Some received lots of clothing but didn't have enough food! There was just no one about that seemed to know as much about caretaking as Sam! The poor people truly missed Sam and longed for his return.

After Zeke was gone, there was no one to help in settling disputes between villagers. Many of the people were bickering and fighting over whose function was the most important thing in the land, and maybe they should all be winners! Strife ruled throughout the land with Zeke's absence.

Now that Old Joe was gone, people began complaining about their functions. They started forgetting that they were not functioning for themselves, but for the glory of their King! But alas, there was no one to remind them of this!

Out in the land of the foreigners, the four men went to as many people as they could find, but Sam, Zeke and Old Joe were having a terrible time at winning. Sam kept wanting to take care of the needs of the foreigners, Zeke kept trying to make peace when disputes arose, and Old Joe kept telling the foreigners that everyone had a function!! This would have been fine if they were in the Land of the King, but the foreigners regarded them as crazy!

They knew it was time to return home.

When they returned to the village a terrible surprise awaited them! On there way into the village they noticed that people weren't doing anything! In fact, they couldn't seem to find anyone around at all! They looked in the windows of the nearby houses and they were sadly empty. They looked in the livery near the horses, and there was no one there. As they walked into the village square, their mouths dropped open in shocked surprise!...

There, standing before them... was the King!!!

"Your majesty!" the four men stuttered as they bowed low before Him.

The King told them to rise and didn't say anything for a moment, but just looked at them.

Tom got up the courage to ask, "Your Majesty, where are all the people of the village?"

The King gave them a stern look, "They are all out being winners."

"But, what about the livery, and the village meetings, and the bakery, and the dry goods store...?" Sam asked.

"As I said, they are all out being winners."

"But, they aren't winners, they have different functions!" said Old Joe.

The King gave each man a withering look. "Exactly!"

The four men all hung their heads in shame, especially Tom.

Tom gave a small moan of sorrow, "Oh, Your Majesty, I have been so selfish and prideful. I was thinking how wonderful it was to be a winner and thought everyone should be one. I never considered my brother's function as important as mine was." Tom knelt before the King, "Please forgive me, Your Highness. I have not been regarding my brothers higher than myself, but have esteemed my function above others. I truly am sorry."

Sam, Zeke and Old Joe all bowed their heads in sorrow. Old Joe spoke for all three of them, "Your Majesty, we ask your forgiveness that we have not been doing the functions that you have intended for us to do. We have not been kind to the other villagers in that we didn't put their needs above our own vain imaginations. It is our fault that everyone is away, and not doing what You intended for them to be doing. Please forgive us."

The King lovingly smiled at them, "Of course you are forgiven. When the people come back from ..." the King cleared His throat, "...winning, please make sure that you all function in what you are to do! Remember, each of you are important and you are to regard everyone's function as highly important. Even esteeming others higher than your own..." as he gave a firm look directly at Tom.

The King bid the men a fond farewell and went on to check on His other villages.

After a while, all the villagers came back after they found out that they were not traveling winners. They all heard about the visit from the King, and each esteemed one another before themselves and lived on functioning in what they were each called to do, with kindness and compassion, one towards another!

Charity

Lesson One
CHARITY

READ: 2 Peter 1:7

PARENT: We have learned many things about being kind to our brothers. Today we are going to start on a new character trait. We are going to talk about adding CHARITY to our BROTHERLY KINDNESS. Have you any idea of what charity is? Some people think that charity is when you give clothes or items to a "charity" organization. We had better find out what CHARITY means since it is very important to the Lord. CHARITY is the last thing on the list that the Lord gave us of traits we are suppose to obtain. Let's first look up charity in the Strong's Concordance...

STRONG'S: Charity

(Greek # 26; love, affection, benevolence. From Greek # 25; to love, in a social or moral sense; beloved.)

DICTIONARY: Charity

(1. An act or feeling of benevolence; good will; or affection. 2. The love of man for his fellow men; brotherly love. 3. Mercy. 4. The provision of help or relief to the poor.)

PARENT: According to these definitions, charity means love. It is love that we are to have for one another. We are to love one another with a great love, just as God loves each of us! What is love? What is charity? Let's read 1 Corinthians 13 and it will give us a pretty good idea of how we are to have charity.

READ: 1 Corinthians 13:1-3

QUESTIONS

If we speak with the tongues of men and of angels and do not have love, what are we like? (We have become as sounding brass, or a tinkling symbol.)
What does sounding brass and tinkling symbols sound like? (They are tinny sounding and have no depth.)
What if we have the gift of prophecy and have no love? (We are nothing.)
What if we understand all mysteries and have no love? (We are nothing!)
What if we have all knowledge and still have no love? (We are nothing!!)
What if we have all faith, so that we can remove mountains, but still have not charity? (WE ARE NOTHING!!!)
What if I give all I own to feed the poor, but have no love? (This feeding the poor does me no good.)
What if I give my body to be burned through persecutions, but still do not have love? (This will not profit us ANYTHING if we do not have love!!!)
What is the most important thing to have? (Love!)

READ: 1 Corinthians 13:4

QUESTIONS

If we have love, do we just take so much from people and then put a stop to their bothering us? (Charity suffereth long.)
Do we grudgingly let people bother us and come over to our homes? (No, charity is kind and is willing to have people bother us and put us out. Charity is all what kindness is, and more!)
Are we to envy other people? (No.)
What if they know God better than us? (We are to regard all men higher than ourselves. Charity envieth not.)
Are we to always make sure that our SELVES are taken care of and that WE have enough of everything without giving thought nor concern of our brother's welfare? (No. We are kind.)
Are we to consider ourselves better than anyone else?

What if we are very Godly and obey God in all things? (Charity vaunteth not itself and is not puffed up.)

READ: 1 Corinthians 13:5-7

QUESTIONS

Are we to have one type of attitude for people to see when we are within "seeing" range, and another for when we are in the privacy of our own homes? (Charity doth not behave itself unseemly, EVEN when no one is looking!)
Are we to make sure WE have the biggest piece of cake, and give others the smallest? (No, charity seeketh not her own.)
When we see people doing wrong to ourselves or others, are we to get angry and yell at them? (No, charity is not easily provoked.)
What about when our little brother or sister is just "terrorizing" us? (Charity is NOT easily provoked.)
When people do us terribly wrong, are we to hope God "gets" them? (No, charity thinketh no evil.)
When someone is very successful, and they are living their lives in the lust of this world, are we to be happy for them? (Charity rejoiceth not in iniquity, but rejoiceth in the truth.)
When the Word of God is accepted by a person, what should we do? (REJOICE!)
What if a believer wants to constantly borrow something of ours and never returns anything we lend them? (Charity bears all things.)
What else does charity do? (Charity BELIEVES all things, HOPES all things and ENDURES all things.)

READ: 1 Corinthians 13:8-13

QUESTIONS

Will charity ever fail? (Never.)
Will prophecies fail? (Yes.)
What will happen to tongues? (They will cease.)
What will happen to knowledge? (It shall vanish away.)
What will last forever? (Faith, hope, and charity.)
Which is the greatest of the three? (Charity!)

ACTIVITIES

Have the children make a list of all the attributes of charity.

Lesson Two
CHARITY
Following Charity

PARENT: God has made it very clear throughout the Word of God that CHARITY is a very important thing we MUST have. There is not a choice in this... We must have charity towards one another as this is pleasing to our Father. If we do not have love but have other things in the Bible, such as prophesying or knowledge of mysteries, these things are of non effect, as we do not have the IMPORTANT thing... CHARITY! Today we are going to read more scriptures that talk about charity.

READ: 1 Corinthians 14:1
1 Corinthians 16:14

QUESTIONS

In Chapter 14, what are we to follow after? (Charity.)
What does it mean to "follow after"? (Strong's says it means to pursue. We are to pursue charity. This also goes right along with the passage in 2 Peter, that tells us to add charity. It is something we willingly do.)
Why is it so important that we have charity? (It is so important because CHARITY is the most important characteristic. The Bible says

FAITH, HOPE and CHARITY are things that will abide, but the greatest of these is charity. If we have charity we will truly treat our brothers as we should!)
In 1 Corinthians 16:14, what are we to do? (We are to let all our things be done with charity.)
What does this mean? (That every single thing we do we do it with love.)
Who are we to love? (God!)
When we do things, ANYTHING, who sees all we do? (God.)
Can He see us in a dark place? (The Bible tells us His eyes see in the DARKEST place.)
Can He see what we do when there is no one else around? (Yes!)
Should we want to do things because God sees what we do? (No! We should only want to do things pleasing to Him because we love Him.)
What type of love are we to do all things? (In the love of God! Doing all things to the pleasure of our Father!)

READ: Colossians 3:12-17

QUESTIONS

What are the elect of God to put on? (Bowels of mercies, kindness, humbleness of mind, meekness, longsuffering.)
How are we to treat others? (Vs. 13, Forbearing one another, and forgiving one another.)
What is above all these things we just talked about? (Vs. 14 says, and above all these things put on charity, which is the bond of perfectness.)
What is the bond of perfectness? (Charity!)
What is to rule in our hearts? (The peace of God.)
Do you think this is the same type of peace the world has? (No! This is the peace of the Lord which comes from Him!)
What is to dwell in us richly? (The Word of God.)
What are we to do to one another? (We are to teach and admonish one another.)
How? (Through psalms and hymns and spiritual songs, singing with grace in your hearts to the Lord.)
What are we to do in the name of the Lord Jesus? (We are to do ALL that we do in the name of the Lord Jesus!)
How does this relate to charity? (We are living our lives and doing everything because of the love of God!)

READ: 1 Thessalonians 3:6

QUESTIONS

What did Timotheus tell the believers about those in Thessalonica? (He told them the good news of their faith and charity.)
What did the believers have there? (They had faith and charity!)
Should we be known for these things also? (Yes!)

READ: 2 Thessalonians 1:3

QUESTIONS

What did Paul, Silvanus, and Timotheus thank God for? (For the believers.)
What happened to the believer's faith? (It grew exceedingly.)
What about their CHARITY? (The charity of every one of them toward each other abounded!)
Should we also? (YES!)

✼✼✼✼✼✼

Lesson Three
CHARITY
Charity Above All

PARENT: The Lord has shown us that the most important thing of all is CHARITY. We are to pursue charity above all else. If we have charity we will then treat others as the Lord wants us to. We are to put above mercy, kindness, humbleness, meekness, longsuffering, forbearance, and forgiveness, ... CHARITY!! God knows that if we have charity, we will treat others right. When you love someone, you want the best for them.

READ: 1 Timothy 1:3-5

QUESTIONS

What was the commandment Paul had to tell Timothy? (Vs. 3, that he might charge some that they teach no other doctrines, nor give heed to fables and endless genealogies, rather than godly edifying which is in faith... DO SO.)
What was the end of the commandment? (Vs. 5, "Now the end of the commandment is CHARITY out of a pure heart and of a good conscience and of faith unfeigned.")
Where does charity come from? (It comes from a pure heart.)
Where else? (Out of a good conscience.)
And where else? (From FAITH.)
If a person believes in God, what does He have? (He has a love for God.)
Why do we do all that we do? (Because of our love of God.)
Would it be a pure heart if we are only "loving" someone because of what God is going to DO for us? (No, this would be selfish motives.)
Is this a part of charity? (No, charity seeketh not her own.)

READ: 1 Timothy 2:15

QUESTIONS

What are women to continue in ? (Faith, charity and holiness with sobriety.)
Where comes charity? (From a pure heart that BELIEVES!)
If you do not believe in God, can you have true charity? (No, you will only have worldly love.)
Where does true love come from? (It comes from God.)
How are women to be? (Full of charity.)
Are just women to continue in charity? (No! ALL believers are to continue in charity.)

READ: 1 Timothy 4:12

QUESTIONS

How was Timothy told to behave himself? (He was told to be an example to the believers.)
Should our lives be an example? (Yes, to believers and to nonbelievers.)
How was Timothy to be an example by his word? (We are to speak kind things, and things that edify or build up others.)
How are we examples by conversation? (The Bible says that our communication is to be pure. We are not to speak evil of others, but speak things that befit a child of God.)
How else are we to be an example? (In CHARITY!!!)
Are we to be an example in our charity towards God and others? (Yes.)
How? (By how we love our brethren.)
How else? (In spirit!)
And how else? (In faith and in purity.)
So how are our lives to be? (We are to be an example in ALL we say, in charity, in spirit, in faith, and in purity in ALL that we do!)

READ: 2 Timothy 2:22

QUESTIONS

What are we to flee? (Youthful lusts.)
What are we to follow? (Righteousness,

faith, charity, peace, with them that call out of a pure heart.)

What does it mean to have a pure heart? (It means that we love God for the simple reason that we LOVE Him, not because we are going to gain in any way from loving Him.)

READ: 2 Timothy 3:10

QUESTIONS

How did Paul live his life? (In the doctrine of the Word, in faith, in longsuffering, in CHARITY, in patience, in persecutions and in afflictions.)
Did Paul know God? (Yes!)
Should we follow his example? (Yes.)
What do we need? (Charity!!!!)

✺✺✺✺✺✺

Lesson Four
CHARITY
We are Commanded to Have Love

PARENT: We have been reading over and over again, that God wants us to have CHARITY. He talks about it all throughout His Word! Paul commanded Timothy to be an example in CHARITY. So should we be an example to all that we love. In our day and time, we live in a society that says that love is leaving others alone in whatever THEY choose to do. They think it is giving ACCEPTANCE to whatever one does, even if what they do is WRONG! This is not love. This is what psychology, the study of self, has brought to our school systems and is what the world's public education organization has taught many people. This is not God's love, but is humanism. God does not wish us to accept things that are against His Word. He wishes us to speak truth in love, and if you love someone, you will love them enough to tell them the truth! This is CHARITY that is spoken of in the Bible.

READ: Titus 2:2

QUESTIONS

How are the aged men commanded to be in God's Word? (They are to be sober, brave, temperate, sound in faith, in CHARITY, and in patience.)
What is the greatest gift of all? (Charity!)
Why are the aged men commanded to have these things? (Because they are an example to the younger. It is also the aged that TEACH the younger, for example dads are to teach their sons.)

READ: 1 Peter 4:8

QUESTIONS

What are we to be fervent in? (CHARITY!)
What does FERVENT mean? (According to the dictionary it means 1. Having or showing great emotion or warmth; passionate; ardent. 2. Extremely HOT!)
Do you remember a scripture in Revelation where Jesus commands us to be HOT? (He says to be not lukewarm, but either HOT or cold, preferably HOT!)
Why are we commanded to be fervent in CHARITY? (The Word says because CHARITY shall cover the multitude of sins!)
How is this? (Because if you love someone, you are always hoping for the best, and when they do wrong you WANT to forgive them. When you love someone, you just can't turn off that love, but you work with people through their imperfections as Jesus is patient with us!)

READ: 3 John 5-7

QUESTIONS

What are we to do faithfully? (Whatever we do to the brethren and to strangers we are to do it faithfully.)
Are we to be charitable to strangers? (Yes!)
Are we to be faithful towards strangers? (Yes!)
Who has borne witness of his charity in this scripture? (The brethren and strangers.)
What does this mean? (It means they see his charity.)
Should our charity be known to all men? (Yes!)

READ: Jude 12

QUESTIONS

What type of feasts did the believers partake in? (Feasts of charity.)
What do you think these feasts of charity were? ...
(Many people believe they were meals the believers shared with one another, distributing together to all who had need and always making sure everyone had enough to sustain themselves.)
Should we too have feasts of charity? (If they did this as New Testament believers, then we should do as they give us example to do, always doing what the Bible tells us to do.)

READ: Revelations 2:19

QUESTIONS

What did Jesus say to the church in Thyatira? (That He knew their works, and CHARITY, and service, and faith and patience.)
Should we also be known by Jesus for these things? (Yes, Jesus is commending them for the good things they are known for.)

Lesson Five
CHARITY
God's Love

PARENT: We have read many scriptures where God has told us that we are not to love the world, nor the things thereof. When we have been studying this we have found that God wants us to walk after His Spirit, and not after the lusts of our flesh. These two things war with one another and there is no way you can have both! God has wanted us to walk lives that are pleasing to Him, because we love Him. But did you know that God loves the people in the world? He loved them so much that He sent His Son to die for each and every one of them. This is true CHARITY, or LOVE!

READ: John 3:16-21

QUESTIONS

Did God love the world? (Yes, God so loved the world.)
What did God do in His love? (He gave His only begotten Son.)
Why? (So that whosoever believeth in Him should not perish.)
What does this word perish mean? (It means to be destroyed.)
Instead of perishing, what will happen to those that believe in His Son? (They shall have everlasting life.)
Did God send Jesus into the world to condemn it? (No, so that the world might be saved by Him.)
Is this LOVE? (Yes. It is true love.)
Are those that believe in Jesus condemned? (No!)
What about those that do not believe? (Vs. 18 says, he that believeth not is condemned already.)
Why are they condemned? (Because God has given a way for salvation, and they choose to ignore it! Because He hath not believed in the name of the only begotten Son of God.)

What is condemnation? (Vs. 19, "And this is condemnation, that light is come into the world, and men loved darkness rather than light, because their deeds were evil.")

STRONG'S: Light

(Greek # 5457; to shine or make manifest.)

Who is the light? (Jesus!)
Do people that do evil like the light? (No, they hate the light.)
Do they hate Jesus? (Yes.)
Why? (Because they neither come to the light lest their deeds should be reproved.)
Who comes to the light? (He that doeth truth, vs. 21.)
Why? (That his deeds may be made manifest, that they are wrought in God.)
Will we sin? (Yes.)
Do we hate the light? (No! Jesus is the light.)
What is the difference then? (Because we do not like to sin. We are at war with our flesh!!! And when we do sin we ask our Father God for forgiveness!!! We do not willingly go around sinning. It is not our pleasure to sin, but makes believers grievous.)

READ: John 21:15-19

QUESTIONS

What did Jesus ask Simon Peter? (If He loved Him.)
What was Peter's answer? (Yes!)
What did Jesus want Peter to do? (He wanted Him to feed His lambs and His sheep.)
Who are Jesus' lambs and sheep? (WE ARE.)
Did Jesus love Peter? (Yes. He loved all His disciples. And not only did He love His disciples, He loved the WHOLE world that He went to the cross and made a way for them to go to His Father.)

READ: Romans 5:5-11

QUESTIONS

Does God love the righteous? (Yes. He does.)
In Vs. 8, when did He love us? (When we were yet sinners.)
When Jesus died for us, what state was the world in? (It was all sinful.)
What did He do? (He brought a way to God through the cross!)
How long has God loved us? (Forever. Even in our sins.)
Does God want people to perish? (NO! God is not willing for even ONE to perish.)
Will men perish? (Yes, sadly enough.)
Why? (Because they willingly reject their salvation, Jesus Christ.)
Is God a loving God? (YES!)

Lesson Six
CHARITY
God's Love For Us as a Parent Loves His Child

PARENT: How much does God love us? ... He loves us so much, that even when we were in sin, He sent His only Son to die. This is a very great love. And then, out of love, and because He conquered death, God raised His Son from the dead! We have learned that God is our Father. He is a wonderful Father and we have someone who is faithful and true to His children. He is also the perfect parent. The Bible tells us that God disciplines His children. Did you know that discipline is a part of love also?

READ: Hebrews 12:5-11

QUESTIONS

In Vs. 5, what are we not to despise? (We are

not to despise the chastening of the Lord.)
Does the Lord CHASTEN us? (Yes, He does!)
What does chasten mean? (The dictionary says that chasten means 1. To punish, either physically or morally. 2. Refine, purify!)
Will God do this to us? (Yes, when we need it.)
Is this good? (Yes, it is.)
What else does it say God will do to us? (He will rebuke us.)
What does REBUKE mean? (The Strong's says rebuke means to admonish, or tell a fault, to reprove.)
Who does God do this to? (To those He loves.)
What else does God do to whom He loves? (He scourgeth every son whom He receiveth.)
If you are a son or daughter of God, will you be scourged? (Apparently so!)
What does it mean to be scourged? (It means to flog, which means to beat harshly with a whip or a rod.)
Are we to endure this from God? (Yes.)
Why? (It says, "If ye endure chastening, God dealeth with you as with sons; for what son is he whom the Father chasteneth not?" vs. 7.)
What if God does not chastise us? (Then He is not our Father. We are without a Father.)
Is it JOYOUS to be chastised? (The Word says, "Now no chastening for the present seemeth to be joyous, but grievous.")
But what happens afterwards? (It yieldeth the peaceable fruit of righteousness unto them which are exercised thereby.)

PARENT: *God has made it very clear that He loves us. And as a parent, He will treat us even better than our own parents do. God has given us some wonderful advice on how to raise our own children, and He follows by the same instructions He gave to His children, US! Let's read some scriptures on parenting...*

READ: Proverbs 13:24

QUESTIONS

Does a person that does not spank their children, love them? (The Bible says that he who SPARES, or does not use, the rod HATES his son.)
What does a parent that loves his child do? (He CHASTENETH him betimes.)

STRONG'S: Betimes

(Hebrews # 7836; to dawn; be up early at any task with earnestness; to search for with painstaking; to do something betimes, early, seek diligently.)

So, how often is a person to chasten their son? (As often as they need to. A parent is to do this diligently and earnestly.)
Does God do this to us? (Yes.)
Does He chasteneth us because He hates us? (No, if He DIDN'T chasten us He would hate us.)

READ: Proverbs 19:18
        Proverbs 22:15

QUESTIONS

When we chastise our children, what are we not to do? (We are not to despair because of their crying.)
Does God feel bad when we cry from His chastisement? (No, for it is for our own good!)
What is bound in a heart of a child? (Foolishness.)
What will get rid of the foolishness? (The rod of correction!)
Will God chastise us with a rod? (Yes, it says He scourges us which means to beat with a rod.)

READ: Proverbs 23:13-14

QUESTIONS

If we are chastened with a rod will we die? (No.)
Are we to withhold correction from our children? (No!)
Will God withhold correction from us? (No! We are His children, and He wrote the commandments so how much more faithful will He be to correct us?)

READ: Proverbs 29:15, 17

QUESTIONS

What do the rod and reproof give? (WISDOM!)
What happens to a child left by himself? (He will bring his mother to shame.)
What will happen when we correct our children? (He will give his parents rest.)
What else will he be? (A delight to his parents soul.)

PARENT: God's Word has told us that we are to correct our children because we love them. Even so, God LOVES us! We are each His children, and He will raise us and train us in the Way we should GO! This is a part of God's LOVE!

✵✵✵✵✵✵✵

Lesson Seven
CHARITY
Loving Our Enemies

PARENT: There is something that Jesus brought to us that was totally a new concept to the people of His day. The Old Testament saying was "An eye for an eye!" and when Jesus came He commanded that we were to LOVE our enemies. We are not only supposed to love our brothers and sisters in the Lord, but we are now commanded to love our enemies. We are to do GOOD to those who persecute us. We are to pray for those who USE us. We are now to love even the unloveable. Let's read some scriptures which talk about this.

READ: Matthew 5:43-47

QUESTIONS

What did Jesus say was the common saying of His day? (Thou shalt love thy neighbour, and hate thine enemy.)
What did Jesus come to tell them? ("But I say to you LOVE your enemies!")
What are we to do to those who curse us? (We are to BLESS those that curse us.)
What are we to do to those who hate us? (We are to do GOOD to those that hate us.)
What about those that despitefully use us? (We are to PRAY for them.)
Why? (This will show who our Father is. We will be showing HIM and His attributes.)
How does God treat those who do not love Him? (God makes His sun to rise on the evil and on the good. He sends rain on the just and on the unjust.)
Are we to love those who love us? (Yes, but we are to go beyond that. We are to LOVE our enemies.)
What is the message it is trying to get across? (That even the world loves those who love them. There is nothing special in that... But we are to love our God as He loves, and He loves and is kind to those who do NOT love

Him.)

READ: Matthew 22:36-39

QUESTIONS

Which is the greatest commandment in the Law? (Thou shalt love the Lord thy God with all thy heart and with all they soul, and with all thy mind.)
Which is the second commandment, according to Jesus? (Vs. 39, Thou shalt love thy neighbour as thyself.)
How important are these two commandments? (On these two commandments hang all the law and the prophets.)
How will we treat others? (We shall do to others as we would do to ourselves.)
How do we love ourselves? (Very much. Most people seek to pleasure SELF first.)
So, we know how we want to be treated, so how should we treat others? (Very well.)
What if our neighbor is unkind? (We should treat them well.)
What if our neighbor is evil? (We should treat them with love!)
How does God treat those who are evil? (He still bestows blessings on them.)

READ: Romans 12:14-21

QUESTIONS

What are we to do to those who persecute us? (Vs. 14 says to bless them, and curse them not.)
When someone does evil to us, can we do the same thing back to them, such as an eye for an eye? (No, Vs. 17 says recompense or pay back no man evil for evil.)
How are we to live with all men? (If it be possible live peaceably with all men.)
Are we to take REVENGE? Can we AVENGE ourselves? (No, vs. 19 says dearly beloved, avenge not yourselves, but rather give place unto wrath.)
Who does vengeance belong to? (The Lord.)
What are we to do to our enemies? (If our enemy hungers, feed him, if he thirst, give him drink.)
What will this do to him? (It will heap coals of fire on his head.)
Are we to be overcome by evil? (No! WE are to overcome evil with GOOD!)

✼✼✼✼✼✼✼

Lesson Eight
CHARITY
Loving God

PARENT: *God wants us to LOVE Him. He desires only that we love the Lord our God with ALL our hearts, ALL our souls, and ALL our MINDS! When we love God, we want to do things that are pleasing to Him! Our pleasure is to please our Father! This is love.*
Let's read what the Bible has to say about the Love of God...

READ: John 14:15-21

QUESTIONS

What does Jesus say to do if you love Him? (Vs. 15 says, "If you love me, keep my commandments.")
What did Jesus do for us? (He prayed to the Father and Father God has given us the Comforter who will abide with us forever.)
Who is it that loves Him? (Vs. 21 says, "He that hath my commandments, and keepeth them, he it is that loveth me.")
If we love Jesus who will love us? (Vs. 21 says, "He that loveth me shall be loved of my Father, and I will love him.")
What will Jesus do to those who love Him? (He will manifest himself to him.)

READ: John 14:23-31

QUESTIONS

If a man loves Jesus, what will he do? (Vs. 23, "If a man love me, he will keep my words.")
What will God and Jesus do to that man? (Vs. 23 says, "We will come unto him, and make our abode with him.")
What's an abode? (It is a home.)
Will someone that does not love Jesus want to keep His sayings? (Vs. 24 says, "He that loveth me not keepeth not my sayings.")
When we hear Jesus' words, whose words also are we listening to? (God, the Father's.)
What will the Comforter, the Holy Ghost, do for us? (He will teach us all things, and bring all things to your remembrance, whatsoever I have said to you.)

READ: John 15:9-19

QUESTIONS

What does Jesus command us to do in vs. 9? (We are to continue in His love.)
How are we to do this? (Vs. 10 says, "If ye keep my commandments, ye shall abide in my love.")
What did Jesus do? (He kept His Father's commandments and abided in His love!)
What is another commandment of Jesus? (Vs. 12, "That we love one another, as I have loved you.")
How much did Jesus love us? (So much that He laid down His life for his friends.)
Who are Jesus friends? (Vs. 14, "Ye are my friends, if ye do whatsoever I command you.")
Will the world like us? (No! It will hate us.)
Does the world love those who are of the world? (Yes. The world loves its own.)

READ: 1 John 4:7-21

QUESTIONS

How are we to treat one another? (We are commanded to love one another.)
Where is love from? (Love is from God.)
How was the love of God manifested towards us? (Vs. 9, "In this was manifested the love of God toward us, because that God sent his only begotten Son in to the world that we might live through him.")
How is love made perfect? (Vs. 17, that we may have boldness in the day of judgment.)
How is it made perfect by this? (Because of Jesus we will be able to stand before God, for Jesus has cleansed our sins!)
Is there fear in love? (No.)
Why? (Because perfect love casts out fear.)
If we fear, what is wrong? (We are not perfect in love yet.)
Can we love God and hate our brother? (No!)
How can we love God? (By loving our brethren.)

READ: 1 John 5:2-3

QUESTIONS

How do we love the children of God? (Vs. 2, by this we know that we love the children of God, when we love God, and keep His commandments.)
What do we need to do? (Love the Lord our God with all our hearts and all our souls and all our minds.)
Can we then love our brethren? (Yes.)
What if we do not love our brethren? (We then do not have the love of God, first.)
If we love God, will we want to do what He wants us to do? (Yes.)
Why? (Because it will be our pleasure to please Him.)
What is the love of God? (Vs. 3, "For this is the love of God, that we keep His commandments, and His commandments are not grievous.")
What if a person does not want to obey His Word? (The Bible says they do not have the

love of God, and sadly, they will probably not love their brethren either, which was a commandment of Jesus.)

READ: 2 John 5-6

QUESTIONS

What was the commandment the believers had from the beginning? (That we love one another.)
What is love? (Vs. 6, "That we walk after His commandments.")
Can we separate the love of God, from the love of our brethren? (No!)

READ: Jude 21

QUESTIONS

What are we to keep ourselves in? (The love of God.)
What is the love of God? (To keep His commandments.)
What is one of the most important commandments? (To love one another.)

✵✵✵✵✵✵

Lesson Nine
CHARITY
Loving Each Other

PARENT: We have learned about loving God, about loving our enemies, and just about how important it is that we develop CHARITY! We learned that God wants us to love one another! We are going to read more scriptures on what the Bible says about LOVING our brothers and sisters...

READ: Romans 13:8-10

QUESTIONS

What are we to owe others? (We are to owe them nothing except to love them.)
What does he that loveth fulfill? (The law.)
How does it fulfill the law? (If you love, you will do all of the ten commandments.)
What are the ten commandments? (Thou shalt have no other gods before me; thou shalt not make unto thee any graven image, or any likeness of any thing that is in heaven above, or that is in the earth beneath, or that is in the water under the earth; thou shalt not take the name of the Lord thy God in vain; Remember the sabbath day to keep it holy; honour thy father and thy mother; thou shalt not kill; thou shalt not commit adultery; thou shalt not steal; thou shalt not bear false witness against they neighbour; thou shalt not covet.)
What fulfills this law? (Love.)
How does love treat his neighbor? (Love worketh no ill to his neighbor.)

READ: 1 John 2:8-10

QUESTIONS

What true light shines now? (The knowledge of Jesus Christ.)
What are we to be in? (In the light.)
Is a person that says they are in the light, really in the light, if they hate their fellow believer? (No, vs. 9 says he that saith he is in the light and hateth his brother, is in darkness even until now.)
If we love our brothers and sisters, are we in the light? (Yes.)
Is this love when you let anyone do whatever they want to do and you all just FEEL love for one another? (True love is where we love one another enough to speak truth all the time, gently, and humbly. We are to love one another enough that we can trust each other that if we are in trouble or in error they love us enough to gently tell us. And our hearts will rejoice, because they have shown us our

error! This is TRUE love, not humanistic love.)
What is he that hates his brother "in"? (He is in darkness.)
Can he see? (No, he is blinded because of the darkness.)
How important is it that we love one another? (VERY IMPORTANT!)

READ: 1 John 3:10-14

QUESTIONS

Does a person that does not love his brother know God? (Sadly, vs. 10 says in this the children of God are manifest, and the children of the devil; whosoever doeth not righteousness is not of God, neither is he that loveth not his brother.)
Should we make sure we love our brothers? (Yes, but first we should make sure we love God, for by this will come the love of our brethren.)
Did Cain love his brother? (No, he slew his brother because his deeds were unrighteous and his brother's were righteous.)
How do we know that we have passed from death unto life? (Because we love the brethren.)
What does a person that does not love his brethren abide in? (DEATH.)

READ: 1 John 4:7-13
        1 John 4:20-21

QUESTIONS

Does a person that does not love know God? (The Bible says no.)
Who dwells in us when we love our brethren? (God dwells in us!)
What has God given us? (His Spirit.)
Who will help us to love the unloveable? (God's Holy Spirit!)
Can we do this? (We can do all things through Christ Jesus who strengthens us!)

PARENT: Do you see how important it is that we love one another? We need to know 1 Corinthians 13 very well, don't we?

ACTIVITIES

Have children memorize 1 Corinthians 13.

Lesson Ten
CHARITY
Review

What is CHARITY? (Charity is love, affection or benevolence. It is brotherly love and mercy towards others.)

If we prophecy but do not have love, what are we like? (We are like hollow, sounding brass.)

If we understand mysteries or have all knowledge and have no love, what do we have? (Nothing.)

If we take clothing and food to the poor, but do not love, what are we? (Nothing.)

How important is it to have love? (VERY important.)

Where does love come from? (It is from our Father, God.)

Does charity only be bothered for a little by pesty brothers and then tell them to go away? (No, charity suffereth long.)

Do we look at our calendar when someone wants to come over and visit, and tell them no because we are tired of company? (No, charity is kind and is willing to have people bother us.)

Are we to want what our brothers and sisters have? (No, charity envieth not.)

Are we to consider ourselves higher than others? (No, charity is not puffed up.)

Do we take the cheesiest piece of pizza? (No, charity seeketh not her own.)

Do we get angry and yell at our family because they have done something we do not like? (No, charity is not easily provoked.)

When people despise us and treat us badly, do we want to get even? (No, charity thinketh no evil.)

What if we are used by people? (Charity bears all things.)

What else does CHARITY do? (Charity BELIEVES all things, HOPES all things and ENDURES all things.)

What will abide forever? (Charity.)

What are we to pursue? (We are to pursue charity.)

How are we to do all that we do? (We are to let all our things be done with charity.)

Where does this love start with? (It starts with the love of God.)

If we love someone, does this mean we smile and never say anything that will cause them to not like us? (In the terms of HUMANISM, this is humanistic love.)

What is God's love? (To put others welfare and concern higher than our own. To truly love them more than we love ourselves.)

What is to dwell in us richly? (The Word of God.)

What does the Word of God tell us to do? (He tells us to LOVE one another.)

In the Bible, what were the believers known for? (For their love for one another.)

What should we be known for? (Our love for one another.)

Where does charity come from? (It comes from God.)

Where does it come from us? (It comes from a pure heart.)

Where else does it come from? (A good conscience.)

What is a good conscience? (It is wanting to do what is pleasing to God.)

How was Timothy an example to the believers? (His life was an example.)

How did he speak? (He spoke things which edified and built up other believers.)

Will other people see our charity? (Yes. Charity is not a feeling, it is an action. It is how we treat others!)

How is this? (The Bible says that they knew the believers by their charity. This proves that it had to be seen in their ACTIONS! You can't see a feeling!)

What does FERVENT mean? (It means to be HOT!)

How are we to be in CHARITY? (We are to be fervent in charity!)

When we have charity what does it do towards other believers in regards to sin? (The Word says charity covers a multitude of sins.) How does charity do this? (If you love someone, you are always hoping the best, and when they do wrong you want to forgive them and hope that they will do better!)

How are we to be towards strangers? (We are to be charitable to them.)
How are we to treat our enemies? (We are to love our enemies.)
How are we to treat those who curse us? (We are to bless them.)
What do we do about those who despitefully use us? (We are to pray for them.)
Who is our example in this? (God.)
How? (God causes the sun to rise on the evil and on the good. He sends rain on the just and on the unjust.)
How do we fulfill all the law? (By loving one another.)
Who is our parent? (God.)
If God loves us what will He do? (He will be a Father to us and discipline us when we need it.)
Why does He discipline us? (Because if He didn't we would not be His children.)
Is it joyous to be chastened by our Father? (The Bible tells us that no chastening is joyous during it, but grievous.)
What happens afterward? (It yields the peaceable fruit of righteousness.)

If we love Jesus, what does He tell us to do? (He tells us to keep His commandments.)
What does Jesus say we should do? (We are to be doers of His Word.)
What will we be accountable for? (For doing just what we know to do. We are not going to give an account for that which we do not know. But, we are just to obey as much as we know because we LOVE Him.)
If we love Jesus, who will love us? (He that loves Jesus shall be loved of my Father and I will love him.)
What will Jesus do to those who love Him? (He will manifest Himself to him.)

What does Jesus command us to do? (We are to continue in His love and to love one another.)
Do obeying God's commandments, and loving one another go hand in hand? (Yes. They are intertwined.)
What will endure forever? (CHARITY!)

✼✼✼✼✼✼

Charity

There was once, in the land of the King, some subjects who claimed that they knew and loved the King more than anyone else in the land. These people were devoted to the King and spent all their time, thinking of ways to please Him.

One day, one of the men sat pondering how He could please His King today. "I know, I am going to go and collect as much food as I can to give to the hungry village on the other side of the mountain! This will be a good thing to do to show how much I love the King!"

So the man went to all the people in the village and gathered as much food as his old wagon could carry and started on his trip to the other side of the mountain.

On his way there, he saw one of the familiar faces of one of the people from his village. It was Isaac, the town pauper. Now the man had already given Isaac a loaf of bread last week to feed his hungry family, and he wasn't about to be deterred from his mission!

"Out of the way, Isaac! I'm on a mission for the King! I have to feed the starving people on the other side of the mountain."

Isaac wistfully eyed the cart full of food and went on to try to find work somewhere else in the village so he could feed his own starving family.

The man continued on his trek up the mountain, and on his way he saw an old man and an old woman sitting outside their cottage. They looked very thin and frail . They greeted him warmly and offered him to come in and rest for awhile.

They offered him a cool glass of water, but regretfully told them that all they had to give him to eat was one loaf of bread.

The man said that was fine and sat down and ate the whole thing in a few bites!

He then told them that He was on a mission for the King and was bringing food to the starving people on the other side of the mountain!

As they bid him farewell, they gazed hungrily at the wagon full of food, watching it until the man drove out of sight.

The man, content and full, traveled some more hours until he at last arrived at the village. He delivered his food to the hungry people and then returned home.

After a rest at home, he decided to find something else he could do to please his king.

"I know!" he exclaimed. "I can go and give clothing to all the needy people in the village on the other side of the mountain!"

So he went and gathered clothing that he could hand out to the people on the other side of the mountain, and started on his way.

On the way there he encountered Isaac, the village pauper.

"Hello, there Isaac! How are you doing today?"

"Well," Isaac answered, "I'm not doing so well today. Winter is coming and my family doesn't have any winter clothing or coats to keep them warm."

"Ah, that's just terrible, Isaac! But I'm sure something will turn up soon for you. I've got to run now, because I'm on another mission for the King! I must deliver this clothing to the people on the other side of the mountain." And off the man went.

He drove on and came to the little old man's and little old woman's cottage on the side of the mountain. He knocked at the door, and they warmly greeted him and invited him inside. Now, at this time of year, up on the mountainside, it had already started to get cold. The man noticed how cold it was in their cottage and said something to them about it.

The old man replied, "It sure is cold, but I'm just too old to go out and chop wood any more. We'd be just fine if we only had warmer clothing."

The man nodded his head. "Well I'm sure something will turn up soon for you."

He thanked them for their hospitality and left.

The people on the other side of the mountain were greatly pleased with the clothing and had so much that they even had some left over!

The man went back to his village and couldn't wait for the next time the King visited him! It was going to be a great visit, as the King was going to be so happy with all he had done!

A few days later, the king decided to come and visit the people of the village. The man went up to the King and bowed low before Him.

"Your Majesty, I have great news to tell you! I have been on two missions for you! I have been to the other side of the mountain and have brought the poor people over there food and clothing!"

The King looked down at the man with a slight frown, "I have heard of your deeds. ... But I am displeased with you!"

The man looked at His king in shock.

The King continued, "The most important thing that you can do to please Your King is to love one another! You can do many things in the name of goodness, but if you do not love one another as you love yourself, it is all for nothing. When you passed by Isaac, and when you passed by the old man and woman, it was just as if you passed by me when I was in need! Don't you love me?"

The man's lips started quivering and tears started pouring from his eyes. "Your Majesty! I would never want to pass you by!"

The King saw the sorrow of the man and gently stated, "When you are kind to the least of my subjects, it is just as if you are being kind to me. This is the love of your King."

The man was greatly sorry, and asked His King for forgiveness, and the King readily forgave Him. He then went on to never pass by another person in need, but gave willingly all that He could give, knowing, that as he treated his fellow subjects, he was doing it just as if he was doing it for the King.

Notes

Notes

Notes

Notes

Notes

Notes

Notes

Notes

Notes

Notes

Notes

Notes

COMING SOON...

Our Hope Chest Series for Young Ladies

Please write for an updated brochure.

Christian Character Curriculum

___The Narrow Way Character Curriculum
Also includes a 300 page spiral plus 8 Kingdom Stories ($29.95 plus $3 shipping)

___Volume 1 (Contains 8 Character Building Stories) $15
The Governor's Plot (Homeschooling)
The House the World Built (Public Education)
The Alchemist (women & Children at Home)
The Viewing Box (Television & Entertainment)
You Can't Shoot the Bears (Animal Rights?)
The New Command (Loving others)
The Conquered Village (Denying the World)
The Beauty (Inner Beauty vs. Outward)

___Volume 2 (Contains 8 Character Building Stories) - $15
The King's Request (Perseverance)
The Goal (Work)
The Love of the King (Obedience)
The Bicycle (Materialism vs. Responsibility)
The Governor's Revenge (Socialization)
The Journey (Following God, Not Men)
The Man of the King (Relationship with God)
The Messenger (Regarding Outward Appearances)

___Volume 3 (Contains 8 Character Building Stories) - $15
The King (The Word)
I'll Always have Tomorrow (Procrastination)
The Kite (Blaming Others for our Own Mistakes)
The Fisherman (Being Fishers of Men)
The Baby Cow (Contentment)
The Treasure (True Riches)
One Little Weed (Hidden Sin)
The Gentle Warrior (Speaking the Truth in Love)

___True Womanhood ~ $18.95 (Ages 13+ till 131)
___True Womanhood Companion Workbook ~ $9.94

___Personal Help for Boys ~ $18.95 (Ages 10+ great for dads too!)
___Personal Help for Boys Companion Workbook~ $9.95

___What the Bible says About Being a Boy ~$4.95
___What the Bible Says About Being a Girl ~$4.95

_____Subtotal
_____Shipping
_____Total Enclosed

Name_____
Address_____
City_____State_____Zip_____

PEARABLES
P.O. Box 272000
Fort Collins, CO 80527